FILM
SCHOOL
CONFIDENTIAL

The Insider's Guide
to Film Schools

Most Perigee Books are available at special quantity discounts for bulk purchases for sales promotions, premiums, fund-raising or educational use. Special books, or book excerpts, can also be created to fit specific needs.

For details write: Special Markets, The Berkley Publishing Group, 200 Madison Avenue, New York, New York 10016.

FILM
SCHOOL
CONFIDENTIAL
The Insider's Guide to Film Schools

Karin Kelly
and
Tom Edgar

A PERIGEE BOOK

A Perigee Book
Published by The Berkley Publishing Group
A member of Penguin Putnam Inc.
200 Madison Avenue
New York, NY 10016

First edition: September 1997

Published simultaneously in Canada.

The Putnam Berkley World Wide Web site address is http://www.berkley.com

Library of Congress Cataloging-in-Publication Data

Kelly, Karin, 1961–
    Film school confidential : the insider's guide to film school /
Karin Kelly and Tom Edgar. — 1st ed.
        p. cm.
    "A Perigee book."
    ISBN 0-399-52339-1
    1. Motion pictures—Study and teaching (Graduate)—United States—Directories.
I. Edgar, Tom, 1963– . II. Title.
PN1993.8.U5K46   1997
791.43'071'173—dc21   96-30032
                                                            CIP

Printed in the United States of America

10 9 8 7 6 5 4 3 2 1

Contents

Introduction

This book contains objective and subjective information about schools that offer M.F.A. degrees in film production. The objective information was obtained from the admissions offices of the schools discussed. The subjective information comes from interviews with students, graduates, and faculty from these schools. The views expressed are those of the interviewees, and do not necessarily reflect the views of the authors. You hear us, USC? Catch that, NYU? If you don't like what you read, don't sue the messengers. We're just trying to pass on what we know for the benefit of those who need it most.

Forgive us if we impart a dismal truth right up front. While everyone who goes to film school hopes to direct features after she graduates, the odds of any one student coming out of film school and immediately getting financial backing to direct a feature are very small. They were minuscule when Spike Lee and Phil Jouanou made their first features, and they are even smaller now.

We don't mean to discourage you. If you are determined to make it in film, you will. But the purpose of this book is to fill you in on information that the schools themselves will not. By definition, much of this news will be bad—if it were good, you would read it in the admissions package.

Don't be discouraged. By getting all the bad news at the start, you will be well-prepared to make the most out of the experience. And by hearing how other people have succeeded or failed in the situations you will be facing, you will be prepared to navigate safely through the many obstacles before you.

Film schools do not have the best interests of their students in mind. Unlike almost every other kind of school, they provide little career guidance, few easy ways to make contacts in the industry, and no help at all once diplomas are handed out. They will offer you some classes, which may or may not teach you to make films, and they will lend you some equipment with which to make some films. This is the most you can expect from them.

Since no one else will be looking out for you in film school, our main objective in this book is to help you keep track of your own best interests. We will tell you what you should bring with you into film school, and what you should expect to get out of it. We will let you know what the various film schools seem to look for in applicants—and what Hollywood seems to look for in graduates.

If you are going to film school, you probably want to be a director. We will tell you the things to do in school that will most likely help you to direct once you are out of school. We will tell you the things that students find most helpful, and the things that students find least helpful. We will let graduates from the top schools tell you about the activities you should try to participate in, and the pitfalls you should try to avoid.

Most of all, we will try to give you the career advice that the schools will not. We will tell you how to make film school work for you in your quest for success in the film industry.

So, everybody ready? Quiet on set! Okay! Roll sound. Speed! *Film School Confidential* Scene 1, shot 1, take 1. Roll camera. Mark!

And — Action!

Film Schools and Hollywood

Twenty-five years ago film schools were campus jokes. Though some universities had been offering courses in film since the twenties, the programs that existed were underfunded and taken even less seriously by administrators than, say, History of Consciousness programs. A few directors working in Hollywood in the early 1970s had attended film school in the sixties—notably Martin Scorsese, who studied film as an undergraduate at NYU—but for the most part, film school graduates had no more recognition, and no more power, than anyone else in the industry. That changed in the mid-seventies when a new generation of filmmakers came out of Southern California film schools and turned the film industry inside out.

The 1960s had seen the most revolutionary changes in the film industry since the advent of sound. The omnipotent studio system that had ruled Hollywood for six decades devoured itself, taking with it the Hayes code that had dictated much of the content that could be put into films. Filmmakers were suddenly free of the cheerfulness and wholesomeness that had been forced on them for as long as anyone could remember, and they gleefully began to see how much pain and despair they could pack into their films. For ten years most of Hollywood's product was rooted in existential despair. From Roman Polanski to Sam Peckinpah to Stanley Kubrick the era's greatest directors explored painful, emotionally charged subjects that their predecessors could not—and, more important, they explored subjects that their new competition, television, could not even hint at. Granted, some terrific films were made in the late 1960s and early 1970s, but few were what you would call rollicking good-time entertainments.

But then along came a pack of graduates from Southern California film schools. Most of these guys did not have a whole lot to say about the world, but all of them knew how to have fun. The early films of Francis Ford Coppola (UCLA), Steven Spielberg (Cal State Long Beach), and George Lucas (USC) were largely brainless but hugely entertaining—and audiences ate them up. After fifteen years of being subjected to cinematic explorations of oblivion and nothingness, not to mention the numbing oblivion of television, audiences felt that they were discovering real entertainment for the first time. It is hard to appreciate today the startling, energetic impact of *American Graffiti* (1973) when that film came out. And it is hard to appreciate how liberating the portrayal of clearly defined good guys and bad guys was in *Star Wars* (1977) when it was first released. And no one appreciated this energy and freedom more than the new generation of young filmgoers, who were bored with television and disillusioned with rebellion, and who desperately wanted to be distracted from the sobering upheavals of the day.

All these elements came together at once, and these films made more money than anyone in Hollywood had ever imagined was possible. No one had ever seen audiences wait in line for five hours to see a movie before, and yet enormous crowds lined up to see *The Godfather* (1972), *American Graffiti, Jaws* (1975), *Star Wars,* and *Close Encounters of the Third Kind* (1977). Hollywood recognized that young filmmakers could make a lot of money and started signing on more to make films.

Universities, too, began to recognize the benefits of turning out alumni who could create such hugely popular entertainments. In the short run these luminaries gave their schools academic cachet and free publicity. Ultimately, film programs paved the way to generous donations from wealthy Hollywood alumni. As the existing film programs grew, new programs cropped up at colleges and universities everywhere.

University administrators and Hollywood studio executives were not the only ones awestruck by the young filmmakers. Newspapers and magazines were quick to publish stories about the new *auteurs,* complete with glossy pictures of the twenty-five-year-old millionaires in jeans and tennis shoes striking poses of directorial authority on glamorous movie sets. And suddenly millions of high school students had a new goal in life—they wanted to become filmmakers.

If public interest in film as an art form grew a little in the seventies with the unprecedented celebrity of directors like Spielberg and Coppola, it exploded in the early eighties when anyone could become an authority on film for about three hundred bucks. With the introduction of the Betamax it was suddenly possible to see *The Third Man* (1949) without having to go to seedy art houses in bad parts of town. It was suddenly possible to see *Lawrence of Arabia* (1962) without commercial interruptions or *Citizen Kane* (1941) in a crisp new print without scratches or breaks in the film. And it was possible to study that film over and over again in the comfort of one's living room. Interest in film skyrocketed and became the main topic of conversation at parties. People who once discussed TV or sports now discussed the works of David Lean or Sam Peckinpah or Stanley Kubrick.

With video copies of great films replacing Readers Digest Condensed Books in bookcases everywhere, and with all the publicity about film school graduates in torn jeans becoming millionaires overnight, it is no wonder that more and more college students wanted to study film.

But by the time the next generation finished film school, the industry had changed. Whereas the huge success of *Star Wars* had been a fabulous surprise to studio executives in 1977, by the early eighties success along those lines—success beyond anyone's dreams—was expected. *Star Wars* had completely changed the way Hollywood made films. Prior to *Star Wars* a hit movie was one with broad appeal, one that people of all ages would see once. After *Star Wars* a hit movie was one that teenage boys would see fifteen to twenty times. Even now, twenty years after that film's release, Hollywood still puts most of its money and effort into films that aim no higher than to stimulate the pleasure center in a sixteen-year-old boy's brain. *Star Wars* also changed Hollywood's business priorities; while the film grossed around $350 million in domestic ticket sales in its original release, toys and other *Star Wars* products have grossed more than four billion dollars.

Needless to say, after *Star Wars* studios were no longer interested in intelligent low-budget films that made respectable profits. They only wanted the next mega-hit; the next *Star Wars,* the next *Raiders of the Lost Ark* (1981), the next *E.T.* (1982). Film students were still hired to make films, but if their first films weren't huge hits they rarely got a chance to make second ones. During this new era of blockbusters and marketing campaigns, Hollywood executives developed a pack mentality. When a film school graduate's film failed, it didn't mean that that individual filmmaker was not yet a mature artist—it meant that audiences no longer wanted to see film students' movies, that film school graduates were no longer marketable. Film students, whose youthful energy had given Hollywood unprecedented success, eventually became passé. Whereas they were once recruited directly out of school, they now had trouble even getting meetings with executives, producers, or agents.

Frustrated film school graduates looked for other alternatives, but the Southern California film schools didn't prepare their students for any kind of filmmaking except Hollywood filmmaking. These schools taught students how to pitch a script and take a meeting—not how to write grants or raise funds from charitable organizations. So the next generation of film students to make features were not graduates of USC or AFI—they were students who had learned down-and-dirty filmmaking techniques from schools that specialized in down-and-dirty filmmaking, like NYU. Following the lead of independent filmmakers like Albert Brooks and John Sayles, film students like Spike Lee and Jim Jarmusch raised their own funds and made challenging, personal films on extremely small budgets. These film school graduates made daring films that became critical successes and made money on a smaller scale. They were not the blockbusters that the studios had come to count on from young filmmakers, but they were profitable. And with Lucas and Coppola releasing big-budget flops like *Howard the Duck* (1986) and *One from the Heart* (1982), even modest profits started to look good again to the studios.

This low-budget heaven lasted for a couple of years in the late eighties, when the economy was strong and wealthy investors were willing to risk their money on films. But with the recession that began to spread across America in 1989 and 1990, film students coming out of school found that no one was interested in them anymore. Independent filmmaking came to a near standstill as even proven filmmakers found they could not get financing to make their films. By 1995 things began to improve, but only after thousands of film school graduates had finished their films and found themselves deeply in debt and essentially unemployable.

When the economy showed signs of recovery, film production

began to pick up again. New technologies that were similar to film emerged, demanding new kinds of directors and writers, people with experience with both acetate and silicon. Interactive CD-ROMs, computer-generated imagery, even the World Wide Web demanded creative, technically aware people with a knack for visual storytelling. Film schools quickly added new media to their film and television programs, and soon film school graduates were more employable than they ever had been before.

As of this writing the problem is not one of too little production—rather of too much. So many movies are being made that audiences can't possibly keep up with them all. Ten years ago a slight but original film like *She's Gotta Have It* had a chance of finding an audience. Today, with a dozen new films opening every weekend, and with hundreds more vying for spots in film festivals, the same film would probably never even find a distributor. Disney recently announced that they would cut their film production in half, and it seems likely that other studios will soon follow suit. With a little luck a balance will be found with new films being made but competition being a little less brutal.

You may think we are overstating the case, that there aren't *that* many good independent films being made, that there aren't *that* many that will never be distributed. If so, we suggest an exercise. Go to a film festival and watch a few independent films. You will see some very good films—films with heart, with intelligence, with great writing and directing, and with luminous performances. Leave the theater and see if you ever hear of these films again. You won't.

As far as content goes, Hollywood and film school graduates have reached something of a middle ground. The hype is over. Film students no longer can film whatever they want and earn recognition as brilliant cinematic prodigies. And the backlash that forced them to make crappy kiddie-exploitation films and then labeled them overrated, undertalented brats is also over. Some studios and large independents are willing to back risky projects by first-time filmmakers as long as the money involved is small. A good example of this is John Singleton's *Boyz N The Hood* (1991), which was a small, low-budget film that paid off handsomely for Columbia Pictures.

On the other end of the spectrum is Disney, who has made a business of hiring first-time directors for many of their terrible kiddie-exploitation films—films like *Three Ninjas* (1992) or *Blank Check* (1994), or those Pauly Shore films they keep releasing. For these low-budget, high concept movies Disney hires first-time directors because they ask for little money and are not confident enough to stand up to Disney executives who dictate directorial decisions. These unfortunate souls are paid to put their names on films they have no control over, and are made to take responsibility when those films fail. As a final insult, when then–Disney studio head Jeffrey Katzenberg struck a deal to co-produce films with Merchant-Ivory productions a couple of years ago, he announced that young filmmakers today are simply incapable of making films of the same quality as Ismael Merchant and James Ivory. The poor man seems to really believe that film school graduates are responsible for the dreck his studio puts out, and that there is nothing young filmmakers would rather do than make drivel like *Monkey Trouble* (1994).

Disney may be good at exploiting young filmmakers, but they are only imitating an earlier master of the art. Roger Corman has been hiring film students and other energetic youngsters to make his discount exploitation films for more than three decades. While Corman is less reliable and less wealthy than Disney, and while most of his crews curse him for his cheapness during production, many of the people once exploited by him are now in the top ranks of Hollywood directors. Corman and Disney do about the same thing—both shamelessly exploit young filmmakers. But Disney does not have the track record that Corman has, and Disney would like people to believe they are more reputable than Corman. Don't believe it for a second.

Independent features go through phases like the rest of the industry—which films are picked up for distribution often has more to do with content than quality. After *sex lies and videotape* (1991) became a huge hit for Miramax, suddenly only independent films with sex in them got distribution deals. Then there was the strange trend toward impossibly low budgets that favored films made for less and less money—*Laws of Gravity* (1992) cost less than $20,000 to make. *My Life's in Turnaround* (1994) cost about $30,000. *El Mariachi* (1993) cost $7,000 (although the studio spent a million dollars fixing the sound before it was released). Why this trend? It probably had something to do with free publicity: at that time, in the worst of the recession, the press liked to print stories about filmmakers making films with no money.

Executives and technicians who work in the industry are still openly hostile toward film school graduates. It is generally believed that film students are stuck-up without having the talent or experience to justify their arrogance. Producers see film students as troublesome upstarts who may have skills but who do not have the experience to make good films. Technicians see film students as usurpers who expect to jump ahead of them in the line waiting to direct—and *everyone* is in line waiting to direct.

Hollywood is now, as ever, a harsh place for a film school graduate. There are opportunities, but they are scarce, and every year ten thousand more film students graduate and move to Hollywood to compete for a handful of jobs.

What no Hollywood executive wants to admit is that Hollywood needs film schools. Young filmmakers are and will continue to be the key to the young audiences who account for the largest portion of the filmgoing public. These young filmmakers need to learn the art and craft of film somewhere, but the studios are not willing to pay for that education as they once did through apprenticeships and assistantships.

While executives today gripe about film students, the fact is that the studios are getting the best end of the deal by far. What other industry in the world can get away with requiring new workers to take $75,000 worth of education before they can find even a menial job, and can get away with refusing to pay for a cent of that training? Well, okay, the same thing has happened in law and business. But in law and business there is a virtual guarantee of highly paid work at the end of the education—which is, in effect, the same as paying for the education. Most film school graduates do not find work at the end of school. Most wind up paying off their student loans years or decades after graduation, often with money they earn outside the film industry.

So while the film industry is the single largest beneficiary of film education, it does not pay a penny toward it. This shortsightedness is what brought Hollywood to the sad state it is now in, and it is what will cause Hollywood's continuing downward slide. Studios will argue that profits are now higher than ever, but they will not mention that their share of the profits is, in fact, dwindling. Better films are being made not only at independent production companies in the U.S., but all around the world. Better-quality entertainment can often be found on television, of all places, thanks to new cable networks. Hollywood is no longer the source of either the highest quality, or the most entertaining films. Look at the Academy Awards in recent years, where independent films have received most of the nominations in the top categories, while Hollywood's films have been left to compete for awards in sound editing and special effects. Look at Hong Kong's film industry, which often makes films ten times more entertaining than anything Hollywood puts out. Hollywood now has some stiff competition, and with nothing but poorly trained filmmakers making lowest-common-denominator entertainments to save it, it seems doomed to continue to lose out, and ultimately waste away.

This is where you come in. Yes, you, who are destined to save cinema from the many powerful forces working to ruin it. Always remember that you have this responsibility on your shoulders. Your goal must not be image or wealth; your goal must be to make great films. If your only goal is success or wealth, you will either fail or you will succeed by cursing the world with more of the same bad movies that we already have too many of. But if you aspire to make great films, you will make the world a better place, and success and fame will come to you. Plus, you will rescue film. It is for this reason you will go to film school. You will learn to speak in the Language of Cinema, and you will use it to say the things that must be said. You will not make films that feature hyper-intelligent monkeys or star alumni of *Saturday Night Live*. You will not make a Pauly Shore vehicle. You will make powerful, intelligent films that no one but you could ever make. You are the future of this industry, the future of this most visceral of art forms, the future of entertainment. Welcome aboard! We can't wait to see your first film.

Before You Go

If you are like most film school applicants, you have toyed with the idea of going to film school for some time. If you are bothering to read this book, then you are now considering film school seriously enough to actually throw some time and effort into research. At this critical juncture, there is a lot you should know about film schools—the different kinds of film schools, how much they'll cost, how long they'll take, what you can expect to get out of them. This chapter will give you the lowdown—everything you should know before you decide to go, and everything you should know to determine which school will be best for you.

What You Should Plan to Get Out of Film School

Film school provides an environment where you can learn how to make films. This much is obvious. But what good is that skill when you graduate? If you flash your diploma at a studio executive, will she give you money to make a feature? Is a degree enough?

Of course not. The only thing an M.F.A. will do for you is make you eligible to teach. To direct, you need to come out of school with proof of your talents. The graduates who have come out of film schools and made features in the last few years always have two things in common: a good short film that they wrote and directed and a good feature-length screenplay that they wrote and hoped to direct. If you want to direct, one of these is not enough. The film is proof that you have talent; the screenplay is proof that you have more to offer than one short film. Neither one is worth anything without the other.

A Good Short Film

The most important single reason for a young director to go to film school is to make a film. You need to make a fabulous, stunning film that shows off all your talents. This is the only thing that will make producers or investors have enough faith in you as a director to give you financial backing. No one is going to let you direct a feature based on a degree alone, so if you come out of film school without a film, you might as well not have gone to film school at all.

Filmmaking is like kissing. You can read about it and discuss it and watch other people do it, but you'll never really learn how until you do it yourself. The best a film school can do is give you equipment with which to go out and make your own films. If it also offers classes in editing and lighting and producing, so much the better. But you have to make a film if you want to become a director. This has to be your prime consideration in choosing a school.

Some schools allow anyone who pays tuition to make films with the school's equipment. Other schools only choose a handful of students to make films, making all the others work as crew on these few films. If you go to one of the latter schools, you have to be aware that there is only a slim chance that you will have the opportunity to direct a film. You don't want to find yourself two or three years older, sixty or seventy thousand dollars poorer, and no nearer a job in the film industry than you were at enrollment.

Many students decide to make feature-length films for their thesis projects. Most who do this learn the hard way that it is a bad course to pursue. The first problem most run into is that they just aren't ready to write and direct a feature-length film, and that their films just aren't very good. They do not yet have enough feel for structure and rhythm to create a captivating 100-minute-long film. But even if a student does make a good feature-length film, she will often find that no festival will program it and no distributor will look at it. While students can sometimes get these films into festivals, it is rare that the films ever see a profit or a wide audience. Student-made features, while intended to be feature length, usually end up being about sixty or seventy minutes long—too short to fill a feature slot but too long to fit into a program of shorts at a festival.

In short, a stunning short film packed with good writing, good direction, and good performances will usually benefit a filmmaker more than a merely watchable feature-length film.

A Good Feature-Length Screenplay

As important as the thesis film is, it is unfortunate that film schools place so much emphasis on it and so little on what comes afterward. Even if the film you make is the best student film ever made (and there are a couple of those every year), it is still little more than a calling card. Like a good resume in another field, the best it can do is open a few doors. If you don't have a screenplay to follow it up, those doors will close just as quickly as they opened.

Always remember that several thousand hopefuls are only semesters away from opening their own doors. For every Phil Jouanou who gets to make a film right after graduation there are thousands of nameless, no-less-talented film school graduates still struggling for their break. So if you are lucky enough to receive phone calls from agents and producers who loved your thesis film, you have to have at least one screenplay to show them—immediately. Without that screenplay, you might as well not have made the film.

The film industry is full of big ideas, but it is almost completely devoid of good new screenplays. There are tens of thousands of screenplays out there, but few of them are even remotely original or good. If you write a good one, then you have power. If you also have a short film that has won awards in festivals and is showing as filler on cable TV, you have even more power. Neither of these alone is enough power to get you a deal. But together they can be enough to convince producers and agents to take a chance on you.

Things to Think About When Applying

Allow us to generalize for a moment. Ready? Okay. Here is our generalization: There are three kinds of film schools: industry, independent, and experimental.

The industry schools, most typified by USC and AFI, train students to insinuate themselves into the Hollywood system with the expectation that producers will give them large amounts of money to make feature films. The independent schools like UCLA, NYU, and Columbia train students to strip down their filmmaking to the barest essentials and then raise their own money to make their films, independently of the Hollywood system. The experimental schools like Cal Arts and the San Francisco Art Institute don't teach students to raise large amounts of money or to make feature films. They teach students only the art of film and encourage them to make art without any thought of the business of film.

None of these is better than the others; it's a matter of personal preference. Independent feature filmmaking is hard work and financially risky, but it gives you complete artistic control within the limits of your financial backing. The industry is hard to get into, and it restricts creativity to whatever is marketable, but once you are accepted you can be financially secure for life. Experimental filmmaking is a calling, not a living. Its chief practitioners do it because they are driven to, not because they expect to make money doing it.

The independent schools encourage independence both in school and out of school. They provide their students with equipment, but the students have to come up with their own money to pay for film stock, transportation, food, and so on. The students have a great deal of freedom to make the films they choose, but the financial burden can be staggering.

AFI and USC provide a substantial amount of funding for the films their students make. This reduces the financial burden on students considerably. But the students pay a high price in other ways; every student wants to write and direct a film, but at USC the faculty only chooses a handful whose films the school will fund. As a result, students spend most of their first few years trying to divine what the faculty wants. Students write scripts to appeal to the faculty. Instead of creating an original work with an original viewpoint, students make practice films to show off their flashy technique, not to experiment with new techniques (and risk failure) in order to learn how best to tell a story in an appropriate way. Another drawback is that industry schools like AFI and USC claim ownership of every film made with their equipment. Students might be allowed to keep copies for their own use, but they are not allowed to enter their films in competitions or to distribute them without the schools' express consent.

Each kind of film school reflects that part of the real world in microcosm. The independent schools are microcosms of independent filmmaking—these filmmakers never have quite enough money for what they want to do and help one another out as best they can. The Hollywood-style film schools are a microcosm of industry filmmaking, where there are fabulous riches to be had, but only for a few lucky people, and the students compete furiously with one another to try to get their hands on it. The experimental schools are full of quiet, artistic people who mostly work alone on shadowy projects that few eyes ever see. As such, film school can teach you more about the filmmaking way of life than about the technique of filmmaking.

More people are applying to film schools now than ever before. The most popular film schools now have to turn down twenty applicants or more for every one they accept. Every year thousands of people are graduating from film schools and trying to make a living in the film industry. Is this a good thing? Colleges won't ask this question; the more students they accept, the more tuition they bring in and the better the odds that one of their alumni will succeed and make a large donation to the school. The film industry won't ask this question; studios don't want to have to invest in training new filmmakers, and making the kids pay for their own training is a great solution for them. Film students won't ask this question; they might not be in film school if fewer were accepted. Since nobody else is willing to tackle this question, we are going to have to do it here and now.

Filmmaking is not an easy career. Save for the one or two lucky people in any given year who get to direct something, almost everyone who comes out of film school has to find work outside of the industry. Unfortunately, a degree in film production is not much help—most film school graduates wind up temping or doing other low-paid, low-skilled labor to survive until their luck turns around.

Our recommendation is this: If you want to study film, wait until graduate school. Do not get a bachelor's degree in film production. It is very important to have a well-rounded education no matter what industry you work in, and if you have to find other work to support yourself for a few years before you can work in film, an academic degree will help you much more than a film degree. But an academic degree will also help you to make films. You need to know how to write a story before you can write a screenplay. You need to know about psychology and sociology, political science and economics if you want to create complete, realistic characters. You need to know about other cultures and ways of life if you want to put your own in perspective.

Film is a language, and like all languages it's not much good if you don't have anything to say. A well-rounded education will build your vocabulary of experiences and enrich your life. We strongly recommend that you study literature or history or political science, or an exact science, or just about anything academic as an undergraduate. We also recommend that you see some of the world, whether by traveling through it or working in it, and experience some of what it has to offer before you go to film school.

There are filmmakers out there right now writing screenplays and directing films who have not seen anything of the world other than what they have seen in movies. As a result, many of the films being made now are not about life; rather they are about what the filmmakers think life is like based on movies they have seen. This is unfortunate for audiences, who have to sit through these empty, pointless films, and it is unfortunate for the filmmakers, who may have learned great technical skills, but who will never make a great film.

Film school will give you a powerful voice with which to speak, but it will not give you things to say. You need to bring your own views and opinions with you when you start. Learning enough to form opinions is what undergraduate study is for. We recommend you use it that way.

At any rate, it is because we feel so strongly about this that we are only discussing graduate schools in this book.

Yeah, we hear you asking, But why are we only covering M.F.A. programs? Why not all the M.A. programs that are out there? We are only covering programs that offer a Master of Fine Arts degree because the M.F.A. degree, unlike the M.A., requires students to make a creative thesis—a film. The M.F.A. is a terminal degree, not unlike a Ph.D., which requires students to make a film rather than write a dissertation. As we have already asserted, a good film is the most valuable thing you can get out of film school. Also, the M.F.A. degree, unlike the M.A. degree, is a teaching degree: after you graduate you can teach at the university level, which significantly raises your chances of finding gainful employment that uses your skills.

How Much Is This Going to Cost?

Film school is expensive. Once you have paid your tuition, which can be more than $20,000 a year for three years or more, and once you have paid for room and board for up to four years, you may still have to buy film stock, rent extra equipment or vehicles, feed large casts and crews, pay for locations, or reimburse people for damaged equipment or property (don't laugh—there is always damaged equipment or property).

Most of the schools purposely play this aspect down. And for good reason: if you knew at the outset what you would have to spend by the end of film school, you might very likely chuck the whole idea.

Which is not to say that it cannot be done relatively inexpensively. There are ways of saving money. There are inexpensive schools, and there are ways of getting through the expensive schools at a discount rate. For each school we will provide a rough estimate of how much the program costs and give hints on how to save money along the way.

There are schools that are unbelievably expensive, and there are schools that are unbelievably inexpensive. But beware—the cheap ones are not always a bargain, and the expensive ones are not always a rip-off.

As mentioned, the most important thing you can get out of film school is a completed film. The cheapest way to do this is to find a public university with a small, little-known film program that has the equipment necessary to make a film. There are quite a few of these schools—universities that offer basic film classes and access to some rudimentary equipment in exchange for a couple of thousand dollars a year tuition. Probably the most attractive feature of these schools is the idea of spending the money you would have spent on tuition at, say, NYU and putting it all into your films. If you are self-motivated enough so that all you need is access to equipment and an accident-insurance policy (insurance is expensive, but it is absolutely essential), this kind of school might be for you. In many cases, it would cost more to rent filmmaking equipment from an equipment house for two weeks than to pay a public university's tuition for an entire year. But beware—there are inexpensive schools with great equipment, and there are inexpensive schools with terrible equipment. While we have tried our best to detail in this book the equipment available at each of the schools, we can't guarantee that the equipment we describe will be available or working by the time you get there. If you decide to go this route, be sure to visit the schools you are considering and ask to see their equipment. And be sure to talk to some current students—grill them about how well the equipment works, how accessible it is, and how efficient the maintenance staff is when the equipment goes down.

The inexpensive schools will give you the solitude and freedom to do your own thing. But you will be as much on your own after school as during school. You will not have a large network of alumni to call on for advice or assistance, and your school will do nothing to promote you or your work. On the other hand, if you have a good film, and if you have the chutzpah to promote it, to enter it into festivals and to show it to producers and agents, then you will be better off than the film students at the bigger schools, who often patiently wait in vain for their schools to promote them and provide them with contacts.

The most expensive schools are big schools—schools with too many students and not enough equipment. These schools have to ration their equipment—they may have good equipment, but they will only give it to you for a week or two per year, which may or may not be enough time to shoot your film. And you may find yourself editing from two to six in the morning on Sundays because the editing machines are reserved for all the other times. These schools will surround you with a diverse and supportive community of filmmakers. You will work on your classmates' films, and they will work on yours, and through this interchange you will learn everything you need to know about filmmaking. These schools will provide better chances of making contacts in the outside world and better exposure after graduation. Whether the contacts and exposure are worth the extra tens of thousands of dollars is a difficult call.

There are other advantages and disadvantages that are hard to quantify. For instance, some schools have more cachet in Hollywood than others. If you tell a producer you went to USC, she'll probably smile grimly and change the subject. Because of the school's size and location, USC alumni—graduate and undergraduate—make up a large portion of the film community in L.A. You can't throw a rock in Hollywood without hitting a USC graduate, and chances are the one you would hit has never made a film. So producers will often be impressed if you tell them you graduated from any school other than USC—from Columbia, or Florida State, of the Chicago Art Institute, or AFI. But, on the other hand, they are only impressed by schools they have heard of: you won't wow anyone in Hollywood by telling them you went to Ohio or Carbondale or Milwaukee.

Still, if you made a great film at Ohio or Carbondale or Milwaukee, and won awards, and had it shown at major festivals, then you won't need to wow them with your degree. A great short film is worth more than a certificate from the best film program (especially when it is accompanied by a great feature-length screenplay).

Student loans are available to most students. But while other expensive fields of study like medicine or law give a virtual guarantee of lucrative employment after graduation, making it possible to pay off loans fairly quickly, film programs offer no such guarantee. Indeed, the vast majority of film school graduates are unemployed for some time after they graduate. New York and Los Angeles are already stuffed with M.F.A. graduates from respected institutions who write screenplays in the evenings while they temp or wait tables or fill out unemployment forms during the day.

It is important that you know this from the start. We have done our best to include cost-cutting tips for each school, but it will still be a very expensive undertaking. And don't say you haven't been warned: unless you are independently wealthy, deciding to go to film school is essentially deciding to be in debt for the next ten years.

How Long Will This Take?

The major film schools are remarkably dishonest about the time their programs require. USC calls itself a three-year program, but in fact it takes four, or five, or six years. NYU calls itself a three-year program, but no one has ever graduated in less than four years. On the other hand, some schools call themselves two-year programs and really are two-year programs.

Each school has different time restrictions: some kick students out at the end of classes, others allow students to continue to haunt the school, wandering the halls like the undead, as long as they keep paying to matriculate. In order to make this as clear as possible, we have included information for each school on how long the program will really take.

Will Film School Bring You Closer to Your Goals?

Many people who want to go to film school don't have a specific career in mind, only a general desire to be in the movies. This can be unfortunate, as many ultimately decide to pursue a career that is not helped by a degree.

For instance, we know of several people who finished three years of graduate film school only to decide that they wanted to be film editors. It is likely that, had they known three years earlier that they wanted to be editors, they could have gotten jobs as assistant editors and worked their way up through the ranks for three years. Not only would they be much closer to their career goals at the end of the three years, but they also would have been making money, rather than spending money they didn't have on tuition.

Compared with directing, fields like editing, sound, cinematography and producing are not hard to get into if you are certain you want to get into them. You can start as a production assistant on any shoot, befriend the technicians in your chosen field, and get them to hire you as an assistant on their next film. It will be a few years before you work your way up to a position of any influence, but even that will certainly be sooner than it would take to finish film school and then pay off all your loans.

If you want to be a cinematographer, film school has a lot to offer. Directing students always need good cinematographers, so if you are good you can shoot your classmates' films as much as you want, get all the practice you can stand, and put together an impressive reel without spending a cent of your own money beyond tuition. And if any of the students whose films you shoot get a chance to direct a feature, you might be hired to shoot it. On the other hand, you could be doing this without paying tuition—all you need to do is hang out with the tuition-paying students until they ask you. Also, it is not that difficult to become an assistant cameraperson in the real world. Once you are in that position, it might be a few years before you get to shoot your own footage, but it is almost certain to happen, and getting there is sure to be a lot less expensive than film school.

Are You Keeping Up with the New Technology?

The high-technology revolution that has reshaped so many industries has only relatively recently found its way into the film industry. It started slowly, when Japanese high-tech firms developed small, high-quality video cameras and recorders that replaced the 16-mm film cameras of television news programs. Then consumer electronics firms adapted the technology to consumer video camcorders to replace the super-8 film cameras of amateur filmmakers. Then movie camera makers like Arriflex and Cinema Products started to put microprocessors inside their film cameras.

But for all the changes in camera technology, they still work about the same way as the old ones: you point, you shoot. Where high technology has really changed is in post-production. In the entertainment industry, most editing is now computerized. When you make a film the old-fashioned way, you shoot your negative, pay to have it processed, and then have a workprint made of the negative. Workprints are expensive: you essentially buy another roll of film, have it exposed from the negative, and then have that film processed. You then have to buy a lot of magnetic film and transfer your sound onto it. When you have your workprint and mag film ready, you rent expensive editing equipment to cut it, and when your cut is finished you rent time in an incredibly expensive mixing studio to mix the sound tracks. The new technology has made workprints, flatbed editing machines, and expensive mixing studios unnecessary; you now telecine your negative directly to video, and then digitize the video and audio tracks into a computer. Once digitized, you edit your footage and sound tracks entirely on computer. When you are happy with your cut, the program will spit out an Edit Decision List. A negative cutter can then cut your negative according to the EDL while you are still at your computer, putting the final touches on the sound track.

This is a startling change. Editing, sound design, and mixing of a twenty-minute film used to cost thousands of dollars, even tens of thousands of dollars, in materials and equipment rental. Now, you just pay for the processing of the negative and the telecine. If you go to a school that has this equipment, you can do everything but the negative cut and the answer print for free.

The fields of sound editing and sound design have changed almost beyond recognition thanks to digital audio technology. Digital audio is higher quality than analog audiotape or mag film, and it is much easier to manipulate and mix. And audio can be manipulated on a computer in ways that were unthinkable only a few years ago; camera noise, once the bane of sound technicians' existence, is now easily removed from recordings using digital audio workstations. Audio effects that once took hours of tinkering to get right can now be manufactured in seconds and saved to disk for future use. Where mixing eight sound tracks used to mean stringing up eight different mag film tracks on enormous dubbers and praying they stayed in sync and that the mag film didn't break while you were mixing, a digital workstation can easily mix *hundreds* of audio tracks at once.

Many schools are taking this technological leap, but not all. Students at some schools still edit their films on Moviola or Steenbeck editing machines, cutting and taping picture and sound tracks by hand. And many film students still mix their films on banks of magnetic film dubbers. These methods still work perfectly well for the making of a film, but they are labor-intensive, expensive, and are used less and less outside of school. Already many students find that the methods of filmmaking they learn in school are no longer marketable skills in the industry. Students who excel in editing are not able to get editing jobs because they do not know how to work an Avid or a Media 100. Students who excel in sound design are not able to find work in the industry because they do not know how to use Pro Tools.

So when you ponder applying to schools, be sure to take into account this new technology. While we have identified which schools have digital systems, this technology and its availability to students is changing faster than we can keep up with in a published book. Before you apply to a school, be sure to call and ask what equipment they have. Verify that they have Avids or Media 100s or D-Visions or Matrox systems. The higher your level of technological awareness when you are in school, the better your chances will be of finding work when you get out of school.

If you really want to go to a school, and that school does not have nonlinear editing systems, there is another option. Because computer prices continue to plummet while their capabilities multiply, there are now nonlinear editing systems affordable enough for almost anyone to buy. Many off-the-shelf computers can, with the help of a video accelerator board and a few pieces of software, edit video and record and mix sound. This means that you can own an entire post-production facility and use it in your living room for a fraction of the price of a year's tuition at one of the more expensive schools. It would in fact be cheaper to go to an inexpensive school and bring your own low-end nonlinear editing system than to go to USC or NYU, where you would be lucky to get time on the Avid anyway. So why even go to film school if you can own the whole studio? Well, unfortunately, movie cameras are still terribly expensive. As are tungsten lights and high-quality sound-recording equipment. As is insurance, in case any of those tungsten lights explodes.

Also, while a desktop computer can do a lot of the same things as a fifty-thousand-dollar Avid system, it is not a fifty-thousand-dollar Avid system—and in order to get a job as an editor after school, you will need to have experience on a real Avid. So buying your own nonlinear editing system is not a replacement for going to film school. But it is an option that can make film school a lot easier, and a lot less expensive.

The biggest problem with nonlinear editing systems is that they are incredibly complex pieces of machinery, and it can take a long time to learn how to use them. Where the old film and tape method of editing was pretty easy to learn, the new method requires considerable knowledge of computer hardware and software, of video formats, film formats, and how film formats transfer over to video formats, of RAM and SCSI, of data busses and disk arrays. A lot of schools are buying these machines, but many are finding that they don't have the extra staff required to teach students how to use them properly—or even to learn how to use them properly themselves. Most schools find they have to hire extra technicians to maintain the systems and to educate everyone else about how to use them. The schools that can't afford the extra staff will sometimes set up the equipment, let the students figure out for themselves how to use it, and then ask the students to show the faculty what they have learned. For the technically aware this can be an exciting opportunity, but for everyone else it is likely to be maddening.

Beyond editing, new technologies have also opened up whole new fields for those who want to work in visual media. Digital effects work has become huge business in recent years, and digital animators are in such demand that they are recruited directly out of school like lawyers or MBAs. Interactive games on CD-ROM often contain as much live-action footage as a movie, and many filmmakers and film technicians are as likely to work on a CD-ROM shoot as a movie shoot. And even the World Wide Web, for all its limitations, is proving to be a fascinating new visual medium. Today, young people who are technologically proficient and skilled in visual storytelling can easily find challenging, well-paid work in almost any of these fields—and new fields are opening up all the time.

But in order to work in any of these fields you will need to choose a school that can teach you the new technologies.

Are You Throwing Your Money Away?

In this strange culture that is America in the nineties, most people seem to feel that paying someone to tell them they can do something is just as rewarding as actually doing it. It is of course much easier to spend fifteen bucks on *Men Are from Mars, Women Are from Venus* than to actually work on improving one's relations with the opposite sex—but we now seem to believe that it is every bit as noble. Likewise it's much easier to throw money at books on how to be a screenwriter, or on screenwriting software, or on ludicrously expensive screenwriting symposia—or even on film school—than it is to put some time and effort into writing a screenplay.

It pains us to see just how wealthy Robert McKee, John Truby and their ilk have become teaching courses in and selling books about screenwriting. Quick—what was the last movie you saw that was written by one of these guys? You can't name one because none of them has ever had a screenplay made into a film. There are two reasons why you will never see any movies written by these guys: 1) because they don't know how to write, and 2) because they have learned where the real money is. Each has learned that people like us might pay seven fifty to see a movie he wrote, but that we will pay twice that for a book, or dozens of times that for a seat in a big meeting room in a hotel near the airport to listen to him tell us that we can be screenwriters.

The film schools are also guilty of this kind of hucksterism, if a little less cynically. "Look at our past graduates," they seem to say in the materials they send out. "Pay us twenty grand a year and you can be just like George Lucas, or Spike Lee, or John Singleton." There is never any mention of how hard these filmmakers had to work after they got their degrees to get where they are now, or of how lucky they had to be. There is no suggestion that film school was only a small piece of a very big picture. In the schools' materials it is always a simple equation:

$$\text{You} + \text{Your Savings} + \text{Our School} = \text{The Next Martin Scorsese}$$

We would be remiss in not pointing out that we, too, are profiting (a bit) from stroking your ego—You bought our book, didn't you? But we're not going to tell you that, having bought our book, you will now become the Next Big Thing. (If you ever see either of us teaching a $300 symposium on how to be a film student, just shoot us, okay?) Filmmaking is hard work, and we're not about to tell you otherwise. Writing is, in some ways, even harder. There is no book or symposium or school that will turn you into a filmmaker or writer. Nothing but hard work will do that.

It would be bad enough if the John Trubys and Robert McKees were just swiping money from those who don't know better. But they are also spewing a simplistic dramatic theory that has wreaked havoc on the state of writing in Hollywood. By emphasizing the three-act-and-two-plot-point structure *über alles,* they have, more than anyone else alive, strangled dramatic writing in Hollywood. Sure, three-act structure is a proven template for dramatic story-telling. But it's not the only structure, and a good writer knows that structure is dictated by content, not the other way around. It is because of these simplistic teachings that Hollywood executives now read screenplays by glancing at page 30 (the first plot point) and page 90 (the second), and then tossing them away—anything that departs from this structure is dismissed as bad writing. It is largely because of this that there is so little good dramatic writing in movies today: writers are punished for trying any sort of experimentation but are rewarded with obscene amounts of money for repeatedly doing the same old thing.

A friend showed us a screenplay recently that was essentially in two parts. He complained that he was having trouble finding a way to fit these two parts into the standard three-act structure. We suggested that, in fact, the story might just be a two-act drama. This suggestion was met by a long silence and an uncomprehending gaze. The mere suggestion that there might be such a thing as a two-act drama was so unusual—so subversive—as to be unthinkable.

Pop quiz:

Q: How many acts are there in *Hamlet*? *Romeo and Juliet*? *Julius Ceasar*? *King Lear*?
A: Each has five acts.
Q. How many acts in *Long Day's Journey Into Night*? *The Crucible*? *Waiting for Godot*?
A: Four, four, and two.

Clearly these hacks, these so-called writers named Shakespeare, O'Neill, Miller, and Beckett know nothing about dramatic structure. If they were real dramatists they would know that a drama can only be in three acts. It's a shame this Shakespeare guy isn't alive. If he were, he could plunk down a couple of hundred bucks and learn from Robert McKee the correct way to write a drama.

Are we ranting? Sorry. Here's our beef in a nutshell: You can learn a lot more about dramatic structure and character by going to the library and reading a bunch of plays than by listening to someone tell you why *The Godfather* or *Star Wars* is the greatest example of the screenplay ever written. Not that Mario Puzo and George Lucas aren't reasonably good hacks—it's just that Ibsen and O'Neill and Shaw are a lot better. Why bother to learn from the B-student (Puzo or Lucas), or from the B-student's B-student (McKee or Truby) when you can learn directly from one of the masters? And best of all, the masters won't charge you a cent.

Speaking of hucksterism, there are institutions that offer a few weeks' worth of intensive classes for a few thousand dollars. You may have seen ads for them in magazines like *Premiere* and *Entertainment Weekly*. Businesses like the New York Film Academy don't offer degrees, but they do offer the opportunity to use their equipment to make a short film for much less money than a real film school. They are exploitative by nature: they always locate themselves near well-known schools, and they give themselves names that sound like well-known schools. The New York Film Academy, for instance, has no connection to New York University's Film School, and Columbia College Hollywood has nothing to do with the film programs at Columbia University or Columbia College in Chicago.

These places do offer an inexpensive alternative to accredited film schools: they provide access to equipment, and they allow students to make short films. But, like the aforementioned screenwriting teachers, they operate not by teaching students the art of filmmaking but by telling students that they can be filmmakers and sharing a few basic elements of the craft. The message is that students are already geniuses who only need access to equipment to become genius filmmakers. Now, there may be one or two people in the world for whom this is true, but for the vast majority of us film school is the place where we go to learn how to tell stories in a visual medium, to learn to communicate in the language of film. It may be possible to learn the technical end of filmmaking in a couple of weeks, but it is not possible to learn the art and language of filmmaking in that time. That takes years of study and experimentation, and it is those years of study and experimentation that accredited universities offer. Saying that you can learn the art of filmmaking in a six-week technical program is like saying that you can be a great writer by taking a course in how to use a word processor.

This is not to say that the New York Film Academy is necessarily a bad place. It's just not a film school and should not be confused with one.

Preparation

There are some things you can do before going to film school that will help you to get in and give you a head start once you are in.

Take Some Writing Courses

Most film schools have come to the realization that if they are going to teach their students directing, lighting, editing, camera, and sound then they will not have time to teach them to write. At many schools this realization has led to a policy of only accepting applicants who already demonstrate writing ability. Consequently, we recommend that you work on your writing skills as much as possible now.

Writing is an indispensable skill in film school, and in the industry. When you apply to school, if you can show the ability to write an original story you are miles ahead of most of the other applicants. In film school, if you can write good short screenplays, then you are miles ahead of most of your classmates. After film school when you are out in the real world, if you can write good feature-length screenplays, then you are miles ahead of everyone else in the industry.

Screenplays represent power. Every person in the industry— actor, director, producer, cameraman, designer, and so on down the line—flatters herself that she is a creative genius. But in truth, if the film she works on is badly written, then her genius will never be noticed. It is the writer who creates the characters for which the actors take credit. It is the writer who creates the settings for which the designers take credit. It is the writer who creates the story and situations for which the director takes credit. All the other crafts merely build upon what the writer creates. So while nobody will ever admit it, a screenwriter is the most creative person in the industry. And good screenwriters wield power. (If you don't believe this, remember that the only person who ever publicly told off Michael Ovitz and got away with it was a writer. Well, okay, it was Joe Esterhasz. We didn't say it was a *good* writer.)

We cannot encourage you strongly enough to take courses in writing, write stories and screenplays, keep a journal, and generally polish your writing skills as much as you possibly can.

Take Some Acting Courses

If you want to direct, you must take acting courses. Actors have a language of their own, and directors must be conversant in this language to be able to direct them. Audiences don't watch movies to see cool camera angles; they watch movies to see characters they can empathize with in situations they can relate to. The actors who portray these characters are the most important element in your film, and if you know how they work, how they talk, and how they feel, you will have a great advantage when it comes time to direct them.

It is a common mistake for first-time directors to concentrate on camera angles and effects and forget about the actors. This is unfortunate as actors can be an emotional and contentious lot. They need to be coddled and flattered if they are going to give good performances. When a director does not give an actor a script, when a director makes an actor sit around for hours with nothing to eat while the crew sets up lights, when a director's only instructions to an actor are "Okay, in this shot I want you to walk over to that railing and look out at the sailboats with a sad, yet whimsical smile," the actor gets cranky and looks unhappy on screen. And if the actor looks uncomfortable, then nobody will be interested in the story and nobody will care if you have cool camera angles or neat effects.

If you take acting courses you will have a valuable appreciation of the actor's craft, and you will avoid a number of the worst mistakes that first-time filmmakers make.

Make Some Films

The best way to learn how to make a film is to get out there and do it. If you have a friend or family member who has a video camera or a super-8 film camera, you should borrow it and make as many films as you can.

When we say you should make films, we don't mean you should shoot bar mitzvahs or Little League games. Rather, we mean you should sit down and write a five- or ten-minute story and find friends to act in the roles you write. Then make people watch your film. When someone sits and watches your work you will find yourself saying, "Hey, that scene would have been better if I'd shot it in close-up," or, "There's too much going on in this scene. I should have simplified it," or "Gee, my sister is a lousy actress—I'll have to cast someone better next time." That is how you learn to make films: by making mistakes and then figuring out how to do it better next time.

If you are an undergraduate at a school that offers film courses, you would do well to take one or two courses that allow you to shoot films or videos. This is a great opportunity to experiment with writing and directing, and get feedback from a receptive audience of classmates. Some film schools like to see examples of work from their applicants, so this could also help you in the admissions process.

While You Are There

Let's say you are accepted into film school. You move to that school, enroll, pay your tuition, and start taking classes. Now what?

The first thing you will discover is that you are spending more money than you had planned. Here are some suggestions for how to deal with that.

Save Money

The single best way to save money (and at the same time make money) is to become a teaching assistant. Most universities pay part or all of their TAs' tuition and, on top of that, a stipend. Because TAs work closely with the faculty, they can often get more equipment than they deserve when it is time to shoot their films—so they do not have to spend money on renting additional equipment. And when a school decides to give out a cash award to some lucky student, it almost always goes to a TA.

You can also save a lot of money on housing by becoming a resident assistant (RA) in a school's dormitory. RAs get free housing and all the free dormitory food they can stand. Rent and food are so outrageously expensive in New York, for example, that you could probably pay for all your films just with the money you save by being an RA. Rent is cheaper in other cities so, depending on where you are living, being an RA may not be as good a deal. But no matter where you are in the country, free room and board is nothing to scoff at.

When it comes time to make your thesis film, do not make the common assumption that expensive effects or complicated shots will make your film good. Many students have made films for next to nothing that were shot entirely in their own apartments and have gone on to wide acclaim. These students knew that the secret to a

good film is not in the technology but in the writing. If the characters are vivid, if the situations are realistic and intriguing, then fancy
camera shots are not necessary. It costs nothing to write a good
story, but no amount of money will make a bad story into a good
film.

You can save money on film stock. There are companies in New
York and Los Angeles that buy unused stock from professional film
shoots and resell it at a significant discount. This is a great way to
save as much as 25 percent of the going price of raw stock.

One more thing. There is a way to save money at film school before you even start: Take some film classes at your local college or
university. Most schools will allow you to transfer credits from
other institutions. So if you can come into a film school with twelve
credits of basic film production already under your belt, you might
be able to save yourself a whole semester's worth of tuition and living expenses.

Make Money

There are a number of ways to make money while you are in
school. The first thing to do is apply for financial aid—if you can
get an all-expenses-paid fellowship, you will not have to worry
about money at all.

Most schools offer work-study programs where students are paid
close to the minimum wage for working as projectionists or in the
equipment room. These are a better deal in the less expensive parts
of the country than in New York, San Francisco, or Los Angeles. In
these large, expensive cities work-study hardly seems worth the effort—the pay is usually less than what jobs outside the school pay,
and the work is usually pretty dull. The main benefit of a work-
study position is it might get you closer to the faculty, and thus into
a better position to get a teaching assistantship

Wherever you go in the country, wages and living expenses will
dictate what are the best ways to make money. In New York wages
are high, but so is the cost of living. If you can find a word-
processing job that is either flexible or on a swing-shift schedule,
you can make $20 an hour—more if you know graphics, desktop
publishing, or multimedia. Bartending is lucrative and flexible,

though you have to learn to deal with drunken New Yorkers. Waiting tables is another possibility, though then you have to deal with hungry New Yorkers, which is even worse than dealing with drunken New Yorkers. Los Angeles is a less expensive city, but wages are much, much lower. Temping is not as good an alternative in Los Angeles—you will have to commute hours every day to earn between $9 and $12 an hour, which is very hard to live on in this fairly expensive city. If you can stand it, restaurant work in Los Angeles is flexible and fairly lucrative.

It is also possible to work in film in many of the cities where there are film schools. New York, Los Angeles, Miami, Chicago, San Francisco, and Washington, D.C., all have regular film production—both local work, like commercials and industrial films, and the occasional feature. Production companies will sometimes post notices on school bulletin boards looking for people to work as production assistants. PA work will generally pay from $75 to $150 per day to start, and as you get better at it you can ask for more. In Los Angeles work in the film industry is more plentiful, but you will have to compete with perky undergrads who are still living off their parents, and who can thus afford to work for very little money. PA work is a good way to learn how a real film shoot operates (as opposed to a student film shoot), and to learn about gaffing and grip equipment (which is something you won't learn much about at most schools). The drawbacks of PA work are gruelingly long days (which always seem to conflict with schoolwork) and stultifying work (you will spend most of your time stocking the crew's snack table with donuts and coffee).

Film vs. Video

The use of video has grown astoundingly in recent years. In one decade video has displaced film as the medium of choice for most productions.

There are many reasons for this. One is that most productions nowadays are only intended to be seen on video. Be they television shows, commercials, music videos, corporate films, industrial films, or multimedia presentations, these productions will never be seen on anything but video monitors, so there is little benefit in shooting them on film. Thanks to the high cost of the silver hallides used in motion picture film, and of the chemicals required to process them, film is much more expensive than video. And with video there is no lag time between shooting and screening. If a Director of Photography on a set is worried about how a take looks, she need not wait until dailies return the next morning to find out— she can just rewind the tape and look at it, and if there is indeed a problem there she can immediately get another take.

Which is not to say that film is doomed. While video has many advantages over film, it still has a problem of image. Video looks mechanical. It is a prosaic medium that captures images with little grace or artistry. Film is more expensive, but it provides a much nicer image and looks both more lifelike and more artistic. And best of all, unlike video, film has an image so fine that it can be projected on huge screens in enormous theaters without appearing grainy.

Of course, video manufacturers have been trying to break into theatrical production, which is the last part of the entertainment industry that still uses film almost exclusively. Some feature films have already been shot on High Definition Television (HDTV). While the final results are admittedly difficult to discern from film, it costs about the same as film, requires the same amount of effort to produce as film, and ultimately has to be transferred over to film in order to be projected in theaters. Because HDTV does not offer any significant economic advantages over film, it has yet to make a real dent in film's hegemony. This may change when HDTV televisions start selling in this country and television stations start broadcasting HDTV signals. But for now, HDTV does not provide enough benefits to be a worthwhile medium for feature film production.

While no DP will shoot ordinary video with the intention of ultimately distributing it on film, many DPs will shoot film with the intention of distributing it on video. Video, when transferred to film, looks grainy and washed-out, and it retains those ugly video lines. But film, when transferred to video, retains much of its crisp look. Many television shows are shot on film—especially the one-hour dramas where the creators want a gritty real-life look. But all sitcoms, talk shows, and news programs are now shot on video; for these shows a good look is less important to the producers than a low budget. If you want a good look at how video and film differ, take a look at HBO's *The Larry Sanders Show*, which alternates between video and film: Larry's television show is shot on video, and the intrigues that go on backstage are shot on film.

Up to now we have been discussing film and video only as production media. Post-production is an entirely different matter. Video workprints have replaced film workprints as the editing medium of choice. Nearly every production made now—whether shot on film or video—is edited on video. This is because nonlinear editing systems on the market now cost about the same as film-editing systems, but they provide huge benefits in convenience and speed.

Perhaps the single greatest advantage of video over film in the editing process is that in video nothing is actually cut. On a film-editing machine the editor physically cuts the film and uses modified Scotch tape to attach it to the shots before it and after it. If a cut does not work, the editor may have to pull the shot out of the film and tape it back in its original place to make sure it is available for later use. The film editor has to be careful: she runs the risk of ruining a piece of the workprint by indiscriminately cutting and re-cutting it. And if she does ruin a part of her workprint, it can be expensive to have shots reprinted from the negative. In video editing nothing is literally cut, and editors are thus free to experiment with cuts as much as they like without running any risk of causing damage that requires expensive repairs. Also, on a film-editing machine the sound tracks are separate pieces of film that have to run in sync with the picture, and thus have to be cut at the same time and in the same precise way as the picture. This is a painstaking process where a mistake of a couple of frames can throw an entire sound track out of sync and take minutes or hours to locate and correct. In video the picture and sound track are one—when the picture is cut, the sound-track is cut with it, so there is no danger of losing sync and wasting time.

And now there is the new generation of digital nonlinear video editing machines that offer still more speed and more amazing features. Editing machines like the Avid are completely computerized editing workstations, where sound and picture are digitized and stored on high-capacity hard disks. Editing a film with one of these machines is analogous to editing a story on a word processor—shots and sound tracks can be moved around freely by clicking and dragging with a mouse, and sequences can be previewed instantly. A scene that might take days to edit on film, or hours to edit on video, can now be edited in minutes—and sound editing and mixing that took weeks using flatbeds and mag-film mixing studios can now be completed in a few minutes on the same machine.

In film school you should plan on shooting film rather than video. We say this because you will want the largest possible audience to see your work, and at the moment the largest audiences for student films are at film festivals. If you shoot video you will be limited to smaller screens at smaller video festivals, and perhaps to some cable television outlets. If you shoot film you will have access to all these venues, whether film or video. But while you should shoot on film, we recommend you edit on video. If you edit your film on video, you will learn how to use these editing systems—and will thus have a marketable skill after you graduate. If you edit on film, you will find that film editing is a skill that is in little demand outside of school.

Bring a Computer

You need to have a computer. Most schools have computers you can use for free, but you will be spending so much time on the computer that it makes much more sense to buy one.

Why will you spend so much time on the computer? Well, to write your screenplays for one thing. Screenplay format is rigid, and people won't take your screenplays seriously if you don't stick to it. It is much easier to set up standard screenplay format as a style sheet in your word processor than to remember all the tab stops on a typewriter. Your screenplays will be changing, too, as you get comments from classmates and professors, and making changes is a lot easier on a computer than on a typewriter, as you surely know already.

There are a number of computer programs that are specifically designed to make filmmaking easier. There are dedicated screenwriting programs that will automatically break down a screenplay into scenes, shots, and shooting schedules. There are programs that will help you budget, create call sheets and crew contact sheets, and help you keep track of all the little bits of information that pile up during pre-production, production, and post-production.

And lately computers have become indispensable in the actual making of films. Desktop computers can be nonlinear editing systems, CD-quality sound editing systems, special-effects production systems, animation studios, and recording studios for music sound tracks.

Most universities offer special prices on computers for students. If you do not own a computer now, be sure to take advantage of these bargains when you start film school.

Befriend the People in the Equipment Room

If you want to make films while you are in school, these people are the best friends you can have. They are probably nerds or jerks, but you have to forgive that because they are your lifeline to the equipment you need. If they like you, they will lend you the best equipment available. If they really like you, they will bend the rules for you and lend you equipment that isn't supposed to be lent out at times when no equipment is supposed to be lent out. They will help you out in a pinch.

On the other hand, if they do not like you they will make your life very difficult. They will give you their worst equipment. You and your films will suffer immensely. Even if they merely feel indifferent toward you, they will still give the best equipment to the people they really like and you will wind up with the camera that scratches film sometimes or the Nagra that often doesn't quite run at speed.

Once you have befriended the people in the equipment room, you can bug them for equipment any time you want and make the films you want to make without interference from the school. The more films you make, the more you will know the craft of filmmaking. And the more you know the craft of filmmaking, the better off you will be when it comes time to make your thesis.

If you get into one of the big film schools, the equipment is almost constantly in use, so there isn't much opportunity to get equipment on the sly. But the people in the equipment room can still be very helpful with the quality and quantity of the equipment you receive when you are allowed to borrow it.

This may be the most important thing we say in this book, so keep it in mind: Wherever you are, and whatever you do, always be nice to the people in the equipment room.

About the Schools

We have broken down our descriptions of each of the schools into three sections: The Program, The Price, and The Lowdown.

The Program describes the basic facts about the school and the film program—what the focus is, how long it takes, how classes are organized, what the specific requirements for graduation are, and so on.

The Price includes a rough estimate of how much the school will cost and some specific suggestions on how to save money and make money. The calculation is only a very rough estimate based on many variables, including tuition, length of stay, approximate rents, approximate film budgets, whether or not you will need a car, etc. Apart from tuition, we have based all these calculations on anecdotal information—average rents and film budgets according to the students we spoke with at the schools. *These figures are not the final word on how much each school will ultimately cost, only a very rough indication for the sake of comparison.*

The Lowdown includes the nitty-gritty information about the school—comments and advice, complaints and recommendations from students who have gone there. This section includes a discussion of schools' best and worst features, information about the schools' equipment and facilities and what the schools look for in applicants.

We also use the following icons to provide a way to quickly compare programs:

Equipment. We rated equipment on a four-star scale, both in terms of quality and accessibility. Some schools have great equipment that students can rarely use; others have modest equipment that students can use almost anytime. We felt these should be rated separately.

Equipment		
	Quality	Accessibility
☆	Barely good enough to make the simplest film.	The school tells you how much time you get with the equipment, and it's not enough.
☆☆	Good enough for most uses.	The school tells you how much time you get with the equipment, and it's enough to complete a good project.
☆☆☆	Good enough to make a great-looking film.	The school allows students access to equipment, as long as they reserve it in advance.
☆☆☆☆	Equipment like you would find on a Hollywood set.	Students can get cameras anytime they want.

Cost. These icons reflect the overall price of a school, based on the estimates we detail in the schools' The Price sections. Each dollar sign indicates $25,000, as follows:

$	Under $50,000
$$	$50,000 – $75,000
$$$	$75,000 – $100,000
$$$$	$100,000 – $125,000
$$$$$	Over $125,000

Focus. This indicates the kind of filmmaking in which the school specializes:

Industry schools prepare students to navigate their way through the Hollywood hierarchy, dealing with agents, producers, and studio executives.

Independent schools train students to make more personal films, and prepare them to raise their own funds by writing grants and getting investors independent of Hollywood.

Experimental schools teach students to experiment with film, and to make personal films regardless of their commercial viability.

American Film Institute

The American Film Institute
Center for Advanced Film and
 Television Studies
2021 North Western Avenue
Los Angeles, CA 90027
(213) 856-7628
http://www.afionline.org

Equipment Quality: ☆☆☆☆

Equipment Accessibility: ☆☆

Cost: $$$

Annual Tuition:	$14,700
Enrollment:	28 per year, 36 total
Deadline:	January 6
Focus:	Industry

The Program

The American Film Institute is much more than a film school. It is a large organization with three purposes: preservation (through the National Center for Film and Video Preservation), advocacy (through lobbying, and through the sponsorship of restorations, special screenings, and film festivals), and training (through the Center for Advanced Film and Television Studies). The Center for Advanced Film and Television Studies is in Los Angeles, housed in Spanish-style buildings that once belonged to a parochial school at the eastern end of Hollywood.

The program consists of six divisions: Writing, Producing, Directing, Editing, Cinematography, and Production Design. (A seventh division, focusing on New Media, is promised in the near future.) Each division accepts twenty-eight students per year, except for Editing, which accepts thirteen and Production Design, which accepts five or six. Applicants have to apply to each division separately.

AFI offers a two-year program. After the first year the school only invites a few students in each discipline to continue on into the second year where they work on big, impressive thesis projects which are largely paid for by the school. The other students are sent on their way. As you can see, the stakes are high during the first year, so competition can be brutal.

At the beginning of the first year, students introduce themselves by screening films they have already made. This is followed by what the school calls boot camp, which is one day of intensive film production intended to level the playing field somewhat, and to get students accustomed to working together. After that, classes begin and each student sets to work on the first of her three video projects. These projects are written by the Writing students, shot by the Cinematography students, designed by the Production Design students, produced by the Producing students, edited by the Editing students and directed by the Directing students. Each of these three projects runs about thirty minutes in length, and is shot on video. Each must be shot in four days and edited in four more.

The school provides production equipment and $400 for each project. Students almost always augment this budget to make their projects more flashy. The school asks that students not spend more than $2,000 of their own money on each of these projects, but in reality most of these projects wind up costing $3,000 or more. The source of this extra money varies. AFI is very much an industry school, and these films are produced as if they were industry films—the producer is expected to raise the necessary money while the other crew members focus on the creative end; though crew members wind up putting some money into these projects. Driven to show off in the hope of being among the few invited back for the second year, crew members usually want to make their own work as impressive as possible. So if the production designer wants to show off, she may have to pay for the props and sets herself. Or if the cinematographer wants to use camera movements, she might have to pay to rent a dolly herself. There are also times when the crew members come to hate one another and refuse to put any extra money into their projects at all. The school has strong ties to unions, and students may only cast their films using members of the Screen Actors Guild (SAG) Conservatory, which is also on the AFI campus. Some students find this convenient; others find it limiting.

Did we say that it is a two-year program? While that is what the school claims, it is never true. As we said, at the end of the first year the faculty chooses a few students from each of the divisions to make second-year films (which take two more years to complete) and sends the rest on their way. So the program either takes three years (if you are lucky) or one year (if you are not). A few weeks before the end of the first year, the Directing and Producing students turn in scripts they want to make as thesis films during the second year. These scripts are usually written by the Writing students, but are sometimes written by the directors themselves. Four directors are chosen to direct the scripts they turned in. Four producers are chosen to produce the scripts they turned in. Eight or nine directors and producers are chosen to return without being attached to any scripts. The four producers choose directors from this group of unattached directors to direct their scripts. And the four directors choose producers from the group of unattached producers to oversee the production of their projects. The four or five left-over directors and producers are not allowed to make films, but are allowed to earn MFAs by writing feature-length screenplays under faculty tutelage. The Cinematography, Writing, Editing, and Production Design students are also cut in this way.

That bears repeating—only eight out of twenty-eight students in each discipline get to work on a thesis film. We feel a need to underline that fact, as the AFI application package is cheerfully vague on the subject. So twenty of the twenty-eight students don't get a thesis film on their résumés. These are bad odds, and you should be aware going in that the deck is stacked against you.

The second-year projects are flashy, expensive films with very high production values. When the students who have been invited back return in the fall, they are told when they will get the equipment to shoot their projects. Projects that, in the faculty's eyes, are ready to be shot may go into production as early as November; projects that the faculty feel need more work are assigned slots later in the school year. The school provides the best production equipment available, and students have to cast members of SAG, the actor's union, to star in their projects. Because AFI has a good reputation in the industry, many AFI students get well-known actors to star in their films. The information the school sends out proudly announces that $17,000 is provided by the National Endowment for the Arts (NEA) for each second-year film. But students are usually in the process of budgeting their films when they discover that much of this amount is not in cash but in "goods and services," which may or may not be of use to any one production. Students may get $5,000 worth of services they don't need, and then have to pay out of their own pockets to feed their casts and crews. And much of the money is in the form of matching grants: students only get access to it when the producer has raised the same amount from outside sources. On every project the production team mails out requests for donations to every friend and relative of every team member. Students are allowed to match the $17,000, making the total budget $34,000, but are told not to exceed that amount. (In truth, the budget of most students' projects far exceeds that amount; the school never punishes anyone for breaking the rule.)

Students work on their films through the second year and into the third year. Because so much of the necessary money is provided by the school, AFI does not have the problem of students hanging around for four or five years while they put together the money they need to make their films. When, at the end of the third year, students have completed their thesis films, their final requirement is to put together a gala screening. They print up publicity packages, send out press releases, rent theaters, and send out thousands of invitations for the world premieres of their films.

The school does not put on an end-of-year festival or promote their graduates. The school does, however, claim ownership of every film made with school equipment. Many students are startled to discover that, after all their hard work, they are not allowed to sell their films to distributors, to hold public screenings of their films, or even to enter their films in film festivals. They have to ask the school's permission to do anything with the films they make, and in almost all cases the school cannot be bothered.

There is another important consideration if you are not a U.S. citizen: because of the federally funded NEA backing, AFI only allows U.S. citizens to direct or produce second-year films. If you are not a U.S. citizen, you may be accepted into the program, but you will not be allowed to make a thesis film under any circumstances. One has to wonder how international students at Harvard would feel if the school told them that they could pay tuition but would never be allowed to earn a degree. At any rate, if you are not a U.S. citizen, do not go to AFI. It would be a waste of time and money.

The Price

$14,700 tuition for two years	$29,400
$10,000 a year rent and living expenses for three years	$30,000
$3,000 per year maintenance and insurance on a car in Los Angeles for three years	$ 9,000
On their three first-year films, students spend around	$ 5,000
Most students put a few thousand dollars into their thesis films	$ 5,000
Total	**$78,400**

Tuition will either be $14,700 or $29,000, depending on whether you are chosen for the second year. We have estimated expenses based on two years' tuition and a three-year stay.

You will need a car in Los Angeles. Students with cars can work on any shoot they like, while students without cars are regarded as something of a burden and are, to a certain extent, shunned by their classmates. Expect car insurance alone to cost around $2,000 per year—that's what insurance rates are like in L.A.

The campus is on the eastern edge of Hollywood, in an area called Los Feliz. Housing in this area is expensive compared with other cities but inexpensive compared with the rest of Los Angeles. The streets here are less dangerous than in many parts of town (see USC). Auto theft seems to be the worst problem, so we strongly advise you to get an apartment with an enclosed garage. One-bedroom apartments within walking distance of the school go for as little as $600 a month, two-bedrooms go for around $800 or $900, studios for $500 or less.

A handful of scholarships are available. Student loans are available at rates that are no bargain. It is not possible to hold a job during the first year, but many students are able to squeeze one in during the second and third year.

The Lowdown

For the Directing Division, AFI accepts submissions of films with applications. In fact, the admissions board really only considers applicants who have extensive experience in film. Generally, if you cannot send in a good film that you directed you have very little chance of getting into the Directing program.

The Directing Division is one of the more exclusive film programs in the country. If you don't get in the first time, go make some more films and send the best of them in the next year. If you want to direct, do not apply to one of the other divisions thinking you can switch into Directing later. Switching is never allowed, so students who go in thinking they will switch are subjected to a cruel torture: they have to watch the directors make films while they are stuck editing or doing production design, and as a result become increasingly bitter as time passes. If, on the other hand, you want to study editing or cinematography or production design, AFI is a very good place to study. The tuition is low, the opportunities to work are many, and the equipment is first-rate.

First-year equipment is Sony Betacam equipment. Second-year equipment is the highest quality production equipment available—this is the only film school in the world where students get to use professional quality Panavision cameras and lenses. All projects are edited on Avids.

For the most part students speak highly of the first year, and praise it as a solid year of intense creativity. The equipment is good, and the professors are solid working professionals. The only real problem with the first year is that the second year looms over it; as the year progresses students become increasingly aware that most of them are about to be axed. By the time students are working on their third video projects, many have given up any semblance of artistic integrity, and are purely trying to appeal to their professors. Rather than creating works that come out of personal experience, they make projects that pander to the faculty, hoping to better their chances of being invited back for a second year.

If most students speak highly of the first year, few have good things to say about the second. Because each student only gets her name on one thesis project, and because she invests her own money (and that of her friends and family) on that one project, she wants some control over it. This can make for a very contentious atmosphere, and crews sometimes dissolve into warring factions, fiercely fighting over directorial and editorial decisions. This is such a common problem that the school has official policies governing these feuds. The most important of these rules is that the person who initiates a project has ultimate control over it. So, if the producer who initiated the project doesn't like a director's work, the producer can pull rank and change the film without the director's permission. As a result AFI is unique among film schools in the phenomenon of film students demanding that their names be removed from their student films. The school discourages students from removing their names, and advises those who make this demand to write to the school's lawyer. Many students back down when faced with a legal action, but several students in recent years have actually hired lawyers and sued the school to remove their names from the proj-ects they directed.

This all may sound a little hard to believe—isn't this supposed to be the ivory tower of academia? To be fair this is exactly the way the industry works, and it is somewhat fitting that an unabashedly industry school like AFI should teach filmmaking in this way. How better to learn about dealing with Hollywood producers and agents than to participate in arbitration and legal actions?

If you go to AFI, alumni strongly recommend you avoid the political (and legal) battles, which will exhaust you and leave you unable to work. They also recommend you not try to use your first-year films to pander to professors. Films made this way always lack depth or feeling, and their makers are rarely lauded for their efforts. As at any school, you should work to develop a strong personal vision and a strong directorial voice with which to present it. Forget about the faculty as much as you can, and you may well be rewarded for it. We do not mean to say that students are never rewarded for brownnosing, nor do we mean to say that artistic integrity will ensure an invitation to the second year. But we have found this to be true: It feels better to be rejected in spite of doing your best than to be rewarded for selling out.

Some of the best things about the program: It begins very well, with a screening of all the films the students sent in with their applications and then with boot camp. This is a good way of learning about the kinds of work your classmates have done, and it's a good introduction to the range of talent in your class. The school forces you to perform. From day one you will be thrown into a vortex of intense creativity and humiliating groveling, of ecstatic successes and bitter disappointments, of dear friendships and seething hatreds. Dive in and thrash around as best you can. With a little luck you'll survive the vortex and wash up on the shores of Hollywood a couple of years later with a good film in your hands.

Some of the worst things about the program: Second year. The faculty members are working professionals, and as such are often more interested in their own careers than in those of their students. This sets a bad tone. Don't expect anything from the school when you graduate. There is no end-of-year festival. The gala screening of your film is something you have to put together yourself. They firmly believe that they owe their students nothing beyond the two-year program.

At AFI, as in the real world, you are on your own.

Art Institute of Chicago

112 South Michigan Avenue
Chicago, IL 60603
Department: (312) 899-5100
Admissions: (312) 899-5219
http://www.artic.edu

Annual Tuition:	**$17,760**
Enrollment:	**9–10 per year;**
	25 total
Deadline:	**February 1**
Focus:	**Experimental**

Equipment Quality: ☆☆

Equipment Accessibility: ☆☆

Cost: $$

The Program

The film program at the School of the Art Institute of Chicago is unlike any of the other film schools described in this book. It is perhaps better to think of it not as a film school, but as an art school that teaches film among other media. The school's approach to teaching filmmaking is similar to its approach to teaching painting or sculpture. Like students in those fields, film students earn an M.F.A. in Studio, which is to say they learn through constant one-on-one interaction with the faculty. Students spend more time working alone or directly with faculty advisors than they do in classes.

Between sixty to ninety applications are received each year. Students are admitted according to the number of graduating students. There are never more than twenty-five students total. Formally this is a two-year program, with an emphasis on "new-nonfiction" films (documentary films with an experimental edge). Most students take three years to finish the program, but all work must be completed within four years.

Students must complete sixty credits during their stay, twelve of which (four classes) must be in Art History. Modern Art History must be one of these if never previously taken. The only other required course is Graduate Projects, which must be taken every semester. This is the one-on-one tutorial portion of the program. In these tutorials students discuss ideas for films they would like to make or screen works in progress. Meetings can occur as frequently or infrequently as students feel the need, with a minimum of five meetings a semester.

Students are free to fulfill the rest of their sixty credits with whatever courses interest them. They can even spend their time only studying one-on-one with faculty in Graduate Projects. Most tend to balance the program by taking a good number of the technical undergrad courses as well. In order to receive grad credit in these classes, students usually do an extra assignment or two. Film I, II, III and IV, the school's main series of production classes, are undergrad courses. Film I focuses on pre-production; Film II teaches the basics of production. In Film III students work on film projects in teams. Film IV is a post-production class.

Semester critiques are done in December and April. Students have one hour in which to present their work to a five-person panel composed of faculty members from assorted disciplines.

As students move closer to graduation, they enroll in fewer classes and take on more Graduate Projects. Although there is a strong slant toward the experimental, students are encouraged to make whatever types of films they want to.

Students can make as few or as many films as they want to at the Chicago Art Institute. One artist graduated having made seventeen films in his two years. Another made only one. The average is two to three, all of which are paid for totally by the student. Historically, students have worked predominantly alone on their projects.

At the end of the year, students are required to screen their films in the M.F.A. thesis screening. Each student is permitted fifteen minutes of screen time. Those whose projects are longer will show a trailer or a selected portion of their film.

The Price

$8,800 per semester for 5 semesters	$44,000
$12,000 rent and living expenses for three years	$36,000
Film costs (varies)	$10,000
Total	**$90,000**

Full-time study is twelve to fifteen credits per semester. Tuition is a flat-rate of $8,800 per semester. Students pay the same price no matter how many credits they take. So the more credits you can cram into each semester the shorter your stay will be, and the less money you'll spend on tuition.

Most students receive a grant that covers approximately 40 percent of full-time tuition. Those who fall below full-time receive less. This type of financial aid is the only sort of funding available other than one $1,000 merit scholarship offered to one incoming student each year. Teaching assistants only receive a small hourly wage. But because the class schedule is so flexible, students have no trouble working either in the school or outside. Most have to work.

The school is located in the heart of the downtown area, overlooking Lake Michigan. There is no student housing, so students find their own places outside the Loop. Housing is very reasonable. One-bedroom apartments in the nicer neighborhoods can be rented for around $600 per month. The closer the proximity to the school, the higher the rents. Lots of students share for less.

Public transportation is excellent, and few students own cars. Most students seem to live within a thirty-minute train ride from the school.

The Lowdown

As an applicant to the M.F.A. program you are expected to have experience making films, and are asked to send at least one completed film in with your application. If you are an artist with a body of work in other media, but have no experience with film, you can send in your portfolio of non-film work. The school will consider you, but you will be at a disadvantage. Along with your application and portfolio you will have to send a statement of intent, which weighs heavily in the admissions process. The school looks for dedicated artists with a clear sense of direction, and if they don't see evidence of these qualities in your statement they will be less likely to consider you seriously.

There is not a true sense of community among the faculty. While there are some very committed filmmakers, each operates very much on an individual basis regarding workloads and interest in students. Many faculty seem to be here simply to support their own work and don't want to invest the time in their students. Even appointments with advisors, a very necessary part of this program, are often difficult to schedule. Advisors tend to accept more students than they have time for. But those who do take the time are respected and can impart some invaluable knowledge.

Graduate students have to share most of the school's production equipment with 150 undergrads. The school owns 30 Bolexes, four CP 16s, and an ACL. Two Bolexes and some other minor equipment are set aside for grads only. There are always equipment crunches. It is not uncommon for students to purchase their own cameras. Reservations can be made one week in advance to avoid delays. Equipment is loaned to students for two-day periods, but special arrangements can be made for longer shoots. A recent student had no trouble securing a camera for a three-week location production in Canada.

Post-production equipment is limited and rather dated. It includes three six-plate flatbeds, two transfer rooms, and a very good sound-mixing suite. There are two JK and one Oxberry optical printers and a Bell and Howell contact printer. There's a class that instructs students in the use of this equipment. Self-printing can save a great deal of money. There is one Oxberry and one Mitchell animation stand. A shooting studio with a light grid is used frequently and can only be booked for short periods.

As with the cameras, post-production facilities can be reserved in advance. A sign-up sheet is posted every two weeks. All are accessible twenty-four hours a day. Flatbeds can only be booked for five hours per weekday and eight hours per weekend: twenty hours total per week. One flatbed is reserved for grads. A Media 100 and an Avid are available in the school, but film students must write to the department heads in order to have access. Since there are no deadlines for grads, with proper planning the busy end-of-semester periods can be avoided.

Chicago is a very artistic community. There are wonderful museums and a large number of theaters and thriving art galleries. Quite a few students arrange screenings for themselves at these galleries. Film communities include Chicago Filmmakers, who provides access to experimental and documentary work, and the Film Center, which offers a solid international cinema schedule. There are numerous art houses and revival houses as well as the typical megaplexes. Chicago is home to several respected film festivals: FACETS-Multi-Media and Children's festivals, the Chicago International Film Festival, and the Onion City Festival.

Some of the best things about the program: The flexibility enables students to tailor a very specific program. Each degree will be as individual as the person receiving it. There's a large international population. Class sizes are small, and there's a great deal of individual attention.

Some of the worst things about the program: Flexibility can spell disaster for those who need structure. Many students have a tough time deciding what to do. Students can become discouraged as they trudge through new territory. Film students are the only artists who are not provided with individual studios. The entire film department seems to suffer from a lack of space. The facilities only support traditional filmmaking. The school does not offer courses in digital editing or sound design, a major omission in this day and age.

Bard College

Milton Avery Graduate School
  of the Arts
P.O. Box 5000
Annondale-on-Hudson, NY
  12504
Department: (914) 758-7481
Admissions: (914) 758-7481
http://www.bard.edu/bard1/
  academics/programs/arts/
  film.htm

Equipment Quality: ☆☆☆

Equipment Accessibility: ☆☆☆

Cost: $

Annual Tuition:	$7,296
Enrollment:	3–4; 10 total
Deadline:	February 1
Focus:	Experimental/Documentary

The Program

The Milton Avery Graduate School of the Arts offers an interdisciplinary program. In existence since 1981, the school receives fifty to sixty applications annually for the few openings. While an exceptional young artist straight from undergrad might be accepted, Bard offers a unique structure designed to support more mature artists who might actually have jobs or lives (GASP!), as well as filmmaking aspirations. Instead of asking students to commit to year-round classes, Bard conducts three intensive summer sessions, where artists live and work in a community that supports many disciplines. For the remainder of the time (fall/winter/spring sessions) students live and work away from the school working on independent projects.

Strictly speaking, filmmaking is not taught at Bard. This is a creative environment in which artists with backgrounds in film have a chance to further develop their craft. They try to replicate the true artistic lifestyle. This often means an individual, isolated experience of creation followed up and supported with reviews and critiques.

There are four basic components that make up the Bard program: Conference, Common Seminar, Presentation, and Master's Project. In the *Conference* students meet one-on-one with faculty in their discipline and at least once during the session with the rest of the faculty. In the *Common Seminar* a resident faculty member, visiting artist, or lecturer from a field outside the practicing arts leads sessions consisting of lectures, readings, performances, and shows. The *Presentation* is, as its name implies, a submission by the student to the entire student body of their work for evaluation. All of the above culminates in the *Master's Project,* a film or a series of films presented to the faculty at the end of the third summer session.

Each summer session-in-residence runs for eight intensive weeks. The day-to-day focus is on each student's work-in-progress. All artists also serve as an audience for other students' works-in-progress. Students are provided with individual studios and access to the production and post-production equipment necessary to work on their films. A typical student's day would consist of working in her studio in the morning, conferring with faculty in the afternoon, and attending the work reviews in the evening. Regular meetings with faculty in their chosen field and tutorial meetings with faculty from other disciplines are distinctive parts of the program. Students are required to make two presentations of their work each summer

Summer sessions offer many workshops in all the disciplines, and students are encouraged to attend as many as possible. This is the time when film students shoot and begin editing their projects. If a special circumstance should arise, the department will try to accommodate a student who needs a school camera during the independent-study months. A critique occurs at the end of the first year, where students are reviewed by a panel of three faculty members.

Sixty credits are earned through the one-on-one faculty conferences, participation in seminars, mounting a presentation, participating in another artist's presentation, independent study between residential sessions, and completion of a Master's Project in the final summer session.

On average, students shoot two or three short films and one Master's Project while at Bard. Master's Projects can vary from a half-hour documentary to several short pieces to a feature-length narrative film.

The Price

$5906 each for three summer sessions;	
$1130 each for two winter sessions and studio fees	$20,608
$880 rent for three summer sessions	$ 2,640
Average film costs	$20,000
Total	**$43,248**

All in all, this is not a bad deal—especially since students can continue to work full-time most of the year. The summer sessions and the cost of residing in Annondale for eight weeks are reasonable. There are some fellowships awarded based on merit, financial need, or program-balancing needs. Students must apply for these by writing to the Graduate Committee and stating the reasons for their request. They must explain why their presence at the school contributes to the diversity of the program. Bard Grants of $500 to $2,000 are also awarded based on financial need. The department tries to equally distribute these awards to students during the summer session. Although there is no guarantee of an award, most will wind up with about $1,200 of assistance per year.

The Hudson Valley is an idyllic retreat in which to spend two months. If one has to work hard, there couldn't be a more beautiful place in which to do it. This is a rural oasis, short on distraction and long on vista. For $880 students can reside in a historic mansion located on a nineteenth-century estate on the campus. Some students do rent private apartments off campus in the nearby communities of Tivoli or Rhinebeck, but why bother? They'll only have to contend with upscale New Yorkers escaping to their "country" homes. Those who do venture beyond the campus spend between $400 and $600 to share a house or rent a room.

The Lowdown

Bard is looking for experienced artists who want to make very personal, experimental, poetic, or documentary films. When applying to the program, filmmakers must submit a film, video, or script.

The school wants to know an applicant's history of activity in the arts and expects to see a record of those activities. They are only interested in serious artists who can back up their claims. Applicants must submit a very personal statement in which they express individual concerns, theories, hopes, achievements, and interests. An established artist who is interested in exploring a new medium might be considered for the filmmaking program, and one-on-one technical training would be provided for that student. Students are reviewed and accepted on a singular basis with their individual talents and needs taken into consideration.

While the faculty changes from summer to summer, it is always composed of working artists, many of whom are Guggenheim fellowship recipients. Every summer three to four additional guest artists come to lecture or run workshops. These have included renowned photographers, painters, musicians, or even sound engineers. For film students there are often additional tech workshops in optical printing, field recording, or hand processing. These are all done in conjunction with the regular teaching and workshops. Every evening the school meets as a group for a critique of students' work. By the end of the two months of total immersion in their craft, most students depart exhausted.

Because the program is so small, there is little problem obtaining equipment. The equipment gets much use by both the grads and undergrads, but never simultaneously. Grads only have access during the summer sessions, when the undergrads are on vacation. There are sixteen Bolexes, two CP 16s, an Arriflex BL, and an Arri S. There are half a dozen or so Hi-8 video cameras and five VHS cameras. There are a hand-processing lab, an animation stand, and a JK optical printer.

For post-production there are five flatbeds, a Gen-lock Special-Effects generator, some video toasters, VHS editing suites, film-to-video transfer, and an Avid Media Suite Pro. The Avid gets a great deal of use.

Some of the best things about the program: The intimacy and individual attention. The visiting artists are an inspiration and an asset. Students and professors alike thrive in the completely supportive environment. Most enjoy the different perspectives that nonfilmmakers have to offer. Students find the complete immersion in art extremely appealing. No one has to put her life on hold to attend Bard. Mature students are especially comfortable.

Some of the worst things about the program: The school offers little financial aid. While it's great to have nine months of preparation, the frantic summer pace might not be for everybody. There's a risk that less disciplined students could slack off during the winter. If a student does not have access to a camera, she will be hard-pressed to shoot, process, and edit a film in the all-too-short summer session. Space is at a premium and one of the reasons so few can be accepted.

Make the most of time at Bard by being prepared to work hard when summer session comes around and continue working during the independent-study time. If at all possible, shoot films during the independent-study months and focus on post-production during the summer. It's very difficult to shoot and edit a film in two months. Students who know what sorts of projects they want to make or even have a project in progress upon arriving will be able to best realize their visions at Bard. Many leave the school with a newfound perspective and the option to teach at other universities while they continue with their filmmaking.

California Institute of the Arts

School of Film/Video
24700 McBean Parkway
Valencia, CA 91355
(805) 253-7825
http://www.calarts.edu/Web_
   Docs/BULLETIN/Film_
   Skul/

Equipment Quality: ☆☆

Equipment Accessibility: ☆☆☆

Cost: $$$

Annual Tuition:	$14,600
Enrollment:	About 25 per year, about 80 total
Deadline:	February 1
Focus:	Experimental

The Program

Cal Arts wins the award for glossy presentation. If you need decoration for your walls but do not have much money, you might want to send for the Cal Arts information package—the brochure is suitable for framing and makes a terrific gift. No, seriously, even if you don't want to go to Cal Arts, you gotta *see* this thing.

Cal Arts' film program surprises most people. Applicants read in the highly designed information package that the school was founded in 1971 by Walt and Roy Disney, and that it still receives a great deal of funding from the Walt Disney Company. They note that many students from the animation department are hired by Disney and that the campus is near Los Angeles. And based on all this information, the applicants make what would seem to be the obvious assumption—that this is an industry school like AFI or USC. But, in fact, Cal Arts is one of the most resolutely experimental film schools in existence. The founders of the school, in 1971, looked around at film schools that already existed, the USCs and NYUs that were already offering courses in narrative filmmaking, and decided they didn't want to do the same thing. So they set up the film school as more of an art conservatory for film students and angled it toward experimental film-making.

Cal Arts' graduate film department has three divisions: Directing for Theater, Video, and Film; Experimental Animation; and Live Action (a fourth division, Character Animation, is for undergraduates only). Directing for Theater, Video, and Film is a small, eccentric program that operates in cooperation with the Theater Arts Department—it is more about the interpretation of texts than the art of filmmaking. Experimental Animation is, as you might imagine, dedicated to expanding the art of animation. The Live Action division focuses on nonanimation filmmaking, which is not to say that the films that come out of this division are typical student films—they tend to be wildly experimental.

The program is well equipped, staffed by a large, diverse faculty, and is quite unstructured; students have to take three years' worth of classes, but are free to make as many or as few projects as they like. The school accepts people who have years of film experience, and people who have no film experience, and allows them to learn at their own pace. When students enter the school at the beginning of the first year, they all start an elementary technical course called Film Fundamentals. The first two weeks of this course are devoted to determining how much each student knows about the technology and technique of filmmaking. After these two weeks, all the students who have experience in filmmaking are dismissed from the class and are allowed to jump into any other classes they like while the inexperienced students continue on and learn the basics of film.

Beyond that single class, the school has no set structure and no course requirements. Instead, each student is assigned a mentor: a faculty member whose responsibility it is to suggest a curriculum of courses that will conform to that student's specific interests and goals. A few years ago the school recognized that while many students flourished under this system, others foundered without any direction from the school. In order to try to help those students who clearly needed some kind of structure the school created some general outlines—suggested class lists for those interested in specific areas like narrative filmmaking, lyrical filmmaking, or experimental filmmaking. Mind you, these are not requirements. They are just suggestions for those students who need a little structure in their lives. But they are the closest thing to structure the school has to offer.

The program offers a wide variety of classes, from straightforward writing and production workshops to classes in more offbeat disciplines like video installations. Film students do not have to stick to film classes—the entire school is at their disposal so they can study whatever strikes their fancy, from theater to painting to music to dance. There is a year-long Thesis Workshop to help second- and third-year students complete their thesis projects. At the start of this class, students present their thesis ideas and participate in discussions of the films they want to make. By the end of the year, the students have shot their films and are ready to screen cuts for the class. While this class is helpful, it is not a requirement, and some students make their thesis films without taking it. All that is required of students to begin shooting their thesis films is a mid-residency review, wherein they discuss with the faculty what they have learned so far and what they want to make for a thesis.

For most students the program takes three years to complete, though the classes can be finished in two, and in recent years some students have managed to make their thesis films and graduate in two. Those who finish in two years do so in the interest of saving money; students who return for a third year have to pay full tuition even if they have already completed the required classes. Still, many students do not complete their theses by the end of the third year. When this happens, there is some flexibility: if a student is clearly working hard on her thesis but is not quite done, the school will allow her to use the equipment for another year without paying tuition. But the school has little patience with students who are slow to finish their projects and sometimes banishes those who take too long to finish their thesis films.

When students finish their thesis projects, they screen them for a thesis committee and then participate in discussions of their films. No comprehensive exams and no written theses are required in order to graduate.

The Price

$14,600 tuition for 3 years	$43,800
$10,000 a year rent and living expenses for three years	$30,000
$1,500 per year maintenance and insurance on a car in Valencia for three years	$ 4,500
First- and second-year exercise films cost around	$ 5,000
Thesis films cost around	$10,000
Total	**$93,300**

Because the program is so unstructured, these amounts are especially unpredictable. Some students finish the program in two years, saving a lot of money in tuition, film costs, and living expenses. The film costs are also especially unpredictable. Some students make half a dozen short exercise films and spend much less than this, others make one big thesis film and spend much more. The best thing to do is decide at the start how much you want to spend on your films and stick to that amount. The school will not dictate a spending limit.

Certainly the simplest way to save money is to finish the program in two years. The way to do this is to come into the first year with a thesis script already complete. If you have a good script at the start, and if your mentor approves, you may begin making that thesis within the first few weeks of the first year, and you can easily have it finished by the end of the second year. You can save yourself a lot of money if you do this, but you will not learn as much about filmmaking as you would if you made several films.

Most of the film program's money goes into the equipment. There is very little financial aid available. Cal Arts is a small school, with a total of about a thousand students in all departments, so there is little need for TAs, and little money available to pay for them. Only three teaching assistantships are given out each year in the film program, which pay next to nothing. Most students have to work while they are taking classes to make ends meet.

The school's financial situation has often been tenuous. For most of the eighties, Cal Arts slipped deeper and deeper into debt. A new president brought the school into an abstemious, relatively secure financial state, but that was shaken up in 1994 when the Northridge earthquake did severe damage to the school. As of this writing, millions of dollars of the school's money have gone into basic structural repairs. So don't expect the film program to receive large grants for new equipment or new TAs any time soon.

The Lowdown

Cal Arts receives between a hundred and a hundred fifty applications each year for the M.F.A. program in Live Action and accepts about fifty, figuring that only twenty-five or thirty of those will actually come to the school.

The admissions board does not look at GREs. With your application to the film program you will have to include some written materials and a creative portfolio. The written materials consist of some comments on works (books, films, plays) that you feel have influenced you and a description of projects that you want to make while at Cal Arts.

The creative portfolio is by far the most important piece of the application. We are told that, in general, the admissions board looks for something weird. They like to be surprised by an applicant's strange personal vision. Remember that this is an art school, and the admissions board is basically looking for art students, not specifically film students. They are seeking creative, motivated individuals with a strong personal vision and are specifically looking for these qualities in the work you submit in the creative portfolio. Your portfolio can include up to ten minutes of film or video, writing samples, photographs, slides of artwork in other media, or any other creative work that you feel shows your abilities. Prior experience in film is not required, but those who can send in good film work have an advantage over those who cannot. Every year a number of applicants send in highly polished Hollywood-type film work— computer-generated special effects of planets exploding, well-staged action scenes, and so on. These applicants are knocked out of the running automatically. The school specifically avoids applicants who want to do this kind of work—Cal Arts has little to offer these filmmakers, and the admissions board recognizes that there are plenty of other schools that specialize in this kind of thing. As if the portfolios weren't already important enough, the school also decides who gets financial aid based on them.

As we have already mentioned, the program is unstructured, and how long you take to complete it is largely up to you. Most students who finish take around three years, though some complete the program in two, and some stretch it out to four. Because the school provides little financial aid, most students have to work. Of those who work, many find film work in Los Angeles. Many of these students work their way up in these jobs, adding hours and earning raises until they eventually have to choose between school and work. Most choose the work, so there is a high attrition rate at Cal Arts, and many students never finish the program.

The school's best cameras are nine Eclair NPRs. There are also some Beaulieus, Bolexes, and Arriflex S/Bs, and they have a good variety of prime and variable-length lenses to use with these cameras. For location sound recording there are Nagras and DAT recorders, and a selection of Sennheiser microphones. The school has light kits and individual Mole Richardson heads, assorted grip and gaffing equipment, and a Colortran dolly. For titles and effects they have an optical printer and, in the animation department, a battery of Oxberry animation stands.

Cal Arts owns nine six-plate Moviola flatbed editing machines. Students may also edit their projects on nonlinear workstations or any of a number of video editing stations. The school has a sixteen-track mag film-mixing theater and is currently installing some new digital sound editing and mixing workstations. This is a small enough school that there is plenty of equipment to go around. Students can generally get camera packages when they need them for as much time as they need them.

Cal Arts has always focused on experimental film and animation, and has kept pace with changes in the technology of animation. For most of the seventies and eighties students of experimental animation coming out of Cal Arts struggled to find work. But in the nineties, as animation has experienced a renaissance and as computer-generated animation has made its way into film special-effects work, the studios have looked to techno-savvy Cal Arts alumni to lead the way. Tim Burton (*Edward Scissorhands* [1990], *Batman* [1989], *Mars Attacks* [1996]), Henry Selick (*Tim Burton's a Nightmare Before Christmas* [1993], *James and the Giant Peach* [1996]) and John Lassiter (*Toy Story* [1995]) are all graduates of Cal Arts, and a large portion of the animation departments at all of Hollywood's studios are either Cal Arts graduates or Cal Arts dropouts. As a result, a degree from Cal Arts has a techno-cool aura that you can't get from any other school.

Valencia is a strange place for a college. The town itself is a completely planned community, designed and built in the seventies by the Newhall Land and Farm Company. It has all the advantages you might expect in a planned community—well-maintained suburban neighborhoods, convenient shopping centers, well-tended bike paths and walkways. But it was never intended to be a college town, and it can present real disadvantages for students. Nearly all the housing in Valencia is single-family houses. One-bedroom apartments are all but unheard of near school, and students have to make do with other alternatives. Some students rent rooms in family homes. Others join together into groups and share houses or condominiums. Others find apartments in unplanned communities nearby like Newhall, or twenty minutes away in the San Fernando Valley, or even farther away in central Los Angeles. Commuting from L.A. or the Valley can be a good solution for many students, especially the ones who support themselves by working in Hollywood. But it hardly allows you to feel that you are a member of the Cal Arts community when you have to drive an hour and a half to get there every day. And when the Northridge earthquake knocked down the only major road between Valencia and the rest of Southern California a few years back, a lot of students wished they lived closer.

The school puts on a juried end-of-year show each year in a public space in Los Angeles. While the school offers no official career guidance, there is a large network of Cal Arts graduates in Hollywood who can help out.

Some of the best things about the program: The funky attitude. Students are encouraged to work on all kinds of crazy projects, and they do. Also, with strong programs in such areas as dance, design, and computer animation, Cal Arts offers great opportunities to combine filmmaking with other media and disciplines. The school is situated remotely enough to feel like a small school in a small town, yet the film labs, equipment houses, prop houses and many other film resources of Los Angeles are only about an hour's drive away.

Some of the worst things about the program: On the other hand, Valencia itself is a real problem—students either have to live in this rather depressing town or commute a long way from Los Angeles. While most students appreciate the freedom the program affords, some students get lost.

Chapman University

Department of Film and
   Television
333 North Glassell Street
Orange, CA 92666
Department: (714) 997-6775
Admissions: (714) 997-6786
http://www.chapman.edu/
   comm/ftv/

Annual Tuition:	$9,450
Enrollment:	15; 70 total
Deadline:	Up to one week prior to the start of the semester
Focus:	Independent

Independent

Equipment
Quality: ☆☆☆

Equipment
Accessibility: ☆☆☆

Cost: **$$$**

The Program

While the Department of Film and Television at Chapman University has been around since the seventies, in the last five years or so the program has grown and advanced structurally and technologically. Between 200 and 300 applicants vie for fifteen openings each year. The school offers programs in Producing, Screenwriting, and Film Production.

Chapman employs a rolling admissions schedule. This means students can apply for admission up to one week before the beginning of any semester. Film students should start in the fall (late-August start date), since essential film courses are not offered every semester.

The core of the program is the Production Workshop, taken every semester the first two years. In the first-year Fall Production I Workshop, students shoot several Hi-8 projects: the first one runs about three minutes, the last around fifteen minutes. The lab fee for this course covers all the tape stock. Every film at Chapman is edited on a nonlinear system; students learn in Production I how to edit on the school's D-Vision workstations. Cinematography rounds out the semester and teaches the fundamentals of both video and 16-mm cameras. Typically this class begins by teaching lighting, composition, and film response. The second half of the course involves shooting some short silent exercises, for which the school provides 16-mm stock.

At the end of the fall semester, students submit scripts for narrative projects or proposals for documentaries for the Graduate Location Filmmaking class, offered during the month-long interim break between fall and spring semesters. At least once during their stay students are required to register for this class. The faculty selects several script finalists who must "pitch" their production plan, crew, and package to a panel of two professors. Final approval is then given to three writer/directors to make ten-minute films, which are made at the school's expense. Location Filmmaking projects have taken students to sites as diverse as Cabo San Lucas, Mexico, and Death Valley.

Spring of the first year continues with Audio Design, Production Management, and Production Workshop II. In this workshop students make their first nonsync sound films. These ten-minute films are paid for by the students and run about $1,000.

At the end of the first year, all students must submit scripts for the following semester's Production III class. A faculty committee chooses one script. The author of that script directs it while the rest of the students volunteer for the other crew positions. The school again pays for this film, which runs fifteen to twenty minutes in length. Typically this film is shot in the first month, edited during the second month, and posted with sound in the final month of the fall semester. Along with Production III, second-year students take Directing Actors and Film Theory and Criticism. They have the option of skipping Graduate Location Filmmaking, but most don't.

In the spring, students have a choice of two of the following classes: Scriptwriting Workshop, Film Genre Studies, Visual Perception and Expression, or an internship. In the final Production IV Workshop, students study film styles and use Bolex cameras to make a series of short nonsync films on reversal stock. These films tend to be of the experimental ilk.

The entire third year is devoted to thesis work. Thesis projects must be approved by the faculty. Students who are unable to complete their films in this final year can extend their stay by simply paying the graduation fee (around $50) for each semester they delay. They do not have to register for more credits.

The only film on which the crew must consist of Chapman students is the Production II project. It is not unusual for students to coordinate crews with outside filmmakers in order to get what they feel is the best crew possible, especially for their thesis films.

There are no limitations or restrictions on thesis films. Although the average runs about thirty minutes, students with financing in place have been known to shoot features. Films generally shoot in two weeks. Once completed, thesis films are shown and defended before a faculty committee.

All students usually do an internship for credit. While they have to find their own positions, the school posts numerous notices from L.A. studios and companies looking for interns.

At the end of each semester, students screen their completed films from that semester. There's a Public Showcase in the spring at which any student can screen any of her newest films. At a banquet at the showcase's end, noncash awards are given for technical skills.

Every week there are screenings of 35-mm films in the evenings. The current Monday-night series is French Films. On Tuesdays, films are screened in conjunction with the Film History class. On Thursdays, there is the Weekly Entertainment Arts Forum. Films are presented and industry professionals in attendance answer follow-up questions after the screening.

The Price

$450 per credit for 54 credits	$24,300
$12,000 per year rent and living expenses for three years	$36,000
$2,000 per year maintenance on a car	$6,000
Average film costs	$15,000
Total	**$75,300**

While the tuition at Chapman is reasonable, they offer little financial aid. Except for five $5,000 grants awarded based upon GPAs at the time of admission, most students are on their own. There are no fellowships or teaching assistantships. Lab assistant positions pay $7 per hour, but most students feel it is too difficult to have part-time jobs.

Located just thirty miles from Hollywood, Chapman is in a typical suburban area. While the proximity to L.A. allows students and the school to reap all the big city benefits, it's certainly a safer area than L.A. proper. Living costs are about the same, with shares in the $500 price range and one-bedrooms in the $600 range. Students live off campus. As in any city near Los Angeles, a car is vital.

The Lowdown

Chapman University is not concerned that its applicants have film experience. They prefer students who have been out of school for a while but will consider recent graduates. Anyone who demonstrates creative promise is welcome. This should be evident in the applicant's creative portfolio and statement of intent. More than anything, it is important to demonstrate the desire to make films. The seriousness of this desire should be apparent through a thesis film treatment or proposal which must be submitted with all applications. While students are not held to these ideas in the long run, the school wants to know that applicants have thought about the types of films they are interested in making. All potential students are encouraged to speak with one of the program coordinators before even applying in order to get a clear idea of the nature of the program.

The faculty runs the gamut from Academy Award winners to struggling documentarians. All faculty are working professionals. They are reportedly dedicated to teaching, always available for consultation, and ready to offer lots of support. There are many guest lecturers. Chapman attempts to bring as many film-related lecturers and conferences to the school as possible. They recently sponsored an Independent Film Conference which brought over 250 filmmakers on campus. And with their evening screenings, students have the chance to see feature films and talk with the makers. Robert Zemeckis has visited several times to conduct in-depth workshops.

Considering that is it shared with the undergrad population, the equipment at Chapman is in great shape. From day one students have twenty-four-hour access all year long. There is rarely a problem checking out cameras. Reservations are usually made one week in advance, with grads having priority. Pre-production documents (breakdowns, schedules, equipment lists, etc.) must be presented to the faculty for review before they will approve a thesis reservation. While students are encouraged to purchase their own high-eight cameras, there are twenty in constant circulation. The school also owns several professional Hi-8 cameras, two Betacams, and a studio with a permanent three-camera setup. All production equipment is normally available for twenty-four hour periods, but students have received approval to take equipment out of the area for as long as three weeks.

Cameras consist of one Arri BL, one CP 16, eight EBMS Bolex, and three Arriflex SRs. The SRs are restricted to advanced undergrad and grad projects only. The equipment is well maintained, and if anything breaks down the problem is addressed immediately. Despite the amount and availability of equipment, students still feel the need to rent more for their thesis films.

Chapman emphasizes nonlinear post-production. Three-hour time blocks are reserved twenty-four hours in advance. There are thirteen D-Vision off-line editing systems, two D-Vision on-line suites, and three Roland digital audio stations, two of which are equipped with booths in which to record foley (sound effects) or narration. Two flatbeds are virtually unused. Chapman has two sound stages, one of which has grid lighting. Students have access to an eighty-seat screening theater.

Some of the best things about the program: The faculty is accessible and very helpful. Students select an advisor to mentor them through the entire program. It is a very nurturing environment. The staff go out of their way to ease computer phobias and make everyone comfortable with the technology. The program is designed so that students depart with a film and at least one screenplay under their belts.

Some of the worst things about the program: Chapman is all but unknown. It is not the place to go for people who are looking for a school with prestige. This could change overnight with a few film success stories. It would be nice to have more financial aid in place. With L.A. so close it would behoove the school to initiate an industry screening to get their name out there.

City College of New York

Department of
  Communications, Film, and
  Video
Rm. 473, Shepard Hall
138th Street at Convent
  Avenue
New York, NY 10031
Department: (212) 650-7167
Admissions: (212) 650-6977
http://www.ccny.cuny.edu

Equipment Quality: ☆☆☆
Equipment Accessibility: ☆☆☆
Cost: $$

Annual Tuition:	**Resident: $4,350**
	Nonresident:
	$7,600
Enrollment:	**30 (projected)**
Deadline:	**May 15**
Focus:	**Independent**

The Program

The Department of Communications, Film, and Video at the City College of New York will be offering an M.F.A. in Media Arts Production *commencing* in the fall 1997 semester. They hope to accept thirty students into the first-ever year of this two-year program. Their goal is to provide affordable graduate-level training at an accessible public institution. They intend to balance equal numbers of both narrative and documentary filmmakers.

The program is designed for those with prior experience in film. Applicants must submit a portfolio of creative film and/or video work, a screenplay, or interactive digital media piece. Those with non-film creative work will be considered but might be required to take prerequisite undergraduate courses in film history and theory, screenwriting, production, editing, or directing before they start the program. Any student who intends to write and direct a thesis project in the second year must also submit a one-page story outline for a narrative or a one-page documentary proposal with their application. Those interested in other creative areas such as camera or editing submit a one-page statement identifying the particular area and the reasons for pursuing it.

The program will encourage students to create cost-effective productions that address the issues of the communities from which they come. Although no time restrictions are in place as yet, short films will be strongly emphasized. Work will not be limited to "making movies," as students will explore emerging interactive digital media. Students will work in 16mm, video, and interactive digital formats and will incur the costs of their projects.

As with any new program, the structure and classes will no doubt adapt or change with the passage of time. The faculty plan to focus the first year on technical mastery of film and video production techniques, examination of narrative structures, creating links to the independent production community, and preparation of thesis projects. Projected fall courses include Independent Media Arts, Camera I, Writing for Media Arts, and Interactive Media Production I. In the spring there will be advanced Camera II, Interactive Media Production II, Media Arts Management, and two electives. The electives of Fiction Screenwriting, Directing Fiction Research and Writing for Documentary, and Producing and Directing the Documentary will be designed to help students focus on their thesis genre.

The second year of the program is built around the production of thesis projects. Editing, Sound Design, and Thesis Project Production are planned for the fall, with a seminar in Independent Media Arts and Post-Production.

The Price

RESIDENT

$2,175 per semester for two years	$ 8,700
$15,000 rent and living expenses for two years	$30,000
Average film costs	$10,000
Total	**$48,700**

NONRESIDENT

$3,800 per semester for two years	$15,200
$15,000 rent and living expenses for two years	$30,000
Average film costs	$10,000
Total	**$55,200**

As of now, there are no specific film scholarships or grants other than traditional financial aid resources. But with such a reasonable tuition, rent will probably be a greater concern than tuition.

The faculty will consist of five full-time professors as well as part-time instructors from New York's production community.

The facilities and equipment in the department are state-of-the-art as a result of a $1.4-million renovation and re-equipping which was completed in fall 1996. The department now includes Arriflex SR-II and Sony Betacam SP EFP cameras, DAT field recorders, six Avids, an Audio-vision post-sound suite, an interactive digital media lab, a fully equipped soundstage, and a multi-camera television studio.

The Lowdown

On paper, City College of New York's program sounds promising. For adventurous types who don't mind paving the way of a new program, the payoff could be big.

Who knows? Adventurous students who like the idea of exploring uncharted territory could wind up with a real bargain. The enthusiasm level is high, the equipment sounds great, and the unique multimedia exposure is very timely. This first class will probably be treated like royalty. If students can adhere to the short-film emphasis and have their acts together enough to submit the necessary application film proposals, City College seems like a very economical place to make some films and get an M.F.A.

Columbia College

600 S. Michigan Ave.
Chicago, IL 60605
312/663-1600
http://www.colum.edu

Independent

Tuition:	$16,752
Enrollment:	20-24
Deadline:	January 5
Focus:	Independent/ Documentary

Equipment Quality: ☆☆

Equipment Accessibility: ☆☆

Cost: $$

The Program

Located inside the Loop, in Chicago's urban core, Columbia College offers a moderately priced M.F.A. program that specializes in Independent Narrative and Documentary filmmaking. The program is less structured than some, and the class requirements can take as little as three or more than four years to complete.

The first year is rigidly structured. From the first day of first year students take courses in screenwriting and editing, and are immersed in an intensive introduction to the technical end of film production called Techniques I. Two weeks into the semester, students in this class are already shooting their first short films; by the end of the first semester each student has completed three. The first of these films is silent, the second has simple sound, and the third has sync sound. The school provides enough film and processing for each of these films and asks that students not buy any additional film stock, as learning to work within limits is part of the point of the class. This course is so intense that it actually outpaces the students. Students make sync sound films in this course, but they have not yet been trained in how to use sync sound equipment, and are thus not allowed to touch the equipment they need to shoot with. Instead they have to find either older graduate students or, more often, undergrads who have taken the required courses in cinematography to shoot their films and record their audio for them. The second semester continues with a class on film theory, a class in directing, and Techniques II, which carries on the intensive technical training started in the first semester.

Students in this course make a fifteen-minute sync sound film. At the end of first year students go through what is known as a focus review. They present their second-semester film, a paper they wrote in the theory course, and the screenplay they wrote in the screenwriting course to a committee made up of their assigned academic advisor, the head of the school, and a few faculty members. Based on this material students are given one of three judgments: an unconditional pass on to second year, a fail, or a conditional pass. Most students receive an unconditional pass, but each year a handful of students get a conditional pass, and one or two receive a fail. The students who get conditional passes are required to have a re-review in the middle of second year. Those who are passed unconditionally have no further reviews to sit through.

In the second year students take a video production course and the first of their electives. At the end of the third semester students choose one of two specialties: narrative or documentary. After that they split into two groups, with each student taking either Narrative Technique or Documentary Production. In Directing II students make a larger-scale sound film project.

Students take more electives in the third year. Electives are, for the most part, undergraduate courses that graduates can attend. Classes offered include further work in cinematography, producing, writing, video production, computer graphics, and interactive media, among others. The primary classes a student takes in the third year are again determined by the specialization she has chosen: the third year is dominated by a seminar in (depending on her specialty) documentary or narrative filmmaking. These seminars are devoted to preparing students for the production of their thesis films. Narrative thesis films tend to run around fifteen minutes; documentary ones, around half an hour. At the end of the third year, upon finishing the second semester of the seminar, each student chooses two faculty members to be her thesis advisors. In the months and years following the third year, these advisors approve a student's thesis proposal, offer guidance during those projects' production and post-production, and approve the granting of degrees when the projects are finished.

The faculty feels students should be able to finish classes and a thesis film in around four years, but some students, as at any school, take quite a bit longer. For these students' benefit the school has a firm limit of seven years after initial enrollment by which their thesis films must be completed.

Columbia College offers more career guidance upon graduation than most film schools. The school employs a full time Internship Officer, whose sole duty is to find internships and jobs for students to move into after graduation. The school claims that 51 percent of its graduates are placed in internships upon completion of the program.

The Price

60 credit hours at $349 per credit	$20,940
$10,000 a year rent and living expenses for four years	$40,000
Films tend to cost an additional	$15,000
Total	**$79,940**

Because the program becomes relatively unstructured after the first year, many students find themselves drifting a bit and taking longer than expected to finish the required classes. Even though it is possible to finish in three years, it is not uncommon for students to continue on through the fourth year, finishing up their requirements. Needless to say, the longer you keep taking classes, the more money you will spend. Conversely, the quicker you get done with your course work, the quicker you can find a job to help pay for your thesis production. It's a good idea to plan out your classes in advance and make sure you don't have to take classes beyond three years.

The school has some funding for students, but not an awful lot. They give out ten $5,000 school-wide Graduate Opportunity Awards each year, of which two usually go to grad film students, and there are two $7,000 grants that go to first-year students. (One student complained that he chose the school because he was offered the $7,000 scholarship, and that he was halfway through his first year before anyone told him that the scholarship would end after one year.) On top of that there are a few smaller grants (the largest is $3,000) that are distributed to students at the end of their first year, based on the work they turn in to the focus review committee.

The school offers some student housing near school, but most graduate students opt to live in the relatively quiet, spacious, and inexpensive suburbs. Perfectly livable apartments can be found a ten-minute bike ride from school for $450 or $500. Whether or not to have a car in Chicago is a tough call. While the city has pretty good public transportation, it is spread out over a huge area. Generally speaking, students who live close in to town can get by without and rent vans when production makes it necessary, but those who live farther out in the suburbs tend to need cars anyway. But because most students live a short train ride from school we are not including a car as a necessity.

Because the school is located in the middle of one of the country's largest cities, there are many job opportunities to be had, including many in media. But beware—with employment opportunities always comes the temptation to lose your focus and drift away from school.

The Lowdown

The school receives around two hundred applications every year, from which between twenty and twenty-four students are accepted. Along with the usual application materials you will be asked to send a portfolio of creative work (which may be film or video, painting or other visual artwork, or writing samples) and a proposal for a film or video you would like to make while at Columbia College. Good writing ability appears to be as valuable to the admissions committee as actual film experience: about half of the students accepted each year do not have any experience with film or video, but all show some ability to write.

The program calls itself a "Personal Voice" program. The faculty try to take a group of promising individuals and train them to write and direct highly personal stories ("touchy-feely," in the words of one student; "pretentious, uptight . . . suicide films and vampire films," in the words of another). Students who want to make more Hollywood-style narratives should probably not even apply here. Students in the program are discouraged from working in a mainstream idiom, and those who do so anyway often find themselves punished with conditional passes at the end of the first year.

Many of the courses graduate students take are dominated by undergrads. While the graduate film department is fairly hard to get into, the undergraduate department has an open-door admissions policy. This is nice for the undergrads, but graduate students complain of working hard in classes alongside undergrads who often don't give a damn. They say that while graduate-level classes can be good, undergraduate-level classes are often bogged down by undergrads who don't do homework or who read newspapers in class. On the other hand, because of the large undergraduate department there is a broad variety of classes graduates can participate in. The school offers courses in computer and traditional animation, in various aspects of screenwriting, and in new media and interactive technologies; and students are also encouraged to take classes in the college's other departments. Students say that the quality of the classes varies widely depending on teachers, and that it is a good idea to ask around about teachers before committing to classes.

The school has a wide variety of camera equipment, including Arri SR's, Eclair NPR's, CP 16's, and a number of Arri S's and Bolexes. Audio equipment includes timecode Nagras, DAT recorders and a wide variety of microphones. The school owns a couple of Avids and more than a dozen D-Vision nonlinear editing workstations, as well as a number of flatbed editing machines. There are several analog audio mixing suites and recording studios, and a Pro Tools digital audio workstation. While it's not the kind of school where you can walk in and ask for a camera at any time, students report that, with a little warning, they are able to get equipment with minimal trouble whenever they need it.

This is an urban commuter school, so those who are looking for a college with a peaceful, inviting campus and a cuddly school mascot should look elsewhere. Few students can afford to live close to the school (few would particularly want to), but everyone finds relatively large, relatively inexpensive places to live (relative to other cities, that is) within a few miles.

The school keeps copies of all the films made with school equipment and mandates that all students mention the school in the credits of their films. But they do not maintain any rights to students' films.

Some of the best things about the program: The equipment is good, and is fairly available, and the school is keeping up pretty well with the changing technologies. The school puts a heartening emphasis on developing a personal voice and using the visual medium to explore subjects of personal importance. The large undergraduate program ensures that there are a wide variety of electives for graduate students to participate in. Chicago has a lot to offer filmmakers. It has a variety of urban and suburban locations, and it has not been spoiled for filmmakers the way Los Angeles, New York and San Francisco have. People actually seem happy to have film crews shooting in their homes and businesses, and won't demand huge sums of money from you.

Some of the worst things about the program: On the other hand, Chicago does not have a bustling independent filmmaking community the way New York, Los Angeles, San Francisco or Austin do. And winter in Chicago can be trying for those not used to it.

Columbia University

School of the Arts
Film Division
513-C Dodge Hall
New York, NY 10027
Department: (212) 854-2815
Admissions: (212) 854-2134
http://www.columbia.edu

Equipment Quality: ☆☆

Equipment Accessibility: ☆☆

Cost: $$$$

Annual Tuition:	$22,116
Enrollment:	75 per year; 340 total
Deadline:	January 4
Focus:	Independent

The Program

Located on Manhattan's Upper West Side, the only Ivy League entry in the film school arena accepts seventy-five students from over four hundred applications. Of those seventy-five, 10 to 12 percent never see second year.

Columbia has revamped its three-year program over the past few years. The result is an integrated approach that not only teaches film heritage and the practice of making film, but also encourages individual student growth. Wherever possible, students will develop one project within several classes. A script will be written in screenwriting, rehearsed in directing, shot in the production class, and finished in editing. Techniques and principles taught in class are applied to projects, reviewed by class and faculty, then reapplied on more subtle and demanding levels as students progress. Every student must fulfill every role in the filmmaking process. Years one and two of the program require course work, with the final year devoted to thesis projects.

Students graduate with degrees in Directing, Screenwriting, Producing, or History/Theory/Criticism (HTC).

Columbia's long-standing academic tradition mandates a graduate level of proficiency in critical thinking. Six credits of (HTC) are split over two years. This is also the only film program with a language requirement equivalent to one year of intermediate college-level study or demonstrated proficiency.

The first year is very structured. All incoming students must take Film Workshop, Elements of Dramatic Writing, Being an Actor (Directing, Writing, and Acting), and a theory and criticism course taught by the director of the New York Film Festival. In writing class, students write two short screenplays: a five-minute screenplay that they later shoot on video in Film Workshop, and a ten-minute screenplay that, when complete, goes into a file for production the following summer.

In second semester students take Directing Actors, Writing for the Screen, courses in sound and cinematography, and one or two electives. Directing Actors puts students into a studio with actors and video gear; students rehearse actors in scenes written by students or taken from existing films and shoot the end result on video. In Writing for the Screen students write feature-length screenplays. A popular first-year elective is Introduction to the Business of Film, an in-depth, warts-and-all look at the independent film business taught by independent producer Ira Deutchman.

Students make their first year video projects during the summer after first year. Each student chooses a screenplay from the file of ten-minute screenplays written in Elements of Dramatic Writing and makes it into video. Students cannot direct their own screenplays. Each student gets seven days to direct her project, then works as a crew member on her classmates' projects.

At the end of the first year, students must declare a concentration of study. The majority choose between directing and screenwriting; a handful choose producer and HTC majors.

Second year classes are determined by the students' chosen specializations. Students take intermediate and advanced workshops in the specific concentrations of directing, screenwriting, producing, or HTC. These are complemented by electives offered in such areas as editing, cinematography, and comedy writing for television. Students can take a workshop to develop a feature-length screenplay or adapt a previously existing work into a screenplay. A few video exercises are shot early in the second year, and by the end of the first semester students shoot a three-to-five-minute project on film.

In Directing III directing majors prepare an eight-to-twelve-minute script to shoot on film or video as a second-year film project. Although this is not required of nondirecting majors, almost everyone makes a second-year film. Directors have up to eleven days to shoot their own scripts.

Producers focus on seminars in Development, Producing Your First Feature, and No Budget Filmmaking. Writers who have taken Revision classes over the summer can begin preparing for Master's evaluation by the end of the second year. There are also periodic panels or lectures offered throughout the year. Topics may cover film casting, writer-director collaboration, or gay films.

Most students complete the required sixty course credits by the end of the second year. Third-year students register for Research Arts credit (this costs about $1,000 per semester), which is required in order to have access to school facilities and equipment while they pursue their thesis screenplays or films. This also allows students to take Advanced Editing, thesis-level Script to Screen, and Script Revision workshops. Thesis films tend to run approximately twenty minutes, are shot in two weeks, and cost on average of $20,000. Many students work to save money in this third year. Some don't actually begin working on their thesis projects until the end of the third year, completing them in the fourth year. Research Arts credit can be taken for a maximum of three years. All students must graduate within five years.

The Price

$22,116 tuition for two years	$ 44,232
Matriculation for one additional year	$ 2,000
$15,000 a year rent and living expenses for three years	$ 45,000
Average film costs	$ 30,000
Total	**$121,232**

Gulp. The school operates on a flat-fee tuition rate. Students must take a minimum of five three-credit courses each semester in order to complete their sixty credits within two years. It's not financially prudent to take less. Those with extra stamina can take advantage of this system and take up to the eighteen-credit-maximum full-time allowance. The Film Department gives over $400,000 a year in both cash and credit remission. Some incoming students might receive a merit scholarship of about $1,000. Each year the Film Division also appoints several fellows based on faculty ratings of student performance. Students apply in the spring for these awards. Generally awarded at the end of the first year, most fellowship money is allocated as Merit Awards, ranging from $750 to $3,000.

There are also about two dozen Service Fellowships. You cannot receive a Service Fellowship without also receiving a Merit Fellowship. Service Fellows apply for positions in the spring, and winners assist in such areas as film festival research and screening coordination. One fellowship position involves mentoring high school students in the Panasonic-sponsored Kid-Witness workshop. Kids are taught the basics of videography one Saturday each month. With grad guidance they complete short films which are submitted to national competitions.

Teaching assistantships are usually awarded in the spring to students entering their second year. Those who don't get the Service positions often land one of these. The number of appointments, usually around twenty or so, is dictated by enrollment figures for the course. TAs receive $4,226 in tuition credit and a stipend of $1,240 per semester. Third-year TAs receive a $2,000 stipend and no tuition credit.

Departmental Research Assistants (DRA) are typically year-long positions which require work for the Film Division in exchange for a $10,000 tuition credit and a stipend of $920 per semester. Appointments are based not only on performance but also on a student's qualifications to do the necessary work. Since this is not an hourly job, students are obligated to work all the hours necessary to properly complete the assigned task for the year.

Despite this assistance, New York is a very expensive town in which to live. Finding an apartment in New York can be an absolute nightmare. A livable apartment, *sans* roommate, might cost $1,000 a month. This is the absolute truth—the New York rental market is worse than most people can even imagine.

New York apartments are tiny and unbelievably overpriced, especially in Manhattan. Studio apartments start at about $800 (and this doesn't mean a normal studio apartment; this means an apartment the size of a small restaurant's bathroom). Those willing to commute through some very bad parts of town can get more for their money in northern Manhattan (Washington Heights, for instance) or in Brooklyn or Queens. Here rent-controlled older walk-ups are more moderately priced—at around $400 per month. There are parts of Queens where there is no crime at all—namely, the blocks where the Mafia dons live. Find these neighborhoods, and they can be great places to live, as long as one keeps a low profile.

Upon arriving in town, try to stay with a friend as long as possible while apartment hunting. Do not stay at a cheap hotel in New York. Most students can't afford to live alone in New York, so there is always someone looking for a roommate. Check university or department bulletin boards for notices. Check the listings in the *Village Voice* and the *New York Times,* but be aware that there may be hundreds of people responding to the same ads. Be sure to check the newspapers early on the day the notices come out; if there are any good apartments, they will be gone by noon. Apartment brokers are an option; they often have inside information on good apartments, but they charge hefty fees (one month's rent or more) if they find a place for you.

When it comes to New York apartments, perseverance is everything. Those in need of apartments in this town must make this fact known to all they meet. One never knows who might be aware of a vacancy. The best to hope for is a shared apartment with moderately sane people.

Columbia's graduate student housing is a great alternative. The apartments are larger than most, are close to school, and are relatively inexpensive: around $500 for a share, $650 for a studio. For incoming students who live more than 200 miles from the school, housing is guaranteed. Leases begin on June 1 and expire May 31. The second you are no longer matriculated, you are ousted. Some students continue matriculating and delay thesis submittals just to hold on to the housing.

International House, which is nominally affiliated with—but is not run by—the school is worth looking into. This multicultural city-within-a-city is a short walk from the campus and is a fascinating place to be. Although bathrooms are shared, the small rooms rent for about $630 per month.

Columbia boasts historic buildings and a campus that, although located in the bustling city, feels somewhat separate. That's a plus because the "Upper" in Upper West Side does not mean ritzy or posh: the campus is only blocks away from Morningside Park—one of the most dangerous places in New York City. But then again, in New York who can afford posh? The cheapest lifestyle possible in the Big Apple can lead to bankruptcy.

There is an abundance of part-time and temp work in New York. Although the school does not encourage working, about 50 percent of the class must do so.

The Lowdown

Writing is key. In your application, you must provide a personal essay, a dramatic writing sample, and two film treatments. Weak writers will have a difficult time making the grade. Personal essays go a long way in the Columbia application review. The essay almost matters more than any other creative material submitted. With their strong independent focus, the school is not interested in students with Hollywood visions but rather strong, personal perspectives. They prefer students who are not directly from undergraduate programs.

Many students feel that the faculty is the best thing about Columbia. All tend to be working professionals. The ones who aren't are devoted to teaching. All provide useful criticism, have accessible office hours, and are not troubled by home phone calls. As in any other school, some professors are stronger than others. Upperclassmen will clue newcomers in on whom to avoid. There is a real effort made by seasoned professionals to challenge students with different points of view and styles. The producing teachers have been singled out as very strong. Many nonfilm students flock to take their classes. Writing teachers receive some kudos as well. The directing teachers are considered the weakest.

Columbia's equipment is notorious for being old and tempermental. Columbia is fighting back with the appointment of a new equipment manager, who is seriously trying to maintain and upgrade the equipment for the first time in the school's history. In the past, video equipment was a real sore spot with students. Serious directors often purchased their own Hi-8 cameras. Other students rented digital cameras for their projects. Sometimes groups of individuals united to pool their resources to rent a Betacam to shoot final projects.

The school swears that this situation is changing. Sixteen new S-VHS video cameras have just been donated by Panasonic. These packages come with basic grip, sound, and lighting and should eliminate some of the availability problems. There are plans to upgrade to digital cameras down the line. There are three Arri SR-1s for non-thesis and second-year films. There is one Arri SR-2 thesis camera and five Arri Ss for pickup shots. Although they are accessorized with basic sound, lighting, and grip support, most students augment packages, especially with grip equipment. First-year and nonthesis students can reserve equipment for eight weeks in advance. Thesis students can reserve equipment twelve weeks in advance.

Students reserve editing time one week in advance. Editing time allotments and sessions vary according to format and class status. First-year students edit on seven ancient three-quarter-inch decks. Because of student overload these machines break down constantly. There is a grant proposal in the works to upgrade them to high-end Beta setups. There are two super VHS video suites for second-year students, and seven Steenbeck six-plate flatbeds and four two-plates. There is also a Telecine film-to-tape transfer.

The school does not own any nonlinear editing systems. They are hoping to rectify this with the much-awaited media lab scheduled to open in spring of 1997. Students will have access to sixteen low-end digital computer editing stations, four of which will be high-end media 100s stations reserved for upperclassman. It is projected that every first-year student will go from video straight to digital editing when the lab is functioning.

Prentis Studio is a small soundstage that is rarely used but can be reserved in advance for twenty-four or forty-eight hours. There is one screening room in which classes are held. Most students rent outside space to screen dailies. There is a minimal sound transfer system.

Each spring there is a week-long film festival. It begins with a night of the best of the first-year video projects, as chosen by the faculty. There is a night of screenplay readings during which selections from students' thesis scripts are presented. For the remainder of the week, thesis films are screened each evening and second-year films are shown in the afternoon. Both the screenings and readings are well attended by agents and industry representatives. The last night of the festival is "Faculty Selects," a program of the top ten or so films selected by the faculty. Films over twenty-seven minutes do not qualify for this screening. There are cash awards and sometimes industry donations of editing time or film processing. In early fall the Faculty Selects is presented again at the DGA (Directors Guild of America) in Los Angeles.

The school is trying to institute an additional night of screenplay readings in February. If successful, authors would have twenty-five to thirty minutes to present a section of their screenplays for faculty and students.

Filmmakers will find no better talent pool than New York. One advertisement in *Backstage,* the local actors' newspaper, can draw hundreds of responses. New York is the training center for truly serious actors, and many start out doing student films.

Some of the best things about the program: This is an intelligent, well-rounded curriculum, led by a strong faculty. Everyone writes. Each student will graduate with a film and a screenplay . . . no matter what her focus. The school maintains a script bank which catalogues feature-length student scripts and summarizes key marketable elements. A twenty-page publication highlighting these elements is sent to development agents on both coasts. Several students have secured agents, met with producers, and even had scripts optioned through this resource. The department library provides up-to-date listings of all film festival and screenplay competitions.

Student screenings are finally being supported and well promoted by the school. Industry contact and exposure is increasing. Students are starting to achieve some recognition on the festival circuit. Several have had screenplays optioned or extended thesis films into feature projects with production companies.

Some of the worst things about the program: Columbia still suffers from gender bias, despite the large number of women students.

In terms of preferential treatment, it's still a bit of a boys' club. Students whose films look the best often get more faculty attention. There is no Avid—this is a real drawback. Several students have invested additional dollars in purchasing their own Avids. Film students need the latest technology at their disposal in order to compete in the job market upon graduation. But at Columbia, technical skills are secondary to the narrative focus. Students historically take a long time to finish.

Florida State University

Graduate Film Conservatory
A3100 University Center
Tallahassee, FLA 32306-2084
Department: (904) 644-0453
Admissions: (904) 644-3420
http://www.fsu.edu/~film

Equipment Quality: ☆☆☆☆☆

Equipment Accessibility: ☆☆☆☆

Cost: $$

Annual Tuition:	Resident: $5,400 Nonresident: $17,700
Enrollment:	24; 48 total
Deadline:	March 1
Focus:	Industry

The Program

About to enter its seventh year of existence, the Florida State Graduate Film Conservatory was initiated by the state in order to actively position Florida as a viable film production location. This is a heavily funded state-of-the-art school with facilities that often equal industry standards. It attempts to replicate Hollywood filmmaking and wants to turn out craftspeople, not artists.

Four to five hundred applications are received for the twenty-four slots that open every fall. The students that do make the cut are an energetic group. And energy is something you'll need to survive this two-year, year-round program that employs a conservatory approach.

Like most schools, there's a general focus on the main production disciplines of writing, directing, editing, cinematography, and sound, and the appropriate in-class exercises that accompany each. What makes this program unique is the interaction between class years and the workshop training atmosphere on major productions. This is a program less about classes than about learning through hands-on experience. All film costs, save craft services and possibly some props for your short class projects, are completely covered by the school. Students will not pay one cent toward film stock, processing, or post-production work. Thesis projects are funded entirely. This also means that all films are owned by the school.

During the first week of school there are no classes. Students meet as a group on the soundstage for a one-week equipment crash course. They learn the basics necessary to rotate crew positions on their first 16-mm productions, Directing I projects. The next few weeks cover filmmaking principles in a classroom setting. These principles are then applied on an individual basis as faculty members meet with students to specifically discuss and plan each Directing I project. Students meet with a writing instructor to work on their scripts. They'll scout locations and talk lighting plans with a cinematography instructor. By the time first-years are catapulted into production, they'll have discussed all aspects of their film with directing, editing, producing, and sound-recording instructors. Each project is shot in two twelve-hour days. At the semester's end the five-minute Directing I projects are completed with each student having written and directed her own project and crewed once in every key position on classmates' films. These films will be posted entirely on film using flatbeds and transferring one-quarter sound tape to mix on mag stock.

Simultaneously with their Directing I work, students are required to assist as crew members on second-year students' Directing III projects. This interaction allows first-year students to progress with more hands-on training while second-year students are supplied with the crew support necessary to create a more advanced showpiece. In the midst of this production work, each week an Aesthetics class screens two faculty-selected films for group discussion.

During the second semester of their first year, students experience their first thesis cycle. When thesis scripts are posted in December, like their second-year counterparts, they choose films they are interested in working on. They then must interview with thesis directors and producers, (whom they already know from the Directing III projects), for below-the-line positions on thesis films. Once they receive their assignments, they attend advanced production workshops to learn their positions. They also attend a nonlinear editing workshop to learn the Avid. By the third week of February the thesis projects are in production, and first-year students will spend the rest of the second semester crewing on two to three projects. All thesis projects adhere to SAG rules. They operate on a twelve-hour-day, six-day-a-week schedule for two-week cycles.

The first-year summer session is for Directing II projects. As in the first semester, students again support one another by rotating crew positions. This time positions are selected by the faculty so that students do not flock to the same people. This is an extremely collaborative program, and the faculty wants students to work with as many different classmates as possible. The other difference is that this five-to-seven-minute film is based on preexisting material. This enables students to concentrate on learning the language of directing actors without having to put the words in their mouths. They are able instead to search for and capture the drama inherent in existing works.

This also provides the necessary free time to start writing Directing III and/or thesis scripts. Students interested in submitting a thesis script must take a summer writing class in which to develop the screenplay. There's also a Production Management course to prepare for Directing III. Once in the can, Directing II films are transferred to tape and edited on Avid. The sound is edited and mixed on Pro Tools systems.

At the end of the first year, students will have explored all the different crew positions. They then meet with the faculty for a review. At this time they are encouraged to pinpoint a focus for the remainder of school.

By the end of the summer, fifty to sixty thesis scripts are submitted to the faculty who selects eight to ten for thesis consideration. The end of the first year also means Directing III projects are right around the corner.

The second-year fall semester is often viewed as the most stressful—albeit the stress being self-imposed by the students. Each Directing III screenplay must be ready the first week of the class. Crew rotation selection is once more in the hands of the students. Those who have decided that directing is not their calling may skip directing altogether and start to specialize. Students with a specialized focus are free to shoot, edit, or produce as many Directing III projects as they can handle.

As in the summer session, during the first weeks students will meet in a workshop forum with cinematography, editing, and sound instructors to plan Directing III projects. Students focusing on producing take an advanced producing course on developing a feature film. Thesis writers go into rewrite class so that their scripts are

completed by the end of the semester. Directing III scripts are delivered and students enter production in October. A composer from
the school of music is assigned to each Directing III. Directors
work closely with composers to create a score for each project. Directing IIIs are shot in two twelve-hour shooting days. By the end
of the fall semester, films have been completed on the Avid, this
time with a full musical score and effects track.

In early December, any student who wants to direct a thesis can
submit a reel of her work. Sixteen to seventeen students generally
apply. After the Directing III film screening, the faculty selects who
can pitch themselves to direct a thesis film. Fifteen usually make
this cut.

Pitching consists of a forty-five-minute interview in which students explain why they should be the person to direct a specific project. These interviews are sometimes lavish presentations with
music and artwork. Students go all out to demonstrate their talent
and connection with a project. Each director can pitch any two
scripts from the pool of eight.

After two days of interviews, the faculty selects five writers
and directors in early December. Sometimes the same person is
chosen for these positions. With faculty approval, the writers and
directors select a producer. The rest of the class interviews for the
remainder of the above-the-line crew positions. By the end of the
week, those have been filled and the first-year students interview
for their spots in early January. Once selected, first-years busy
themselves with their workshops while the thesis films are in pre-
production. Student producers are assigned their budgets (somewhere in the area of $16,000) and proceed to plan the entire shoot.
In late February the films enter production. They shoot in two-
week cycles, again adhering to SAG guidelines. As each film finishes, they begin their post work which will usually carry them
throughout the summer.

Summer of the second year is addressed on a student-by-student
basis. Editors are still working on films. Some students line up internships. Producers are supposed to follow their films through to
completion. They can take an additional class or, with school permission, a nonconflicting internship. There are several classes of-

fered on an invitation only basis. These are designed for students with a specialized focus.

Cinematographers can take advantage of an advanced 35-mm cinematography course. Panavision donates a rig to the school so that serious cinematographers may gain 35-mm experience and obtain footage for their reels. There's a Film Marketing and Distribution class for producers, an Advanced Sound class for sound majors and a Feature Screenplay class for writers.

By August graduation, films have been completed and are screened for family and friends as part of the graduation ceremony. In addition to the graduation screening, Florida State conducts a well-publicized thesis film screening at the Director's Guild in Los Angeles. The dean selects the films that are shown. Film festival entries of thesis films are also made at the dean's discretion. The chosen films are heavily promoted and entered in festivals worldwide. If a film is not school supported on the festival circuit, students can make arrangements and pay for festival entries on their own.

The Price

RESIDENT

$1,800 per semester for six consecutive semesters	$10,800
$9,600 a year rent and living expenses for two years	$19,200
Average film costs (miscellaneous)	$ 200
Total	**$30,200**

NONRESIDENT

$5,900 per semester for six consecutive semesters	$35,400
$9,600 a year rent and living expenses for two years	$19,200
Average film costs (miscellaneous)	$ 200
Total	**$54,800**

Residents can't beat this deal. In order to establish residency, a person must live in and collect a paycheck in the state for one year. Work-study or school-supported employment does not fulfill this requirement. Time constraints make it extremely difficult to have a part-time job, especially outside the department. Determined or desperate students have been known to pursue some minimal job in order to cash in on the lower tuition by second year. One lucky incoming student thought to demonstrate the most potential receives a full scholarship from the get-go.

Even teaching assistants, of which there are usually about ten, have a very tough time meeting their minimum work hours. Luckily the assistant workload is light and the hours are flexible. TAs are completely exempt from work-study hours during thesis cycles. Down the road the school hopes to convert these positions into scholarships to eliminate the work requirement entirely. Until then, most of the TAships go to second-year students who receive a full tuition waiver and about $700 each month per semester. By graduation most students have had an assistantship at some point.

Florida State University has an agreement with the Screen Actors Guild and often features SAG actors in Directing III and thesis films. Other projects make use of the actors in the school M.F.A. or B.A. acting programs. It is not uncommon for the school to sponsor casting calls in Orlando or Jacksonville or even approach New York or L.A. actors who interest them. There is a casting director who works with the school in coordinating local talent searches.

Tallahassee is a safe, quiet state capital. It's a large industrial burg with lots of lawyers but little culture. Nice two-bedroom shares go for about $650. A one-bedroom falls in the $400 price range. School is within walking distance for most. You don't need a car.

The Lowdown

Applications must highlight a history of creative expression. GRE scores matter and statements of purpose are vital. While most submit reels, it's not necessarily the folks with the most experience, but rather those with greatest desire and determination to be part of the filmmaking process who are selected. Every attempt is made to match a class as a whole and they will want to make sure that applicants fit in with their Hollywood paradigm. There is no room for egos.

The faculty is not star-studded, but they do boast Academy Award–winning sound recordist Richard Portman. Several instructors are knowledgeable, enthusiastic, and helpful: the kind that will accept a midnight phone call to talk you through a problem. They could use some more writing talent. It's a mix of working and non-working professionals who really listen to students. The requests of past students have had a real impact on the program that exists today. If students identify a problem, it is usually remedied.

There are quite a few specialists brought in for Pro-Seminar Lectures. These guests range from respected screenwriters to obscure sound technicians. Students say that Dean Ray Fielding, who is one heck of a P.R. man, is prone to favoritism. A special-effects expert, students say he is partial to thesis scripts that spotlight such techniques. He's gone so far as to approve a student-staged special-effects demonstration for Movie Magic on the Discovery Channel. His partiality poses a problem for both thesis film selection and festival entering, according to students. If he doesn't like you or your film, he will not support it. But he energetically promotes the student films he likes, entering them in festivals and issuing press releases to highlight the results.

Florida State's star is on the rise. They work to get the school's name out there and cash in on any publicity to keep it there. Thanks to constant entering of festivals, the school's films are starting to receive worldwide recognition. One of the first films out of the program caught the eye of Quentin Tarantino at one such festival. With his support, the project was developed into the feature film *Curdled,* released in 1996.

As a relatively new, well-funded program, Florida State is on the cutting edge when it comes to all the latest technologies. Equipment is partially shared with the undergraduate department. But since the production schedules are well established, and some equipment is reserved just for grads, there are no conflicts. First-year graduate students use the dozen or so CP 16s. There are ten Arri SRs for second-years. And, of course, there's the Panavision loaner for select students. There are two chameleon dollies and large lighting packages with several HMIs. The sound packages, approved by Mr. Portman, are high-quality DAT and Nagra setups. There are even two grip trucks available for Directing III and thesis projects. Equipment is in a constant maintenance cycle. At any given time, two cameras are being refurbished at Arriflex. If equipment is available, students with the time can check it out on their own.

There's a large mix theater with an acoustically centered mix board and seating for one hundred and forty. Mixing Room B emulates this while Mixing Room C is solely used by first-years for traditional 16-mm film mixing. There's an ADR/Foley room.

There are seven flatbed editing suites, three Avids, several Beta off-line and on-line suites, and four Pro Tools stations with a fifth on the way. Sound Stage A is a 3,000-square-foot space with remote-control grid lighting. Sound Stage B is about half that size.

There's a twenty-four-hour writing lab open to the entire school. It houses ten to twelve Macintosh computers loaded with Final Draft screenwriting and Movie Magic budgeting software. There's also a video library with over five thousand movie titles

Some of the best things about the program: Students get a lot for their money and even more with the school's money. Everyone gets to write and direct something, and graduates depart with employable technical skills. There's a very strong chance of professional level exposure to special effects, usually unheard of on student films. We're not just talking miniatures but matte painting and train wrecks.

Even those who don't direct thesis films could have a strong showpiece in their Directing III film. Without a film budget variable, the student playing field is really level.

This is Mecca for aspiring cinematographers and sound recordists. The equipment is plentiful, well organized, and up-to-date. The classes are tight-knit.

Some of the worst things about the program: The consecutive year-round training can be exhausting. Some students can't hack the boot camp mentality. Some drop out; others have been asked to leave. Film allotments must be strictly adhered to. There's no margin for error or improvisation. Big Brother is watching . . . constantly scoping for the next thesis directors. There's no guarantee to direct a thesis film. This creates a great deal of stress around Directing III projects. And there's always some bitterness after thesis directors' selection. The DGA screenings are a bit political. Because so much assistance is given, students are not prepared for the guerrilla tactics paramount in pursuing independent filmmaking.

The post-school network is extremely active and supportive. Despite his flaws, Dean Fielding is akin to a proud parent. He's a public relations machine, intent on making the industry take notice of his program. There's a snazzy school bulletin that keeps students and alumni posted on everything they could possibly want to know about current and past students as well as thesis films and program updates. Former students have actually created their own Web site. There's a growing L.A. contingent of alums that should only increase and assist recent grads.

Howard University

Department of Radio
  Television and Film
School of Communications
525 Bryant Street, N.W.
Washington, DC 20059
Department: (202) 806-
  7927/7929
Admissions: (202) 806-2750
http://www.soc.howard.edu/
  RTF/RTFFirst

Independent

**Equipment
Quality:** ☆

**Equipment
Accessibility:** ☆

Cost: $$$

Annual Tuition:	**$10,041 (full-time); $533 per credit**
Enrollment:	**10; 38 total**
Deadline:	**Fall: June 30 Spring: November 1**
Focus:	**Independent**

The Program

Howard University is America's leading African-American university. Each year they receive slightly under a hundred applications for their M.F.A. Film Program, which began in 1984. From this group, ten candidates are chosen for admittance.

Before beginning this two-year program, students with minimal or no film background must first fulfill a semester of prerequisites which do not apply toward their degree. These include Film History, Scriptwriting I, Cinematography I (a nonsync 16-mm production course), Blacks in Film, and History of Documentary Film. Experience mandates whether all or some of these courses will be required. These undergrad-level classes are available during any semester, but it's a good idea to take them in the spring before the "official" fall start of the two-year curriculum.

Classes are offered in a progressive order once a year starting with that fall semester. Howard tries to accommodate students' lifestyles and financial constraints, so they do permit them to veer off the department recommended schedule and even pursue part-time study if necessary. This is accepted, but not encouraged. Skipping a required course in the fall or spring means waiting a whole year until it is offered again. This will needlessly extend the program and immerse the student in a serious game of "catch-up."

If at all possible, stay on track and follow their suggestions exactly in order to graduate anywhere near on time. Part-time study is inadvisable. Each student is assigned an advisor at the start of the program. Students should consult with individual advisors when problems or questions arise, especially regarding course loads.

Although nine credits is considered full-time, in order to keep on track, take fifteen credits per semester. This is tough, because in addition to production work, classes will require written projects as well as tests. Try to get syllabus copies prior to the start of the semester to get a jump on projects. At the very least, plan accordingly when professors provide due dates at the start of the class. Of sixty required credits, six are electives, normally taken in the last semester.

First semester follows up the undergrad prerequisites with Scriptwriting II, Cinematography II, Film History, and Film Editing. In the second semester there's Cinematography III, Film Analysis, Critique and Theory, and Cinema Sound. At Howard, the first cinematography courses are actually production courses in which films are made. In scriptwriting courses, students are encouraged to complete feature-length screenplays. Most settle for shorts with only those focusing on screenwriting pursuing a feature-length project.

In Cinematography II students make a sync-sound group project. They jointly decide on a short student-written script, then rotate crew positions scene by scene. Every student gets a shot at every position during this typically weekend production. If well done, this unedited project is then handed over as an editing exercise to the following year's editing class. If not well done, as was the case during this writing, the editing class is given a traditional, much-used elementary editing exercise known as "The Robbery." Cinematography III is not a production course. Students instead choose a cinematography-related topic which they must research, write a paper about, then present as a lecture to the class.

The fall of the second and final year progresses with African-American Cinema, Scriptwriting III, Directing II, and the first elective opportunity. Since there are few film classes offered beyond the required courses, most students choose electives outside the department. In Directing II students finally make their own five-minute films (the first since the prerequisite Cinematography I class).

By spring it's time for thesis class along with a Production/Distribution Seminar. At this juncture a focus is selected and students pursue either Advanced Film Directing or Screenwriting IV. In this final directing course students shoot a short video, not film. This is done so that cost is not an issue and students can concentrate on the process of directing. Different professors teach this course in different ways. Sometimes students direct different sections of the same script. Other times, they choose a short scene from an existing script.

A three-to-one shooting ratio of film stock and processing (or videotape where applicable) is provided for all class projects. This varies according to the approved film length per class (five minutes for Directing; fifteen minutes for thesis films). Students who exceed these allotments absorb the additional costs. In the past, some students made extremely long thesis films that took forever to finish, if at all. For this reason future thesis projects may have to meet with department approval before film stock is provided. With department approval, school equipment is available, to make as many additional films as one can afford and find the time for. Most students don't make additional films.

All films shoot on weekends or Tuesdays or Fridays, when there are no classes scheduled. The school does not pay for or require students to take their films through to completion or answer print stage. Once processed, most projects are transferred to video. This is often as far as most make it. Students retain their negative to match at a later date if they so choose. Although the school does at least partially pay for film costs and thus "technically" owns copyright, this has never been an issue challenged by either the school or students.

The thesis requirement is met through either a feature-length screenplay or a short thesis film. In the past, screenplays have been the preferred route. For those who choose to pursue a screenplay thesis, Scriptwriting IV must be taken as an elective. Once course requirements are fulfilled, students need only register for one credit each semester to maintain matriculation while completing a thesis.

While each graduate student is encouraged to participate in the end-of-semester screenings, undergrad films make up the majority of this two-day offering. Grads are usually not finished in time to make the deadline. The Paul Robeson screening, held in late spring, is primarily for grad students. Students must submit their films to be judged for acceptance into this screening. The winners are shown for this university-attended function. There are some cash or film prizes. Plans are in the works to start extending invitations to the public. If this goes well, an industry screening could be next.

Talent to perform in productions is usually gleaned from the school theater department. Students have to initiate this search as there is no solid communication between departments. Most advertise in local papers. Howard does have a relationship with several local casting companies which often help supply actors. It is not uncommon to resort to fellow classmates for casting.

The Price

$10,041 per year for two years	$20,082
Matriculation for one additional year	$ 1,066
$7,200 a year rent and living expenses for three years	$21,600
Average film costs	$10,000
Total	**$52,748**

The good news is that all graduate film classes are only offered in the evening. Classes usually take place after 4:00 P.M. and wrap up around 9:00 P.M. This is ideal because most grad students need to have day jobs. And although D.C. is not a cheap city in which to reside, luckily the job pool is significant. The bad news is all graduate classes are offered in the evening. This is because Howard is not in an economically prosperous neighborhood. While living in nearby group houses may be cost efficient, this is a high-crime area.

Like many inner-city campuses, the university is not at all separated from the neighborhood. The locals, friend and foe alike, will be sharing your campus.

You could choose to commute from another neighborhood, but you will still need some street savvy traveling the metro and walking in the streets. Public transportation is good, so you can get by without a car. Graduate housing is limited and expensive, so most students live off campus. Off-campus rents average in the $400 range for shares to $600 for one-bedrooms. If you do have a car, you might want to consider living in Virginia or Maryland, which are only a short commute away and offer more and often better housing options. Regardless of where you reside, be sure to take advantage of the many resources and cultural venues of Washington, D.C. There are numerous institutions with large film collections and information. The Smithsonian, American Film Institute, the National Geographic Society, the National Archives, and the Library of Congress are at your disposal.

Five to seven teaching assistants are selected by the faculty each year. Students apply for these coveted spots and are chosen based upon their academic performance and level of skill as evaluated by the faculty. Candidates are interviewed, and those selected receive full tuition remission and an $8,000 stipend for one year. In return, they will assist professors or teach labs to undergrad students. Other than the film allotments, there are no additional cash grants to aid students with the cost of their films.

The Lowdown

Howard wants to groom independent filmmakers. A film background is not important for acceptance. In the statement of purpose they'll be looking for motivated, intelligent, committed students who demonstrate some purpose beyond personal gain. Applicants should possess a strong social awareness. A film portfolio is not necessary, but feel free to include any creative work relevant to the course of study.

Professors tend to be working professionals. While they are accessible and committed, they are limited in number. Students repeatedly take classes with the same teachers, thus limiting different film perspectives and styles.

The financial limitations of Howard make themselves apparent in the equipment area. While the minimum necessary to make films is available, the equipment is not well maintained and most of it is shared with undergrads. This means it breaks down a lot and repairs take forever. Last summer most equipment was sent out for repair and was inaccessible for three months.

There's an abundance of super-8 cameras, (virtually unused by grads), three Arri SRs, eight Bolexes, and an old, loud Mitchell 35 SR that no one uses. The best Arri is reserved for grads. There are Nagra sound recorders and basic microphones to accompany cameras.

Supposedly booking two days in advance can usually reserve an equipment package, but five days is better insurance. There is a hierarchy of preference for equipment availability. Class projects take precedence over any other. These are followed by thesis projects, grad students, undergrads, and special projects. Students complain that they barely have the time and equipment access to do little more than meet class deadlines. Creativity and aesthetics often suffer. Equipment is only available for checkout on a daily or weekend basis. Suffice it to say, weekend slots go very fast. Without proper planning, equipment can be unavailable on weekends. It is not uncommon to experience a shortage of cables, lights, and accessories. Students frequently adjust their schedules to share packages in order to complete work on time.

There are seven post-production editing suites. These hold two six-plate, one eight-plate, four four-plate flatbeds, and a Moviola. These suites can be reserved for two-hour time slots. Unfortunately, at any given time, several of these suites tend to be indefinitely commandeered by thesis students' works-in-progress. At this writing five were in this state. Thesis students permanently fill these rooms with their own materials and films, essentially making them unavailable for anyone else. The school is supposedly looking to expand the number of editing suites. They also need to consider banning this "possession is nine-tenths of the law" ownership policy in the interim.

There is no Avid. There is an S-VHS editing suite, several three-quarter-inch editing suites, and Telecine film-to-tape transfer. There are definite plans to expand their video post, especially regarding digital formats. And although there are no plans to purchase an Avid in the near future, they are aggressively searching for a donor to provide one. This is another reason why students often resort to film-to-tape transfer. Some students would like to try to complete their films entirely on video, pending department approval.

Howard's most basic problem is lack of resources. Students say that the professors are good, but there just aren't enough of them. The equipment is functional, but again, there isn't enough.

Some of the best things about the program: Students will receive the basics necessary for a film education with the bonus of a greater understanding of black cinema. Howard is not at present recognized for its film program, but the school has a fine reputation. Students will have the freedom to make whatever kinds of films they choose. The program is a nurturing environment designed for people of color and offers an impressive collection of research material in African-American history and culture.

Some of the worst things about the program: Because Howard is interested in developing independent filmmakers there's no real Hollywood network or access for students who would like to pursue that venue. Students can wind up stuck in the program for a very long time if they don't push themselves. Projects are not always completed on film, and many are never completed at all. There's no exposure to the technology that is changing the film industry and creating jobs. The program doesn't allow for serious specialization.

Some classes are ill defined. Cinematography and Directing are often more like extended production classes rather than courses that teach the specifics of each craft. There are few faculty members so students will not be exposed to a large scope of perspectives. A great deal is expected from each course in a short amount of time, despite the fact that facilities are minimal. Registration is a disorganized and frustrating process. There need to be more financial subsidies to help with film costs. Previous alumni are disgruntled and hesitant to assist the school.

There is a job corps office that invites television and film representatives to Howard for student interviews. This same office is trying to overcome years of alumni disinterest and dissatisfaction in order to rekindle connections and solicit much-needed support from grads. Upon graduation, it is up to students to maintain connections with classmates and find their way into filmmaking.

This two-year program can be completed in two and a half years by students who work nonstop and choose to write a thesis screenplay, or those whose thesis films the gods of finance smile upon. Three years is the standard. Switch to part-time and years could be added.

New York University

Department of Film and
   Television
Graduate Division
721 Broadway, 9th floor
New York, NY 10012
Department: (212) 998-1780
Admissions: (212) 998-1918
http://www.nyu.edu

Independent

**Equipment
Quality:** ✮✮✮✮

**Equipment
Accessibility:** ✮✮

Cost: $$$$$

Annual Tuition:	**$21,625**
Enrollment:	**36; 85 total**
Deadline:	**December 15**
Focus:	**Independent**

The Program

New York University is a big school in the crowded heart of a big city. The Tisch School of the Arts Graduate Program feels small by comparison. Thirty-six students are chosen from over one thousand applications each year. This number drops through attrition by the second year. This is an expensive and demanding three-year commitment.

Within the last five years NYU has gone through a complete metamorphosis. Stronger support systems have been initiated, and the number of students accepted has been decreased by more than half. Many of the old professors were purged and replaced with a completely new crowd. Classes have been restructured and split into smaller sections to allow for more interaction between professors and students. New courses have been added, especially in the screenwriting area. Most of the changes can be credited to the new dean, Cheryl Antonio, and the department chair, Christine Choy. These two women have tried to address the needs and requests of students that for years went largely ignored. The end result is a more dynamic, albeit staggeringly expensive, graduate film program. The school attempts to provide students with a realistic vision of the field they have chosen and train employable graduates who can pay back those students loans (of which there will be plenty), in film-related positions after school.

Initially, there is little room for personal choice at NYU. All first-year students follow the same, jam-packed schedule. While there is a very heavy class load for both first and second year, first year is by far the most difficult.

All production courses are taken alongside the appropriate aesthetics courses each semester. In the first semester, Aesthetics of Silent Film is taken with Motion Picture Camera Tech, Fundamentals of Screenwriting, Editing, Directing Silent Films, Production Management, Location Sound Recording, and the Actor's Craft. To ground students with equipment, each directs four MOS one-to-two-minute exercises on 16-mm B&W reversal film. Four hundred feet of film stock and processing is provided. The semester concludes with one four-minute nonsync film. No classes are taken during the two weeks students work in groups of six to create their four-minute MOS films. With the support of the group, each student directs her own film in two days. Six hundred feet of B&W reversal stock and developing and 1200 feet of 16-mm mag stock is provided. It is common for students to augment their allotments. Projects are completed by January.

In the spring semester it's more Motion Picture Tech and Actor's Craft, along with the Aesthetics of Documentary, Writing Dialogue, Editing/Sound Mixing, Documentary Directing, Production Management, and Sync Sound Recording. Four hundred feet of B&W negative, processing, one-quarter-inch sound tape, 600 feet of mag stock, and edge coding are provided for an eight-minute documentary film, the production piece for this term. Students work in groups of three this round. At the end of each year, there is a faculty evaluation. Adjuncts are brought in along with regular staff to discuss and evaluate a student's progress.

Before second year even starts, there is an intensive two-week writers' workshop to prepare those without second-year project scripts. Those without a first draft are required to attend this boot camp which meets three times a week from the last week of August through the first week of September. The "official" second year covers Producing Short Films, Aesthetics of Style, Pre-Production Direction, Writing Short Films, Cinematography, Narrative Sound, and Directing Actors. Either Production Design and Editing Dialogue can be taken as an elective. The writing course focuses on creating a thesis film for third year. The first-semester project is a twelve-minute narrative or documentary. There are also additional short video exercises shot in directing. These videos can cover a range of topics, including effective uses of props, casting, blocking, etc.

Spring of second semester continues with The Aesthetics of Genre, Masters Class Directing, Thesis Writing, and Advanced Editing. The Masters Class is a workshop in which each student screens second-year project dailies and rough cuts to the faculty three times during the semester. The purpose is to advise, adjust, and plan for any necessary reshoots. This time Aesthetics deals with the basics of building a solid story. Students begin to post their second-year projects, usually continuing to work on them into third year. Second-year films edit on flatbeds.

In fall of third year, students select one writing class: Thesis Writing, Thesis Alternative Writing, or Thesis Feature Writing. Thesis Directing is also required. The remaining ten credits are electives designed to help the transition to the real world and potential employment. Students choose ten credits of electives from courses like Interactive Writing, Nonlinear Editing, Digital Sound Design, Acting, Exhibition Distribution, and Packaging or internships. A wide variety of internships are available to film students at such companies as Paramount Pictures, Dateline NBC, the Tribeca Film Center, HBO, and a host of independent production and post-production companies.

The writing course continues through the spring along with Thesis Producing and Directing. Six elective credits can be filled with Advanced Cinematography, Nonlinear Editing, Digital Sound, Directing Scenes, Aesthetics of Narrative Structure, or an internship. All directors, except those with special departmental approval, must make a thesis film. Each student has to apply for her thesis. Thesis projects must be green-lighted by writing and production faculty and department chairs. Films shoot for two-week cycles, starting in the spring and continuing through summer and fall. The stipend for this thirty-minute project is $1,950. This is barely a drop in the ol' film budget. Producers, cinematographers, or editors can work on four to five films for thesis credit. Collaboration is encouraged, and it is preferred that directors not edit their films. While working on their thesis films, students continue to have full access to all equipment and facilities for the bargain price of only $650 per semester. Thesis films can edit on Avid. Most students graduate in four years. No one can stay past six years.

There are several unique extracurricular programs in existence at NYU. Third-year students have the option of choosing a mentor for an apprentice sort of experience for two semesters. Students inform the department what areas they are interested in, and the school searches for a mentor match. In order to be eligible to participate, the student must have a prethesis review, after which the prospective "mentee" fills out a questionnaire listing the type of mentor she seeks: director, writer, etc. Each student is interviewed and matched with a mentor. A mentor is expected to consult with the mentee at least twice a month and assist in identifying postgraduate opportunities. There is also a Cinematographer Mentor Program, limited to ten graduate students, and a Commercial Editors Union Mentor Program.

The Directors Series is a weekly screening that provides a venue for a variety of directors, writers, producers, and actors to show their work and answer questions afterward.

The Contact Series is an informal lunch that allows students to relate on a more personal level with film and television professionals. Attendees include faculty and grad and undergrad students. Everyone brings their lunch and listens while the guest discusses her role in the industry. Students must sign up for this lunch, held once a week in the Dean's Conference Room.

Third-year students are invited to the TNT Masters Contact Series every Friday. This is an hour-long opportunity to meet front-rank professionals at Turner Network Television to better understand the TV market.

The Master Workshop is a series of specific training sessions led by a guest professional. The Master Director's Workshop provides third-year grads the unique opportunity of participating in a workshop where a twenty-minute scene for their thesis film script is presented live before an audience of their peers and the visiting master director. Questions and critique ensue. Past guest directors include

Spike Lee, Arthur Penn, and Beeban Kidron. Other workshops topics have included "Cinematography, " "Legal Aspects of Filmmaking," "Independent Filmmaking," and even "The Hitchhiker's Guide to Electronic Post-Production of Feature Films on the Avid." All workshops are videotaped for the archives.

The Price

$21,625 tuition per year for three years	$ 64,875
Matriculation (for one additional year)	$ 1,300
$15,000 rent and living expenses for four years	$ 60,000
Average film costs	$ 30,000
Total	**$156,175**

Luckily, this book can double as a sturdy fan for the faint of heart. When we said "staggeringly expensive," we weren't just whistling "Dixie." And our film costs assume level-headed, relatively trouble-free filmmaking.

First-year students will have to bite the bullet as far as additional financial aid is concerned. Thirteen teaching assistantships are available to second- and third-year students. Assignments are based upon faculty evaluations and the level of skill a student can bring to a position. Recipients work twenty hours a week and receive full tuition remission and a $6,785 stipend per semester.

There are four fellowships and a handful of other scholarships that provide 50 percent tuition. The Mitsubishi Foundation pays one student $5,000 toward her thesis to supervise a Japanese student in the program. There are quite a few post-production awards that are given out on a competitive basis. These usually go to thesis students, and the lowest is around $1,000. Again, the faculty reviews each student's work to determine who receives the funding. The department hopes to develop a fellowship program down the road.

Although the matriculation fee is reasonable, and does postpone repayment of student loans, the reason most students don't graduate within three years is financial. After handing over $64,000 tuition, after paying to make a number of short films in first and second years, and after shelling out to live in overpriced apartments in New York for three years, few students have $20,000 left with which to make a thesis film. This is the main reason stays are extended.

Although it's draining, only those students who have chosen their parents wisely do not have to work. New York offers a great deal of decent-paying temp work. Many students proofread on night shifts. There is always waiting tables.

As at Columbia, students contend with exorbitant New York rents and unbelievably horrible New York apartments. Those coming from out of state will be tempted to apply for university housing. Don't. Rents are outrageous (around $1,000 per month) to share a one-room apartment with a total stranger. What's worse, the school actually makes students sign a one-year lease. Full rent must be paid during the summer even if a student leaves town. Some people manage to sublet their apartments for those months, but it's a very hard sell: these are small, ridiculously expensive places to live. International students often fall victim to university housing. There is a helpful student off-campus housing office that lists quite a variety of apartments and shares.

Check it frequently as the list is updated on a regular basis and the good listings don't last. And, as usual, department bulletin boards and local papers are not to be overlooked. Luckily, a car is not necessary and would actually pose more of a problem than anything else.

New York is the cultural capital of the world. The city pulsates with an energy not found anywhere else. There is tremendous exposure to all the arts. The museum, performance, and music scenes are unrivaled, and for filmmakers, there is something to be said for seeing the world on foot. Different perspectives that often elude those in cars await the streetwise New Yorker. Manhattan is home to a large population of artists and independent filmmakers. It is a tight-knit, supportive environment that respects individualism, and the food ain't bad either. Every ethnic community imaginable has a neighborhood filled with local eateries. These perks almost outweigh the absurd rents. Almost.

At the end of each year NYU puts on a week-long film festival showcasing films from the graduate and undergraduate divisions. There are hundreds of films in all. To make time for them all, each day of the festival begins about noon and ends about one in the morning. Nobody comes to see the films shown before six, and few wait to see the films that begin after ten. The goal is to get a time slot between six and ten. Few people come on Monday or Tuesday night, but Wednesday and Thursday the crowds grow. Friday is the big night: the one everyone wants her film to screen on. Few second-year films get good time slots. For that matter, few thesis films get good time slots. First-year grad films are not accepted into the festival. Second year films cannot exceed fifteen minutes; thesis films can not exceed thirty minutes.

The three best undergrad and three best graduate films are selected by a group of outside professionals. There are some small cash prizes. There are faculty craft and excellence awards. A two-and-a-half-hour program goes to Los Angeles to be screened at the Haig Manoogian Screenings at the DGA in June.

There is always an abundance of talented actors available to audition for NYU films.

The Lowdown

NYU is not looking for people straight out of undergrad programs. They prefer students who have some life experience. The GPA is important because they want only serious, intelligent students. It is best to submit a portfolio that demonstrates originality, not necessarily on film or video. Applicants will also have to include a dramatic story presented as a short story, screenplay, or video, the subject chosen by the Faculty Admissions Committee. NYU seems to base their selections more on writing ability and character than on experience with film. One-third of each first year's class is students of color. Over 53 percent of the class is women.

The recent overhaul has resulted in a significant change in faculty. The staff is more unified. They strive for more personal interaction with smaller numbers of students. They are skilled professionals who want to impart their knowledge. While none are reported standouts, they are certainly competent at leading students through the program. And they are more culturally diverse than most institutions. There are six African-Americans (including Spike Lee, who will join the faculty in 1997) and three Latino professors. And because there is such a conscious effort to bring in outside guests on a weekly basis, students really have great exposure to various industry perspectives. There is some politics at play, especially regarding TA assignments and production awards, but nothing like the blatant favoritism that was rampant in the old days. A real concern to the new administration, this was one of the areas that was addressed quite early on in the restructuring. A cross-check system exists to assure that the entire faculty has a voice and administrative levels of command are taken seriously.

Although students are known to complain, the equipment is very good and well maintained. Students are taught to handle and use the equipment carefully, so it remains in pretty good condition. There are sixty work-study students and ten regular staff members who keep things running smoothly in the equipment department. There are even on-site film and video camera repair shops.

The equipment is managed and assigned in a unique, extremely fair system. The equipment manager decides the production schedules for the entire school. Each class is then assigned one to two complete packages tailored for that particular level of production and the amount of time needed for each student to shoot. The faculty and students of those individual classes decide student shooting dates within the preassigned schedule. Everyone receives the same exact package. Because the equipment is in such good shape and each package is available when needed, there is no panic about getting a troublesome rig or no camera at all when needed. Students and faculty determine which films shoot when. There is no hassle with reservations, but rather responsibility for the package. The three thesis packages function in the same way. They are the most elaborate but are still equal across the board. While the schedule evens the playing field during production, it makes it much harder to get cameras outside of one's scheduled time for tests or experimentation. But then again, the schedule is such that who has time?

There are over one hundred cameras shared between undergraduate and graduate students. This includes two dozen grad-only Arri SRs, two dozen Betacams, and two dozen Hi-8 video cameras. Some of the more sensitive equipment is reserved for grads. Cameras for the first year MOS projects are of the Arriflex-S variety. Late first-year, second- and third-years cameras are Arri 16SR's.

These are great cameras that are treated reverently by the students and by the equipment room. The lenses vary in quality from good to great. Second- and third-year shoots are provided with just enough lighting and grip equipment to light a medium-sized room. Second-year and thesis students often rent lenses, filters, and lights. NYU's best dolly is a hunk of plywood on roller-skate wheels that rolls along lengths of plastic pipe. While this is often more than what is available at other schools, students who need smooth camera movement have to spend close to $1,000 per week to rent a dolly from General Camera.

The sound-recording equipment is good. Second-year shoots get a couple of good microphones and a Nagra 3. Third-years get an assortment of Sennheiser shotgun mics, several clip-on mics, a mixer, and a Nagra 4.2.

There is a lot of good-quality editing equipment. There are over two dozen Steenbeck flatbed editing machines, each in its own private room. Graduate editing reservations are made a week ahead. The number of slots allowed changes from week to week depending on assigned deadlines for projects. Students reserve for one of two available six-and-a-half hour editing slots each weekday and two five-and-a-half-hour slots on weekends. For advanced editing there are two Avids (with a third on the way), one D-vision, two Pro Tools and one Sonic Sound Design.

There are a large, very nice soundstage; recording studios; sound-mixing, recording, and ADR studios; several sound transfer rooms; two screening rooms for watching dailies; and two large state-of-the-art theaters.

While the financial burden of paying for a film is enormous, each student owns her own films when she is finished and is free to do with them what she pleases. Most enter their films in festivals and competitions and some even get distribution deals. While the financial return is never enough to recoup the original expense, it is always nice to see some money for all that effort, and the exposure that festivals and distribution provide can help to make contacts and even lead to being befriended by agents and producers.

Keeping one's head on straight is the first way to make the most of NYU. Some students become really full of themselves first year. They seem to think, "If I got into NYU, then I must be really hot!"

People tend to calm down pretty fast, especially once production kicks in. Then students are too stressed to worry about how "hot" they are. And since everyone works for everyone else, everyone has a stake in everyone else's success. By the end of second year, there is a real feeling of camaraderie among the students: one that lasts well beyond graduation.

The amounts spent on films at NYU are much larger than they need to be. While most people spend $20,000 or more on their thesis films, many good thesis films have been made for $10,000 or even less. In a recent year one student spent more than $80,000 on his thesis film. It was long and had lots of impressive helicopter shots, numerous locations, and a car chase; it has not been chosen for screening at any festival outside of NYU. Another student spent $4,000 on his thesis, and it went on to be a regional finalist in the Student Academy Awards and has been screened to great praise in festivals around the world. The former student still lives in New York where he is presumably working to pay back his student loans. The latter now lives and works in Los Angeles where he has an agent

Remember this: The two most important elements of a good short film cost nothing. All a film needs to be good is vivid characters and a good story. With these elements, there's no need for a helicopter shot. We recommend keeping second-year film budgets under $5,000 and thesis film budgets under $10,000. A limited budget is often the key to creativity.

Work on as many films as possible. It's a great chance to learn by others' mistakes and recruit future crew members. Don't hesitate to volunteer to crew for advanced projects. Attend the Directors Series. At the very least, it's a free film; at the very most, it's helpful to hear firsthand battle stories of making it in film. Participate in every mentoring and networking venture available. Make as many contacts as possible. Aim for one-on-one time with teachers.

Some of the best things about the program: The newly restructured program appears to be an improvement over the old one. It embodies the spirit of independent filmmaking. As for technology and facilities, NYU can hang with the best. There is tons of hands-on experience, and the equipment is really good. Many students now leave with a feature screenplay.

Some of the worst things about the program: Although greatly improved, politics are still at play at NYU. There are always some questions about festival time slots and which films are nominated for awards. The program may be too structured for some. Students have to search out guidance. The cost . . . ? Well, 'nuff said about that.

The Tisch School of the Arts has two alumni associations, one on the East Coast and one on the West. This association is for the entire school of the arts, graduate and undergraduate, not just the film school. The West Coast alumni association does little but organize screenings of current films and some networking gatherings. The East Coast is preoccupied with fund-raising.

There are real efforts being made to graduate employable students. So, even if a student is not one of the few plucked from the crowd for stardom, she still graduates with a number of marketable film-related skills. And although it helps to have a great film, a degree from NYU is a very prestigious one. Many people will agree to meet with a graduate solely based upon that association. The festival and DGA screenings can both be real stepping-stones for the chosen few.

<u>Northwestern University</u>

School of Speech
RTF Dept.
1905 Sheridan Rd.
Evanston IL 60208-2270
Room 212 AMS
(847) 491-7315
http://www.nwu.edu/graduate/
   bulletin/programs/speech/
   spch-rtf.html

Equipment Quality: ☆☆☆

Equipment Accessibility: ☆☆

Cost: $$

Tuition:	**$17,184**
Enrollment:	**4**
Deadline:	**January 15**
Focus:	**Experimental**

The Program

Part of the quaintly named School of Speech, Northwestern University's Department of Radio/Television/Film offers a two-year M.F.A. program which takes at least three years to complete. Because the school only accepts as many students as it can afford to give second-year TAships to, it is a very small program. And while the program is quite selective, it's relatively inexpensive.

Students in the M.F.A. film program go through six quarters of classes, and then take at least one additional year to make their thesis films. The first year is fairly intensive, with required courses in Video Production, Film Production, Film History, and Film Theory. In the film production course each student is loaned film production equipment and given 400 feet of stock (and free processing) with which to make exercise films; in the video production course, video equipment and tape are provided. These production courses are attended by both graduate and undergraduate students. The only difference between grads and undergrads in these courses is that undergrads team up and make group projects while each graduate student must make her own.

In addition to these courses students can choose electives in Producing, Screenwriting, Computer Animation, Multimedia, and a host of other technical courses. Students are encouraged to do interdisciplinary work as well, taking electives in departments outside of film. The program is particularly focused on film history and theory. Three two-quarter series are offered (Experimental History and Experimental Theory, Documentary History and Documentary Theory, and Narrative History and Narrative Theory), and students are required to complete two of these three series. The school also encourages students to cook up their own independent-studies projects. For instance, a group of five graduate students recently joined together to do a large video installation, and the school happily granted them independent-study credit.

In the middle of the first year, students choose an advisory committee to evaluate their work. This process is somewhat vestigial—until a few years ago, the committee wielded supreme power to cut students whose work was not up to par. Students are no longer cut after the first year, so the committee and the meetings students have with them are largely a formality. The committee's main purpose now is to oversee students' thesis projects. As a result, many students don't meet with their committees for the first time until the very end of their second year.

In the second year, students are required to take a two-quarter series specifically in Dramatic Directing. This class puts students into a studio environment for one quarter, where they use one another as actors in their scenes. During the second quarter they learn how to express their ideas in visual media. The second year also includes a number of classes in post-production, including nonlinear editing and digital sound design, and courses in new-media technologies like computer graphics, computer animation, and multimedia. Students may take four courses per quarter in their first year but may only take three per quarter in the second year while they work as TAs. One of the best features of Northwestern's program is that every student gets a TAship in the second year. TAships give full tuition remission, plus a stipend of around $10,000: second year is, in effect, free for all students.

Students complete all their class requirements by the end of their second year. Then they begin work on their thesis films. The third year is a strange time for students; they are allowed to use the film equipment and meet with the faculty as if they were students, but they do not enroll as students, and, in fact, the university does not consider them to be students. This situation has advantages and disadvantages. On the plus side, students can focus on their projects and they don't have to pay Northwestern's fairly steep tuition. On the minus side, they do not get any of the benefits enrolled students get (they are not allowed to use the library, student centers, gyms, or health clinics) and, perhaps worst of all, their student loans begin to come due.

For the past few years most students have taken three years after they finished classes to complete their thesis projects, if they finished them at all. The faculty wants students to finish their thesis films by the end of their third year, but they recognize that with little structure and some financial burdens to bear many students take longer. As of this writing, the faculty are discussing making the M.F.A. program a three-year program within the next few years. If this change is enacted, students will have to finish their thesis projects in a more timely fashion and pay at least partial tuition for one additional year.

In order to graduate, students have to screen a body of work for their committee. Generally, the school likes to see about an hour's worth of material, though students who work in computer animation or multimedia are not expected to have anywhere near an hour's worth of stuff when they finish.

The Price

$17,184 per year tuition for one year	$17,184
$10,000 a year rent and living expenses for first and third years	$20,000
Second-year tuition and living expenses are covered by TAships.	$ 0
$1,500 per year insurance and upkeep on a car for three years	$ 4,500
Thesis films tend to cost an additional	$ 8,000
Total	**$49,684**

This really is a very inexpensive school. And given the size and diversity of the faculty and the quality of the equipment available, it has to be considered one of the best bargains of all the film schools. The worst difficulties students face are not financial, or at least not directly so, as we will discuss in the next section.

Evanston is a wealthy suburb of Chicago and, while quiet and pleasant, is a pretty expensive place to live, especially for students. Students who live near the school have to pay five or six hundred dollars a month for tiny studio apartments, or even more for equally tiny apartments in the school's graduate housing. Some students share larger places, but many move south of Evanston, into middle-class neighborhoods in the northern reaches of Chicago where the same money will rent a spacious two- or three-bedroom apartment.

A car is a necessity if you want to make films in Evanston. While Chicago and environs have good public transportation, it is a sprawling urban area and outside of the city center things are spread pretty far apart.

The Lowdown

The school receives seventy or eighty applications per year, from which around four are chosen. The actual number of applicants accepted is determined by how much funding the school has: the school only accepts as many students as it can afford to give full TAships in their second year. In some years this has been as many as six students, but it is usually four. The applications process changes a little each year, so it's hard to predict exactly which materials they will ask to see in the future. As of this writing the school asks for a reel of no more than ten minutes' worth of film or video work, a sample of creative writing, a sample of academic writing, and a proposal for a project to be made at Northwestern. One professor told us that they immediately dismiss any applicant whose essay runs along the lines of "Ever since I was a child I've loved movies and have always dreamt of one day making movies." This is not a program for people who want to be in movies—it's a program for dedicated artists who have a clear vision and a reason for wanting to express that vision through film.

We may be doing a disservice to Northwestern by labeling it an experimental school. While it offers many classes in experimental and documentary films, a few students each year make straightforward narrative films, and a few make more unclassifiable projects. With a variety of specialized classes in documentary, experimental, narrative, video production, video installations, computer graphics, and computer animation, and with new classes in Web site design and CD-ROM authoring, Northwestern actually offers more specializations than they have M.F.A. students in any year. As a result Northwestern offers a great deal of flexibility in the kind of work students can do. So while applicants have to show a clear vision and purpose to get in initially, once they are in the school they are free to explore a wide variety of media, and perhaps find one they like better than the one they started out with.

As we said above, the worst difficulties students face at Northwestern are not directly financial. Since second year is basically free, second-year students have relatively little to worry about financially. But factor in taking full-time classes, working nearly full-time as teaching assistants, and making several films each quarter—students have to work very hard. They complain of being so burned out after second year that they can't even begin to think about their thesis films until well into third year. And by that time, since they are no longer officially enrolled in school, their student loans from first year are coming due and they are often holding down full-time jobs to pay the rent. Some wind up drifting off into full-time work in Chicago and never complete their thesis projects. Those who finish their thesis projects often take the entire three additional years allowed by the school to do it. The faculty recognize that students often get lost in the nebulousness of the post-classwork years and are trying to find solutions to this problem. In the short term, they sometimes find paying teaching gigs for third-year students. In the long term, they are planning to make the third year an official year of school (with classes and tuition) sometime in the next few years.

The equipment at Northwestern is quite good, but because it is shared with a large undergraduate department, it is not as accessible as it might be. Film cameras are great—after finishing the requisite production and cinematography courses students have access to Arri SR-2s, and an assortment of BLs, Eclairs, and Bolexes. Sound-recording equipment includes Nagras and some recently purchased DAT recorders. The school appears to have a fair amount of money for new equipment and is doing an impressive job of keeping up with the new technologies. For editing there are two Avid off-line editing systems and an Integrated Research on-line editing system. For computer graphics and animation there are two Silicon Graphics workstations. For audio post-production and mixing there is a Pro Tools workstation. The school is moving heavily into new media and offers classes in interactive CD-ROM authoring and Web site design, and gives students access to an assortment of Macintoshes equipped with all the necessary software for multimedia work. At present two of the four second-year students in the program are not working in film or video, but in new media. The one area the equipment is lacking somewhat in is grip equipment. Many students find themselves dashing down to rental houses in Chicago to pick up extra grip equipment before their shoots.

There are very few graduate-only courses—almost all the classes graduate students take are also attended by undergraduates. The film and video production courses are large classes attended by both; undergraduates make group exercise films in these classes, while each graduate student makes her own exercise film. While this is understandable given the small size of the M.F.A. program, students say they sometimes feel as if they are just getting another undergraduate degree. Students also say that the fact that the school is on the quarter system makes things very hectic. It is very hard to complete two exercise films in an eleven-week period—particularly while also working a full TAship and taking a full course load in second year. The experience can be exhausting.

Northwestern's RTF faculty governs democratically. There is no all-powerful department head who dictates the rules; instead there is a Production Committee, made up of all of the production teachers, which dictates department policy by consensus. Each member of this committee takes a turn acting as department head. While this is a nice idea in theory, in practice it has proven confusing and frustrating for students, as policies are added, changed, or deleted seemingly at random.

Some of the best things about the program: Northwestern is a good school for dedicated artists who know what they want to do. The equipment is great, access to it is good, and—thanks to the guaranteed TAships in second year—the price is surprisingly low. And the fact that they are already offering courses in interactive media and Web site design indicates that they are dedicated to exploring new media. If you have some experience with film and video, and have a good idea of the kinds of projects you want to make, Northwestern will give you access to great equipment and provides a friendly and inexpensive environment in which to work.

Some of the worst things about the program: The faculty is made up of working professionals who are dealing with their own careers, as well as their many undergraduate students. They can give good advice when asked, but they don't have the time to be mentors to the graduate students, nor to provide them with much guidance.

Ohio University

School of Film
378 Lindley Hall
Athens, OH 45701-2979
Department: (614) 593-1323
http://cats.ohiou.edu/~filmdept

Independent

Equipment
Quality: ★☆

Equipment
Accessibility: ★☆

Cost: $$$

Annual Tuition:	Resident: $8,775
	Nonresident:
	$17,145
Enrollment:	15; 45 total
Deadline:	February 15
Focus:	Independent

The Program

Founded in 1804, Ohio University is a quaint, scenic school around which a town grew up. Most students live within walking distance of its picturesque brick buildings and streets. The M.F.A. film program, established in 1973, receives between 125 and 160 applications for 15 openings each year.

On paper, Ohio appears to be a course-intensive program with a requirement of a whopping 135 credit hours. With 35 credits allotted for thesis work, and independent study credits an option, in reality the workload is not too overwhelming past the hectic first year. Although it is advertised as a three-year program, the great number of requirements means that most students need at least one additional quarter to finish.

The program operates on a quarterly schedule. The foundation of the program is the sequence of Production courses taken over the first three quarters. In Production I-II-III, students make, in the following order: two silent films; a short (30-second) sync-sound piece; and a five-to-ten-minute sync-sound film. Although not encouraged, longer Production III projects are an option. Students incur the entire cost of each of these films and the two advanced films that follow if they choose to focus on directing. Students purchase film stock in bulk and ship off exposed footage for processing to whatever labs offer the best rates.

The first year is fairly structured. Along with your Production courses, students take the Film History I-II-III series. Every quarter students participate in the Film Symposium, in which the entire grad film student body meets for an hour once a week. It's a forum for announcements, feedback, or lectures by visiting artists.

The remainder of courses taken during this first year include Film Analysis, Film Theory and Criticism, a New Technologies class, and an elective course. Because there are so many credit hours to fulfill, department electives are added in toward the end of this first year. The Film Survey course is a popular elective with topics that rotate each quarter. Appealing topics like "Women In Film" or "Film Visionaries" need be taken when offered, as they might be unavailable down the road. Other electives include International Cinema I-II-III, Advanced Film Theory, and Criticism and Media Arts Management. The latter course is offered every winter quarter and entails assisting with the Athens International Film Festival. This can be a labor-intensive internship of sorts, but also a tremendous learning opportunity. Participants can view film submissions, assist with judging, and have close contact with all sorts of independent filmmakers.

At the end of this first year there's an Advancement to Candidacy. This is faculty evaluation at which candidates who have completed a required thirty-two credits present a research paper and screen their answer print. This review supposedly decides whether or not one can proceed with the program. While no one has been asked to leave, students can be put on probation and reviewed again to prove their progress.

During second-year quarters, there's more flexibility regarding class schedules and courses. Independent-study credit is available for crewing in key positions on classmates' films. Cinematography, Editing, Sound, Theory and Criticism, Screenwriting, Directing, Avid Instruction, and Producing are offered along with Symposium. Cognate course requirements (elective credits that must be taken outside of the department) also come into play at this time. Second year also presents the choice of the Masters Class or Second-Year Project.

The Masters Class is taught by an eminent scholar. For the last several years this scholar has been respected Croatian director

Rajko Grlic. Participants are selected by Grlic, based upon first-year reviews and previous work. Usually no more than five students are chosen. This is basically a directing class in which students work closely with the professor to develop a short film of about ten minutes. Often the class joins together to make a longer film comprising these individual shorts. A common topic or thread unites the shorts as a whole. This is an intense narrative film workshop where participants write, do video-storyboard exercises, shoot, and edit a film under the professor's close mentoring.

Students not accepted by or interested in the Masters Class must register for Second Year Project. This is a more-or-less independent class where students can make any genre of five-to-fifteen-minute film or write a feature-length screenplay. Both Masters Class films and Second Year Projects shoot in early spring and are normally completed by fall. Students crew for one another or sometimes recruit people from the undergrad telecommunications program.

At the end of your second year, there's another Portfolio Review with the faculty. This time they evaluate second-year films or screenplays, again with the potential of postponing your advancement.

Third year is mostly devoted to thesis development (fifteen credits per quarter). Depending on previous course loads, most requirements should be fulfilled by this point. One or two courses might be necessary. In order to focus on thesis projects, the remaining credits can be met through registering for independent study. This usually carries over into at least one additional quarter. Upon completion, thesis films or thesis screenplays are defended before the faculty at final reviews.

In addition to required classes, there is a well-received Scriptwriting Seminar offered over Christmas break. A guest lecturer is brought in to conduct an intensive one-week writing crash course. A Producer's Workshop is also offered, in which outside producers lecture on independent film producing. Thanks to the eminent scholar connection, there is also a Croatian exchange program in place. Every year three Croatian students come to the school for these seminars. In the summer, two or three Ohio film students are selected by the faculty to travel at the university's expense for another seminar in Croatia. Interested students must submit a feature-length screenplay to be considered for this exchange program.

The Price
RESIDENT

$195 per credit for 135 credits	$26,325
$7,500 year rent and living expenses for three and a quarter years	$24,375
Average film costs	$20,000
Total	**$70,700**

NONRESIDENT

$381 per credit for 135 credits	$51,435
$7,500 year rent and living expenses for three and a quarter years	$24,375
Average film costs	$20,000
Total	**$95,810**

No one really pays full tuition so you will never pay the amounts listed above. You can apply the thousands you save toward your film budgets, your most significant expenditure. Upon completion of the first year, nonresidents apply for status reclassification and qualify for lower resident tuition.

Athens is a good place to reside and focus on work. The community is slow-paced and there isn't the pressure prevalent at some of the larger institutions. There are very few distractions—except, of course, for students plagued by the bottle. With no less than thirty-eight bars in a four-block radius, this could prove a challenge. It also gives insight into undergraduate pastimes. There's a decent live music scene but few good restaurants. There's one movie theater which does show art films at weekend matinees.

It's very inexpensive to live in Athens—once an apartment is located. Housing is unusually tight if not impossible to find. While a one-bedroom can run as little as $300 a month, only a student's graduation or untimely demise is likely to make it available. One student actually found it easier (and darn cost-effective) to purchase a small house rather than fight the apartment drought. It is highly recommended to arrive well in advance of start of classes to find an apartment. It might be wise to contact current film students before your arrival to procure their assistance in apartment hunting. Living in town won't necessitate a car, but there's no way to get out of town without one. Columbus is only an hour-and-a-half drive away, and it might be nice to have a mode of escape. A car would certainly come in handy on film shoots, but the parking situation is just as severe as housing and spaces are metered. Ticketing is like clockwork.

As a recruiting incentive, at least 50 percent of the incoming class receives a full tuition waiver. Most women and international students count themselves in this fortunate group. You will be notified if you are chosen for this perk upon acceptance into the program. Receipt of this during your first year does not guarantee it will carry over into the following years, but normally everyone in the second year gets some sort of tuition waiver.

Most of each class is also assisted financially through graduate assistantships. The number of positions vary but at minimum seem to comprise five to six full-time positions that are distributed by the faculty. Sometimes this means dividing the positions in half in order to support more students. For instance, ten to twelve recipients receive one-half tuition remission and a $400-per-month stipend (closer to $200 less fees subtraction). At this writing, the entire second-year class was receiving full tuition remission and half stipend. There is no application process or sense of merit-based selection. The allocation varies each semester. The department chair arbitrarily decides who gets what. Most students secure some form of assistantship for at least one quarter during their stay. The work hours vary according to assignments as teacher or assistant. All financial aid is reevaluated every year. Your status can change, without explanation, from one quarter to the next. While more receive financial help than don't, you can't really count on the assistantships or waivers from year to year.

Assistantships are important because it's difficult to find time to work and most of the part-time jobs available outside the university are minimum wage. If you have to pursue this course, temp work is starting to become more available and is the preferred alternative.

For the first time, last year the department reviewed works in progress and awarded three $500 film-finishing grants. This year they also provided every second-year student with two rolls of second-year project film. There is an annual university-wide fellowship competition for which one student is nominated by the film department. Film students have won this grant of $7,900 for the last couple of years. Film students also have a good track record with the Houk Grant, a quarterly competition open to all university students. Winners receive grants of $100 to $750.

First-year students usually screen their silent films for the class at the end of the first quarter, but there is no recognized student film festival as yet. In the past, a nameless screening would surface once in a while. Students have been known to band together and reserve a campus auditorium to hold their own screenings of finished films. Last May the new Production teacher began an end-of-year screening that will hopefully continue. Students can enter the Athens Festival, but they compete for admittance against some independent heavyweights.

The acting talent pool is generally limited to the theater department. It's tough to juggle both department's class schedules and coordinate film shoots. You also have the possibility of contacting local community theaters.

The Lowdown

The school spends a lot of time reviewing applications. They are concerned with finding students who are clearly prepared for a graduate level of study. In the 500-word personal essay they look for extremely goal-oriented persons able to concisely articulate a strong point of view. You need to convince them that once equipped with the skills they teach, you are competent to apply them. Any creative video or film work will help. They want a solid writing sample.

Grad Film candidates at Ohio University tend to be on the young side. Most are fresh from undergrad or in their early to mid twenties. And while you might find a few over-age-thirty students, they tend to feel out of place. For such a small school it does boast a high (24 percent) international population. However, international students are often the least prepared for small-town American life.

It's extremely important to note that the recent departure of the department chair has also thrown the school into a state of flux. In the future, this program could be completely revamped and will certainly undergo some sort of change with the arrival of its new leader.

Students find the quality of faculty very inconsistent. Individually all are nice people, but most have been there for a very long time and don't get along with one another. Students are often stuck in the middle of their squabbles. There is a real division between production-oriented faculty and academics. It is rumored that the departing chair was actually ousted by his co-workers in some dramatic coup. Many professors are knowledgeable but not effective teachers. Classes are reportedly uninspired. And since most of the faculty do not make an effort to involve themselves in students' educations, students find defending themselves and their work at the end-of-the-year reviews unnerving.

The working professionals on staff tend to be the strongest faculty. The new production teacher is well liked but, as a successful cinematographer, is often out working. The faculty is small, with the same professors teaching numerous classes. It makes real sense to take classes outside of the department whenever possible. The Theater Department offers good writing, directing, and acting courses. It's unfortunate that the only legitimate director, Grlic, teaches just one course. Students not interested in the Masters Class will never have the opportunity to work with him.

While the number of incoming students has increased over the years, the amount of equipment has not. Cameras include eleven Bolexes, three CP 16s for first-year students, two Arri Ss for nonsync work, one Arri SR-1 for second-years, and one Arri SR-2 for thesis projects. Someone on staff is assigned to manage equipment, but the burden has really fallen on student equipment managers to keep the department on track.

Cameras can be reserved four weeks in advance for first-year projects, five weeks in advance for second-year projects, and six weeks in advance for thesis films. Some of the advanced students don't like the restrictions, but all students tend to be respectful of one another's schedules and try to work together to avoid equipment conflicts. There's always equipment failure, and crunch times at the end of the third quarter, but there are usually enough functioning items to get by with. Nagra sound packages are comparable to the camera assortment. Many students choose to shoot over weekends but, with approval, they may check out equipment for two and three weeks at a time.

There are three six-plate, one eight-plate, and one four-plate Steenbecks and two Moviolas. Access is twenty-four hours and four-hour shifts can be scheduled two days in advance. Twenty hours is the maximum amount of prescheduled hours per week. Each year has its own room to reserve. Smart students take advantage of winter and summer breaks for editing. This avoids the final-quarter crunches for both flatbeds and the Peterson Sound Studio, where students can mix up to ten tracks of sound with interlock capability. First-year directing exercises are on video so there are video editing suites, but two of these have been inoperable for six months. There's a small twenty-five-seat theater but no soundstage.

Students must elect to take the necessary class to use the low-end Avid. Unfortunately, the course is basic and the Avid is really only used to learn how to do simple cuts, fades, and dissolves. No one actually edits their films on it. The Pro Tools system that complements the Avid is not functioning, so students cannot completely edit their film digitally.

The most can be made of Ohio University by knowing what you need to accomplish. Students who excel know the types of films they want to make before arriving. Arrive early so that the housing situation doesn't add stress during class time. Make sure to take as many electives as possible outside of the department. If you play your cards right, you can usually schmooze your way into getting repeated or concurrent graduate assistantships.

Work closely with other students. The school is small enough that everyone can really get to know one another, and the students are some of its best assets. In them you'll find a sense of camaraderie and creativity that your professors lack. Make sure not to miss a single bonus seminar or lecture, especially those offered by the University Film Conference, which brings world film scholars into town every year. Try to work on the Athens Festival. Push your professors to give you more. You might have to make them take an interest in you. The good teachers can be very good and can really help you. This is especially true of the sound and production instructors, who are excellent troubleshooters one-on-one. With the arrival of a new department chair, you have the opportunity to help reshape the program and address your needs.

Some of the best things about the program: The filmmaking fundamentals are sound. Experimentation with equipment and various genres is supported. Self-motivated individuals can shape the program to suit their needs. There are interesting seminars and a conscious effort to bring industry professionals to students. The Croatian exchange is unique. There's a fair amount of tuition funding to offset film costs. You'll have the opportunity to experience the well-respected Athens Film Festival up close.

Some of the worst things about the program: The remote location limits your exposure to film and culture. If you are not small-town material, you may go out of your mind. The infighting among the faculty is a real concern. Film school is hard enough without having to deal with destructive behavior from your instructors. The faculty reviews and financial provisions are based more on favoritism and politics than merit. Students are frustrated by this somewhat random assignment of university funding. One can only hope this issue will be remedied by the new department chair. With so many credits to fulfill and no strong push toward finishing, students will need that extra quarter of classes, and there's a great possibility it will take much longer to complete the program.

San Francisco Art Institute

800 Chestnut Street
San Francisco, CA 94133
Department: 1-800-345-7324
Admissions: (415) 749-4512
http://www.sfai.edu

Annual Tuition: $16,416
Enrollment: 3–4; 17 total
Deadline: Fall: February 15
Spring: November 1
Focus: Experimental

Experimental

Equipment Quality: ☆☆

Equipment Accessibility: ☆☆☆

Cost: $$

The Program

Twenty to sixty applications are submitted each semester to the San Francisco Art Institute. The number accepted depends upon the caliber of the submissions: the school will accept a handful one semester and none the next. It is intentionally a very small, specific program geared completely to the filmmaker as artist, not director. It should be thought of as an artists' program with film as the medium. Enrollment is kept low to provide students with greater equipment access. The current total of seventeen students is the largest class size in the school's history.

Most students take three years to complete the interdisciplinary two-year program. The goal of the institute is to help students "develop an independent body of work to be pursued throughout their lives." The faculty are more concerned with providing an environment supportive of this goal than a highly structured course load. Classes are more like discussion groups composed of a variety of artists from throughout the school. Under the guidance of a professor, students review and evaluate one another's work and progress. Each program is tailored to meet the individual goals and needs of the artist.

The entire program is centered around four classes taken repeatedly throughout the program. These consist of Studio Critique Seminar, Graduate Tutorial, Theory and Criticism, and Interdisciplinary Studio Seminar. Students are encouraged to seek out like-minded professors in any of the school's departments, and to study a wide variety of creative media outside of film.

Tutorials are one-on-one advisements with a faculty member. These meetings usually occur three to four times over a semester and are intended to provoke discussion and feedback to help the student develop her artistic vision. Graduate seminars meet weekly to discuss and critique student work. Students must intern and/or serve as a teaching assistant for two semesters.

There are reviews and exhibitions of work at the end of the first and second years. Review committees consist of one visiting faculty member, one regular member, and a professor from another division. Students can choose to invite an additional faculty member. This hour-long discussion and critique of a student's work can advance or halt a student's progression toward candidacy. Those who fail must address the reasons given for their failure and be re-reviewed at a later date. Failure of the second review can result in dismissal from the program. The final review at the end of second year is more of the same. Students must be able to successfully defend their work to pass these reviews.

Students pay for all film costs. The number of films made varies widely. Students can literally make as many films as they can afford. Sometimes there's collaboration, but because projects tend to be of a personal nature, most students work alone, handling all shooting, sound recording, optical printing, hand processing, and editing. Any technical training is usually achieved through trial and error or consulting with the equipment staff. There are some tech workshops, but no screenwriting or directing classes.

Instead, the school focuses on alternative uses of film. The department is changing and expanding into conceptual work. Multiple projections, performance-art pieces, and multimedia film-based installations are becoming more popular.

The Price

$16,416 per year for two years	$32,832
$684 per semester matriculation for one additional year	$ 1,368
$9,600 per year rent and living expenses for 2 1/2 years	$24,000
Average film costs	$15,000
Total	**$73,200**

There is little in the way of official funding to assist with tuition costs. Each department at the institute awards one or two merit scholarships to incoming students. Those selected receive $4,500 per year for two years.

In return for the mandatory TA stints, students receive $1,000 in tuition remission. The hours spent earning this remission vary according to the assignment. Six to nine hours per week are required: ten hours is the norm. Kodak grants provide about $2,500 worth of free film that's split among students each year. Film stock is provided to virtually any student who writes the fifty-word proposal to request it. Nearly all students have work-study positions or work outside the institute to defray costs. Some students settle on part-time study to ease the financial strain but maintain access to equipment and facilities.

San Francisco is a very cosmopolitan, livable city. The Art Institute is located in the beautiful Russian Hill section. The bay view is breathtaking, but nearby housing is expensive and hard to find. There is less than a 1 percent vacancy rate in San Francisco. Most students pay about $600 per month to share a space. Lucky individuals who secure a one-bedroom will pay significantly more. Many students choose to live in the Mission area. While San Francisco is relatively safe, some areas are safer than others, so be sure to ask a lot of questions. Cars are not mandatory. It is easy to get around by public transportation. And traipsing up those steep, winding hills eliminates the need for Stairmasters.

Students book lecture halls and screen their work whenever they feel like it. There is a department screening at the end of the semester and a student-organized showing at a local nonprofit art house. The M.F.A. graduate show for the entire school is a big event in the Bay Area, but the film department is not represented at this off-campus exhibit. The division instead sponsors a separate screening on campus.

The Lowdown

Students without prior film experience will have to demonstrate strong skills in other visual media on the application. Creative work is seriously evaluated. Experience has taught the faculty that the best candidates are those who have already begun an artistic journey. The program is more about concept than technique. They do not intend to show students how to make films, but rather support an individual's endeavors. Applicants must be able to demonstrate how they will fit into this distinct program. There are fewer applicants for the spring semester than the fall.

The faculty is largely composed of working artists. Many of the film instructors started working in experimental film in the late fifties and early sixties. They've been around awhile and are not as active as they once were. But most are helpful. Students should consult with classmates and check out faculty before taking classes. There are usually some worthwhile visiting artists whose classes should not be overlooked.

By other schools' standards the equipment at the Art Institute seems meager. Yet students are surprisingly satisfied. Although they share equipment with a small undergrad film population and other artists in the school, they enjoy unlimited access. Experimental film seems to thrive in this rudimentary environment. The filmmakers appreciate the purity versus the technology.

Equipment can be reserved one month in advance, but there is never a problem getting a camera when needed. Most students use the four or five Bolexes. There is also an Arri S, an Eclair NPR, a CP 16, fifteen Super-8 cameras, and a Hi-8 video camera. There are Nagras and cassette recorders and some minimal lighting equipment. One Bolex is reserved for grads.

Post-production facilites are open twenty-four hours, and editing space can be reserved one week in advance. During the overnight hours the facilities are usually empty. The school owns five flat-bed editing machines. One is reserved for graduate use.

There's a large mixing studio with an eight-track DAT recorder and mixing board, and a smaller studio that students use for fun experimentation. There are two classrooms that double as both studios and projection rooms at night and on weekends.

Students can hand-process their films. There is a mechanical processor that is OSHA inoperable due to the small size of the room the machine is located in. They hope to relocate the machine to rectify this. An interdisciplinary center for digital media recently opened along with a Hi-8 editing suite.

The most can be made of the San Francisco Art Institute by students who know what they want and aggressively seek it out. Those who arrive without a clear direction will flounder. Be persistent. Take full advantage of the equipment and make as many films as financially possible. Explore other artistic mediums. Don't delay fulfilling the TA requirement. Teachers have favorites, and students who don't move quickly can get stuck in the worst positions.

Some of the best things about the program: Students are encouraged to take risks. No one tells anyone what to do. Those who feel the need to alter the program in order to serve their vision often get what they want. Students work at their own pace and have tremendous freedom. The extensive feedback from instructors and students alike is extremely beneficial. The world of fine arts will be at students' fingertips. Access to equipment is unlimited. Interested students can check out a camera every single day and edit as long as they want.

Some of the worst things about the program: Students who are not self-motivated will not survive. The lack of structure is deadly for some. The film division is a very small part of the institute. Student funding is severely limited. There is much more support, financial and otherwise, given to the other departments. Sometimes the film program gets lost in administrative hell. There are not all that many specific film courses offered. Students tend to linger in the program longer than they need to.

Many graduates move on to teach.

San Francisco State University

Cinema Department
1600 Holloway Ave.
San Francisco, CA 94132
(415) 338-1724
http://www.cinema.sfsu.edu

Equipment Quality: ☆

Equipment Accessibility: ☆☆☆

Cost: $$

Annual Tuition:	**$1,982**
Enrollment:	**15**
Deadline:	**February 1**
Focus:	**Experimental**

The Program

San Francisco State's M.F.A. film program is an established and well-regarded, but somewhat underfunded, program which strives to overcome its lack of money through pure craftiness. The school has offered B.A. and M.A. degrees in film for more than two decades, but it was only in 1993 that it began offering an M.F.A. This is a very young program, but the faculty who designed it used their extensive experience to make it an unusual and cleverly structured course. While still in its formative stages, it is already a well-thought-out, and well-organized program; students are encouraged to make suggestions to better the program, and many have been pleased to find the faculty actually taking their suggestions seriously and incorporating them into the curriculum.

For many students the program begins even before the first day of the first year. New students have to show that they have already taken courses in film theory and history prior to starting SFSU; the faculty will actually grill incoming students to make sure they really have a firm knowledge of film theory and history. Those who have not taken these courses (usually about a third of each class) are required to take them in the school's summer session prior to the start of the first year.

The goal for the first year is to introduce students to "Film as It Is Now." Each semester, students take an advanced class in theory and history and also a production class where they learn the technical end of directing, writing, shooting, and editing 16-mm film. Students are required to complete a 16-mm film in their first year— including mixing that film and taking it through to an answer print at a lab. Typically about a third of first-year students make documentaries while the rest make narratives. The school asks that these films be no more than eight minutes in length, but most of the finished projects wind up running between fifteen and twenty minutes, and a few run as long as thirty. Students also take a course called Creative Process that requires them to write a number of short screenplays. This course ensures that they build a surplus of written material and has benefits later on: many students continue to polish these screenplays in the second year and wind up using them as the basis for their thesis films in the third year. Students have the summer after the first year to finish their first-year films; each student is asked to screen an answer print of her first-year film in a festival at the beginning of her second year. In reality some students don't have the money to make an answer print of this film, and the school will somewhat grudgingly accept a film if it is ready to go to the lab—if it is a final cut of the workprint with a single mixed sound track and a checkerboarded negative. But, most students do make answer prints of their first-year films.

While this is essentially an Independent program stressing narrative filmmaking, students are at times encouraged to experiment with radically different media and genres. This is particularly true in the second year of the program when the school encourages students to experiment with different media and techniques. While the first year of the program concerns "Film as It Is Now," the second year is about "Film as It Might Be." Students work with faculty advisors to come up with new and different ideas for projects. Some of these projects stick roughly to the narrative mold, while others go far afield; in the first few years of the program second-year students have constructed video installations, staged operas, worked in interactive media and computer animation, and even attempted to tell narratives through installations of found objects. The school encourages students to be as experimental as they can, to explore completely new media and completely new styles. Students and faculty describe the showing of the second-year projects as the most exciting part of the entire program. This two-day event takes place at the end of every year. Strange and fascinating projects are installed and displayed in spaces all around the school, and students hold symposia to discuss and analyze their ideas and works.

In the third year students return to narrative filmmaking. Third-year classes revolve around the making of a single thesis film. In the first semester students take a course that guides them through developing a screenplay and starting pre-production on the project. Each student chooses two faculty members to be her Thesis Committee, and that committee advises her as she develops her project. When the Thesis Committee approves the student's project, she can then arrange to check out equipment and start filming. The school hopes that thesis films will be somewhere between the first-year films and the second-year projects, that students will have learned things from their experimentation in second year that can be applied to their more straightforward third-year narrative films.

Students are encouraged to teach. All students are asked to TA a course for no pay for one semester—after that they can apply for the few paying TAships that are available. Paying TAships do not pay much—they only provide remission of some of the school's already negligible tuition. So a TA at SFSU doesn't get a free ride for a year the way TAs at some other schools do, but this is still a good opportunity for those who want to teach. Students are also expected to do an internship in the beginning of their third year, though at SFSU an internship has a special meaning (see the glossary for what it usually means). The school wants students to find something more like an apprenticeship—they ask each student to find an artist who is doing something interesting and ask that artist to let her hang around and learn. The faculty admits that this doesn't work for everyone, as not everyone meets an artist she admires and not all artists are willing to be followed around by a film student. But for some students it becomes a valuable learning experience.

When a student finishes her thesis film, she has to organize a public screening and hold a question-and-answer session about it. No students finish their thesis films in the third year. They all take at least one additional year to finish. Money is the main hindrance to speedy graduation: the school has only negligible monetary grants to give, so everyone works or writes grant applications, slowly piecing together the money necessary to process and complete her film. Some students manage to finish in four years; others take five or six or seven. After seven years, students are not allowed to use the school's equipment anymore. But even this is not an insurmountable hurdle, as most students are not even using the school's equipment but are editing at the Film Arts Foundation. We'll discuss the Film Arts Foundation later, though.

The Price

$1,982 per year tuition for three years	$ 5,946
$12,000 per year rent and living expenses for four years	$48,000
First-year films cost about	$ 5,000
Second-year films cost about	$ 3,000
Thesis films cost about	$10,000
Total	**$71,946**

The good news is the tuition is incredibly low. The bad news is everything else in San Francisco is very expensive. The cost of living is very high there: one-bedroom apartments in the city are more expensive than most students can afford, so just about everyone winds up sharing two- or three-bedroom apartments with other students. And even a share like this will cost each person $400 or $500 a month.

There are few ways of getting around these costs. The school only offers a handful of TAships, and these only give discounts on tuition, which is negligible to begin with. The few grants the school gives out are for less than $1,000, which doesn't go very far when you are working in 16-mm film and taking it all the way through to answer print. The first year is too intensive to allow for any activities outside of school, but from the second year on everyone works to pay their bills and production costs.

A car is neither necessary nor even a good idea in San Francisco. Few apartments have garages, and street parking is scarce. And if you do find parking on the street you are guaranteed to have your windows smashed and your glove compartment rifled through on a regular basis. Most students find it best to befriend people who have cars and borrow those cars when necessary, or to just rent vehicles. Public transportation in San Francisco and the Bay Area is very good, so when students are not in production they get along perfectly well without cars. One enterprising student brought a van to San Francisco, which he rented out to fellow students, using the proceeds to help pay for his projects.

Almost everyone works in 16-mm film in the first and third years. These films by necessity cost $8,000 or more to complete: there's not much flexibility when you're working with 16-mm film. But the second-year project need not be a film and can thus be less expensive than the other projects. Some students work in video, others in interactive media. Still others create installations and artworks that are more like sculpture or painting than film or video. While the faculty wants these projects to contain a narrative, they are open to a very broad interpretation of narrative, and it is possible to work in inexpensive media like Video, interactive CD-ROMs—or even sticks and stones—and spend very little money.

There is one film-processing laboratory in town called Monaco. Since it has a monopoly, Monaco is fairly expensive, but it is fast and very convenient. Monaco only processes color film, so students who shoot black and white have to send their footage off to labs in Los Angeles, Portland, or Seattle for processing. The school encourages students not to use Monaco, to instead ship their footage off to labs in Los Angeles that offer much better prices, but few can resist the convenience Monaco offers. One solution students have discovered is to band together into large groups and negotiate volume discounts with Monaco.

The Lowdown

San Francisco State receives about two hundred applications each year, from which no more than fifteen new students are accepted. The faculty are very picky about whom they accept and will let in fewer than fifteen when there aren't fifteen that they feel are up to their standards.

With your application you will be asked to send a resume, a personal statement, an example of academic writing, two letters of recommendation, and a portfolio of creative work. Applicants who send films or videos have an advantage over those who don't, but the school will consider applicants with no experience in film if they show both an ability to write and a strong visual sense. Students who have both film production courses and film theory courses in their transcripts are at a distinct advantage. GREs are not required.

San Francisco State's film department recently moved into new digs: a brand new building containing a 2,500-square-foot soundstage, a 150-seat screening room, editing rooms, animation studios, audio recording studios, and audio mixing studios. It is probably on the audio end that the school has the best equipment. There are two audio mixing studios; one of them contains the mixing board on which *Amadeus* was mixed, which Berkeley-based Fantasy Studios donated to the school when they went over to digital technology. It's such a complex piece of equipment that it has taken a few years for anyone to learn how to use it, but now it's used fairly frequently to mix student films. Students who have learned how to mix on this console, including some who graduated some time ago, are hired by current students to mix their films. The school also owns two Sonic Solutions digital audio workstations, and more and more students are doing their audio post-production digitally. There are animation stands, Macintosh computers set up for computer graphics and multimedia work, and an optical printer.

Compared to the audio equipment, most of the school's production and editing equipment is rather dated. Thesis films are shot on Eclair NPRs. The school reportedly owns the camera Maya Deren shot her experimental films with in the early forties—and it's still being used to shoot student films! (We can't decide whether this is incredibly cool or incredibly cheap.) Most production sound is recorded on Nagras, and, though the school now owns a Media 100 nonlinear editing system, most films are still edited on film using flatbed editing machines. Because the school, like all of California's state universities, is poorly funded, there is not enough equipment to go around: the flatbed editing machines are in particularly short supply, and students can't always get the good cameras when they need them.

To get around this limitation, most students wind up joining the Film Arts Foundation. Film Arts, located a few miles away from SFSU in the South of Market area, has flatbeds, audio transfer facilities, screening rooms, and cameras and other production equipment that they rent to members at very low rates. As of this writing

Film Arts is also adding two Avids to their post-production equipment. Though intended as a resource for all independent filmmakers in the Bay Area, Film Arts at times can seem like an extension of San Francisco State's film program. In some ways Film Arts is the savior of SFSU—without the equipment Film Arts provides, SFSU students would be hard-pressed to complete their projects. That Film Arts will now be providing access to high-tech equipment that SFSU can't afford to buy will only make the university more dependent on the foundation.

San Francisco is a nice town with pleasant weather and beautiful surroundings that provide a wide variety of shooting locations. There is an established independent-filmmaking community there, and the town as a whole is very cinema-literate. There are a number of great repertory cinemas scattered around the city, and even the local public television station runs uninterrupted classic films every Saturday night. The only blot on the cinema landscape is the local paper, the *San Francisco Chronicle,* an inexcusably awful example of semiliterate provincial journalism which, for some reason, wields supreme power over the films that people see. If you move to the Bay Area, be sure to subscribe to a magazine or newspaper that prints the work of critics who have intelligence and taste. If you rely on the *Chronicle*'s critics to determine the films you see, you will miss much of what is good and interesting in contemporary cinema.

Some of the best things about the program: The faculty's flexibility. They put few limitations on students, and those few are more like helpful suggestions than strict rules. For example, the first-year films are supposed to be no more than eight minutes in length. Almost everybody makes fifteen- or twenty-minute films, and in retrospect, after spending too much money and too much time on these projects, almost everybody wishes they had kept them under eight minutes as the school suggested. The second year offers tremendous freedom to experiment. And perhaps best of all, you get to live in San Francisco.

Some of the worst things about the program: Though it just invested money in a new building, the school lacks some important filmmaking equipment. The single worst thing about the program is the perennially destitute state of the California State University system. Students and faculty argue that it builds character—by making films with minimal equipment and no money, students get a good idea of what life will be like as independent filmmakers after graduation. But it is also true that sooner or later everyone—students and faculty alike—despairs at having to fight for even the smallest amounts of money or equipment.

Savannah College of Art and Design

P.O. Box 3146
Savannah, GA 31402-3146
800/869-SCAD
Department: (912) 238-2407
Admissions: (912) 238-2424
http://www.scad.edu

Equipment Quality: ☆☆☆

Equipment Accessibility: ☆☆☆

Cost: $$

Annual Tuition: $12,600
Enrollment: 27 total
Deadline: 4–6 weeks prior to the start of any quarter
Focus: Independent

The Program

Established in 1985, Savannah's is a relatively young program. The entire college has only been around since 1977. It is the only school that offers an M.F.A. in Video. The goal of this two-year program is to teach film principles and apply them to the less expensive medium of video. There is also a focus on new technologies and the role that video plays in them.

The school operates on a rolling admissions system—students can apply to enter the program in any quarter of the year. There is as yet no maximum number of students admitted. Traditionally, most students who show any sort of creative promise are accepted. In a recent year the enrollment numbered around eight.

Classes can be taken year-round, including summer, on a full-time basis. Students who do this can graduate in a little over two years. Inexperienced students are first admitted in a provisional program available every quarter. This consists of the following basic undergrad production courses: Introduction to Video, Lighting, Pre-Production, Field Production Techniques, Post-Production and Sound Design as well as Survey of Western Arts I and II. Including the provisional program, Savannah is a three-year, full-time program.

Once the provisional courses have been completed, students must take ninety hours of graduate-level study, twenty of which are electives taken within or outside the department. Every course is five credits, so we're talking a total of eighteen classes. For full-time study this amounts to three classes per quarter during the traditional school year and two classes during the summer session. Graduates can take undergraduate classes as electives, but they are required to do extra work. Students must take two internships. Savannah has seen a recent escalation in local feature film production and students are often able to obtain internships on these films. The school has recently created a staff position that aids students in locating internships.

While there is no established order in which to fulfill requirements, some grad courses are only available every other quarter, so students hoping to graduate on any sort of schedule need to keep tabs on when required courses are offered. Every student is assigned an advisor to assist in planning her schedule.

Graduate courses aim to familiarize students with critical approaches, develop writing skills, and refine production skills. There are several classes that concentrate on production. Typically students make three short videos per quarter in each of these classes. Students provide their own tape stock.

To follow up the provisional program, there are required advanced courses in Sound Design, Post-Production, and Directing the Narrative. Field Production provides students with the opportunity to experience location shooting. Advanced technology classes are technical courses that teach hands-on operation of Steadi-cams, the Panther Dolly, or the school's Mozart twenty-four-track recording studio. Interactive Video is a multimedia class in which students create interactive works with Macromedia Director, or build Web sites to post on the World Wide Web. Writing for Television provides a broad overview of all aspects of creative writing, from commercials to sitcoms. Video in Society is a lecture class that reviews and evaluates the ever-changing role of video and the dominant ideologies that surround it. There is also a required class in Contemporary Art. Some students avail themselves of a newly offered minor in Sound Design or study the basics of Documentary Directing.

One of the last classes students take is Self-Promotion, which tries to prepare students for a successful transition to the real world and (one hopes) employment. Demo reels are prepared and resumes and interviewing techniques reviewed. Once all course work is completed, students have a final review by the dean and faculty. At this time they must present samples of their completed films as well as pre-production materials. There is an in-depth question-and-answer session where students defend their thesis projects. There are no length requirements for thesis films. Projects run anywhere from five to fifteen minutes, with the occasional epic popping up periodically.

Graduate students organize an annual film festival which is juried by the faculty and presents noncash awards in a variety of categories. The school is hoping to sponsor a multimedia festival within the next couple of years. There is also an annual local Arts Festival to which students often submit their films.

The Price

$12,600 per year tuition for three years	$37,800
$6,000 per year rent and living expenses for three years	$18,000
Average film costs	$ 5,000
Total	**$60,800**

Savannah is an economical school, both in terms of tuition and overall production costs. This is good, because there is not much in the way of financial support outside of government loans and grants. There are no paid teaching assistantships. A scholarship is awarded to incoming students who have outstanding creative portfolios. This scholarship amounts to $2,500 toward the first forty-five hours of study and $3,500 toward the second, and is distributed on an individual basis to as many students as the department feels deserve it. There are also two $1,000 fellowships awarded to incoming valedictorians or to the student with the highest GRE score. They offer a free "scholarship search" which any student can apply for as many times as she wants to during her enrollment.

Savannah is a charming, inexpensive city. The college takes up most of the historic downtown district. Gorgeous buildings from the

1800s have been restored and remodeled by the school's Architecture department. Most students live in this area, which is near the school. Rents average around $300 for a one-bedroom or slightly less than double that amount for a large two-bedroom. A car is not strictly necessary—most students get by with bikes. Part-time work is available in nearby stores and restaurants, and many students can be seen waiting on tables in the evenings.

The Lowdown

GPAs count on the Savannah application. And although the GRE is optional, applicants should remember there is a scholarship available for the highest score. Students will need the usual letters of reference and a statement of intent. For those submitting reels, the department wants to know exactly what hand an applicant had in each submission, so that they can decide whether or not a student must begin as provisional. Acceptance is almost certain for those with some talent and drive. Faculty are interested in supporting artistic spirit and energy and have yet to reject a passionate applicant.

Like the school as a whole, the film faculty has been growing. The eight professors onboard are not famous but have worked in the film or video industry in various capacities. They are experienced, production-oriented professionals who enjoy the technology that the school focuses on. Students feel the faculty is one of the strongest elements of the program. They are highly motivated, supportive individuals who enjoy teaching. This makes for a very nurturing environment.

As far as video production goes, Savannah has tremendous video equipment and facilities. All is shared with the undergrad population with students gaining access to better and better cameras as they become more experienced. Because the program is still quite small, there is rarely a problem obtaining equipment. Things get tight around mid-semester, but students can reserve their packages several days in advance to guarantee availability.

There are twelve Panasonic S-VHS cameras for lower-level classes; seven Panasonic M2 cameras for more advanced students and six Panasonic DVC pro digital cameras for grad thesis film and undergrad senior projects. Cameras are reserved up to twenty-four hours in advance and are available for four-hour checkouts. Those shooting thesis films can borrow the DVCs for up to seven hours. Special approval is needed in order to keep equipment overnight or to arrange for longer checkouts for thesis films. There are no Friday classes, so this is always a big production day.

SCAD has sixteen Avid workstations and is an Avid Education Center which offers one-to-three-day industry training seminars to non-students. Students, on the other hand, have an entire quarter to learn this equipment. Those in the Avid classes have priority over the rest of the student population. And since hard disk storage space on the Avids is limited, only the students working in class are allowed to save their projects.

There are twelve lower-end models for beginners and four Avid 1000s for advanced students. Those not currently in class have little if any time on the advanced Avid 1000s. Most students still use the five A-B roll video editing suites to cut their films, and will arrange to do only the final cut on Avid. A-B roll suites are reserved for four-hour slots, with a maximum of sixteen hours per week.

The department is home to a chromakey/blue screen studio, three soundstages, individual post-production suites, a Mozart audio production suite supporting twenty-four-track digital recording, and an audio mix-down suite. They have recently renovated a local thousand-seat movie theater that dates back to the 1920s.

Some of the best things about the program: It is a comfortable, noncompetitive environment. The cost of student productions is amazingly low: a thirty-minute video piece, shooting at a ten-to-one ratio, will only cost a student about $150 worth of videotape. That's about one-tenth the cost of a 16-mm film of that same length. Students are able to and do make a lot of projects at that price. The school strives to be state-of-the-art. Equipment is constantly being updated. Even their catalogue is available on CD-ROM.

Some of the worst things about the program: Very few student videos are entered in film festivals. A professor has recently been assigned to address this problem by working with students to pursue festival entries. There are no courses that work with film, nor is there any film equipment at all. Students say the writing program is weak. If the school wants to support students who are truly interested in writing narrative films, this area needs to be expanded.

Make the most of your time at Savannah by making a lot of projects. Master the equipment, especially the Avid. The school is right on the money regarding technology, and students can graduate as skilled technicians, ready to leap directly into jobs.

Savannah tries to help interested students secure work after school. There are resume and interview workshops and a job-referral bank. School representatives travel to industry conventions like the National Association of Broadcasters and the Independent Feature Film Market to promote students as potential employees.

Southern Illinois University at Carbondale

Department of Cinema and
   Photography
Carbondale, IL 62901-6610
Department: (618) 453-2365
Admissions: (618) 536-7791
http://www.siu.edu/cwis/

Experimental

**Equipment
Quality:** ☆☆

**Equipment
Accessibility:** ☆☆

Cost: $$

Annual Tuition:	Resident: $6,616
	Nonresident: $10,016
Enrollment:	4; 12 total
Deadline:	March 1
Focus:	Experimental/ Documentary

The Program

Carbondale is a tiny, selective program. Forty applications are received annually. The number of applicants admitted fluctuates between four and six each year, depending upon the number of graduating students. There are never more than twelve students total in this three-year program. Students graduate having fulfilled a double major in Cinema and Photography.

Prior film experience is not a requirement, and the program is often tailored to meet individual student needs. There's a core of required courses, including three production courses and some technical, theory, and history classes. Students fulfill sixty credits at their own pace and in a variety of sequences. Most carry three to four classes each semester. Since it is a double major, many students take advantage of the photography courses within their department. Students must complete twelve credits of independent study, fourteen hours of general electives taken within or outside the department, and six hours of thesis project credits. Thesis credits are often extended over several semesters to keep enrollment active while completing thesis films. Cross-disciplinary study is encouraged. All film production costs are incurred by the student.

At the end of the third semester, students are required to select a primary advisor along with a committee of two additional graduate faculty members. The faculty members can be from an outside department. Students consult with this committee several times a semester to develop and review a specific plan of study. Although technically a three-year program, since classes are offered year-round and students register by the credit hour, some graduate in less time, others more. Part-time study is an option, but most students attend full-time.

A good number of classes are taken with undergraduate students. These include all of the history and theory courses and many of the fourteen electives students must take outside of the department. Students with no film background must take Production I, an undergraduate super-8 film course for which they provide their own camera and supplies to make several short films. More experienced students can start with the required 16-mm Production II course. In this class they make a nonsync, four-to-ten-minute film during the semester. Also required are two specific production courses like Sound or Lighting, which can be taken concurrently with Production I. However, students are not permitted to take screenwriting concurrent with either Production II, III, or IV.

Production III/IV is a two-semester course in which students make a ten-to-twenty-minute sync-sound film. Scripts for these films must be submitted and approved by the cinema faculty. Once approved, students shoot their films during the first semester. The next semester is devoted to post-production. Exposed film is shipped for processing to numerous labs, the most popular being in Chicago or Denver. Due to the location, at Carbondale, student filmmakers do some of the more tedious post-production work themselves. They shoot their own titles and perform sound mixing, film conforming, negative matching, and optical printing. There are no length restrictions on student films. A two-minute film fulfills production requirements the same as one of thirty-minutes. Projects in general are of a very personal nature. Crew sizes are small and consist of graduate and undergraduate students. Many students simply check out a Bolex and work solo on their films.

At this point, students can schedule remaining electives and requirements in the order most appropriate for their individual program. Theory classes offer constantly changing topics. At the discretion of faculty, students can explore Science Fiction of the Eighties or wind up studying Soviet Montage. Another class required for two semesters is Graduate Seminar, where all graduate cinema and photography students meet to show their work. It's a forum for feedback and discussion. Each student receives one presentation opportunity per semester.

Since program emphasis is upon artistic development, students may delve into other fine arts, especially photography, as heavily as they want. While the degree title will not vary, the education received will be as specific and individual as each student.

All final creative projects must be exhibited publicly and evaluated at an oral examination by the faculty. There have been cases where a students did not make a separate thesis but instead submitted one or more earlier class films for thesis credit. In the last few years some students have shot part of their thesis projects in video. The final degree requirement is an advertised public screening of a student's thesis work. This is coordinated and paid for by the student.

The Price

RESIDENT

$330 per credit for 60 credits	$ 19,800
$9,000 per year rent and living expenses for three years	$ 27,000
Average film costs	$ 10,000
Total	**$ 56,800**

NONRESIDENT

$500 per credit for 60 credits	$ 30,000
$9,000 rent and living expenses for three years	$ 27,000
Average film costs	$ 10,000
Total	**$ 67,000**

Ignore these figures. No student will pay these tuition fees. This is because every single graduate film student is funded at Carbondale. No kidding. One of the reasons cinema and photography are still a joint degree is that together they receive more funding than either small department would qualify for alone. This is also why they limit the number of admissions. They really try to support their students financially.

While assistantships are usually awarded after the first semester, a highly experienced student might even receive one upon acceptance. At this writing there are actually more assistantships than students. Positions are filled as quarter- or half-time assignments. Both receive a full tuition waiver but vary in the amount of hours worked and cash stipend provided. Quarter-time assistants work about ten hours each week and receive a monthly stipend of $400; half-time assistants work about twenty hours per week and receive $800 per month. Other positions include faculty assistants or equipment managers, or even director of the Big Muddy Film Festival. But the majority of grads teach undergrad classes for their assistantships. It only takes three months to establish residency so if for some unexpected reason you do not get an assistantship early on, you can still take advantage of the lower resident tuition rate.

There is a newly instated Screenwriting Fellowship established through an alumni endowment fund. The exact figure of the scholarship has yet to be decided.

Undergrad and graduate students compete for Kodak film grants. Students submit film proposals which the faculty reviews along with class performance to determine recipients. They can reapply for these grants every year. Otherwise filmmakers usually purchase film stock at a 20 percent discount through the school

Carbondale is a scenic, rural community bordering the Shawnee National Forest. The nearest large cities are Chicago, a mere six-hour commute by car, and St. Louis, just a two-hour drive. This lack of distraction means students put exceptional amounts of time into their films. There is little else to do. It's easy to get almost anywhere in town on foot. But a car would be nice for those cold production days or sanity-preserving weekend getaways.

One-bedroom apartments go for as little as two hundred dollars a month. Though rents are cheap, it's still difficult to live on the quarter assistantship stipend. Since the job market is minimal, most students try to get more than one assistantship rather than seek employment outside the university.

Casting locally for narrative production is extremely difficult. Talent is usually imported from Chicago or found within the university theater department.

At the start of each semester there are screenings of Production II and thesis films. There are also the individual thesis screenings held by graduating students. Carbondale is best known for the Big Muddy Film Festival. Students are discouraged from entering this well-respected independent festival because Carbondale students are in charge of the screening. It's hoped that the newly created Little Muddy Festival, which was designed as a student alternative, will fill this void. Little Muddy is a small student screening and competition judged by university recruits and culminating in an awards banquet.

The Lowdown

Carbondale is searching for creative applicants. It helps to have a film background, but they do try to balance a class of varying experience levels. Any creative work is evaluated and appreciated as a demonstration of your perspective and potential. Only truly focused self-starters need apply. Such large financial investments in their students makes them understandably selective. They try to ensure that their money is well spent.

There is but a handful of faculty. Luckily courses can easily be taken outside the department to avoid inherent boredom. With the exception of one Production teacher, most faculty members are not currently working in film. They are not overly enthusiastic about their positions or students. You must be persistent and aggressively solicit their support.

Although not in the best state of maintenance, the equipment works. There are ten Bolexes, seven Arri Ss, three Arri BLs, one Arri M, one Eclair NPR, one CP 16, and one Arri SR camera. All but the Arri SR and one Bolex are shared with undergrads. You will have to purchase your own light meter. There is only cassette-tape sound acquisition for Production I and II classes. Production III's graduate to Nagras, Sennheiser, and elector mikes, and standard-university-fare lighting equipment. Packages can be reserved two weeks in advance to be checked out for twenty-four hours during the week and weekends. There are no Friday classes, so weekends are popular for filming. With faculty approval, extended shoots can be arranged providing no one else is waiting in the wings. Since undergrads only have a one-week advance, grads do have a leg up on them. Checkout is via the honor system. Graduate students have keys to the equipment room, so they can take equipment whenever they want. There is a reservation sign-up board, so everyone is aware of who gets what when. Most respect this schedule. Equipment privileges are suspended for those who abuse the system.

There are nine six-plate Steenbecks, four of which are installed in editing rooms. Three are in storage for lack of space. There is one eight-plate room reserved for grads. The grad flatbed is considerably nicer than those used by the undergrad rabble, so grads tend to clamor around its availability. There are four Moviolas but no space to put them in. Editing reservations are made forty-eight hours in advance for four-hour time blocks. A 1.2-million-dollar building renovation is currently under way. This is expected to greatly effect the post-production facilities and will certainly provide for extra editing rooms.

The school does have an Avid, which was purchased by the entire Communication Department. It is located in the Radio and Television Department. Apparently there's some bad blood between Radio/TV and the Film Department. Film students are angry because they have trouble even getting access to the Avid. This problem will more than likely be addressed with the introduction of an Avid instruction course in the works for fall '97.

There are four Media 100s on campus. One is located in a newly opened media lab, which also contains top-of-the-line Macintosh computers, all with animation capabilities, multimedia offerings, and Pro Tools. The Cinema and Photography Department is in the process of purchasing their own Media 100, which will be reserved for advanced film-editing projects

There is a sixty-by-forty-foot soundstage which contains track lighting and an El-Mac dolly. Although this space is normally used as a classroom, student projects override all other uses. The stage is also used for Foley and ADR work and recording. The sound-mixing areas are located right off the soundstage. There are two sound suites, the better of which has an eight-channel mixing board with three 16-mm dubbers and two 35-mm dubbers.

The school has film-to-video transfer capabilities. This pleases students who don't want to spend extra finishing money on early projects and also like making free video dubs of their films.

The most can be made of Carbondale by students who have a need to make small, personal films and are sufficiently responsibile to be able to finish the program in timely fashion. Make as many films as possible. Seek out fellow graduate students as early as possible. Learn from their experiences, especially regarding class structuring. It would help to have some savings to cover film costs before beginning. Participate in the Big Muddy Festival.

Some of the best things about the program: Tuition is minimal. Experimental and documentary filmmakers might enjoy the less structured, personal nature of the program. Filmmakers produce all genres and types of films. There's a surprisingly international population. There is a Los Angeles internship program. While more geared to undergrads, it offers the chance to work in and experience the Hollywood film and television industry on a short-term basis without great financial drain. They are looking to expand this program to Chicago. The joint Cinema/Photography setup lends itself to some interesting visual growth and expression. The Big Muddy Festival brings the independent film industry up close and personal.

Some of the worst things about the program: "You went where?" No one has heard of this small school (until of course you put it on the map). The location. Students seeking a hip, exciting learning environment will be greatly disappointed. Of course this leaves plenty of time to heighten self-speculation and awareness. Some students find it annoying that the graduate department is not really separated from the undergraduate. There are no full-fledged graduate film classes. Carbondale is not a haven for narrative filmmakers. It can take a very long time to graduate in such an individualized, slow-paced program.

Some interesting folks have passed through Carbondale. Steve James and Fred Marx, the creators of the Academy Award–nominated *Hoop Dreams,* and Liz Ralston, who worked on animating the world's most famous pig, Babe, are all alumni. There's a fairly active alumni association that tries to keep in touch with former students and point grads in their direction. All alumni seem very supportive of the program. Three student Academy Awards have been bestowed on Carbondale students in both the documentary and narrative categories in the last few years.

Syracuse University

Syracuse University
Department of Art Media
  Studies
102 Shaffer Art Building
Syracuse, NY 13244-1210
(315) 443-1033
http://vpa.syr.edu

Equipment Quality: ☆☆☆

Equipment Accessibility: ☆☆☆

Cost: $$$

Annual Tuition:	$503 per credit hour for 24 hours—$12,072
Enrollment:	5 per year, 15 total
Deadline:	February 1
Focus:	Experimental

The Program

The M.F.A. program at Syracuse University is part of the College of Visual and Performing Arts. It is a division of the Department of Art Media Studies, which includes the studies of Film, Video, Computer Graphics, and Photography. It is a very small program; out of around eighty applicants each year only five are admitted. There are never more than fifteen students in the program at a time.

This is a three-year program, with classes and film production continuing through all three years. In the first semester students take three or four classes, including an introduction to film theory, and a studio course that introduces them to the technical aspects of filmmaking and prepares them to make their first-year films. The scripts that students then begin to write for the first-year film average around ten pages in length. In general the school makes few requirements regarding students' films. They can be any length, they can cover any subject matter, and they can be in any genre. However, there is one rule about this first-year film. The school requires that this film be a "narrative film." By "narrative" they don't mean "Hollywood," or even "conventional." They only mean that a first-year film should tell a story, should use actors, and should make use of a full crew. The school's hope is that by using actors and a crew students will see what it is like to make a film under the most complex circumstances. The first-year film is expected to be in the can by the end of the fall semester.

In the spring semester students edit their first-year films while continuing to take three or four classes. Reshoots are possible—for most students a few pickup shots are a certainty. Syracuse has enough cameras and equipment that last-minute shooting is never a problem. There are a good number of flatbed editing machines, and the university has a nonlinear digital editing system for those who want to explore new technologies. All first-year films must be completed by the end of the spring semester when each student's work is evaluated by the faculty.

Second year is similarly structured. Students are asked to bring a script in on the first day, and during the year they take three or four classes while working to make that script into a completed film. Second-year students take a course in Cinema Acting Directing, which puts them into a studio with a group of actors from Syracuse's drama department. Students direct the actors in scenes from the screenplays they have written for their second-year films and record the scenes on videotape, completing a scene every week and getting a sense of how their screenplays will play out on film. In the second semester students shoot their second-year films. There are no restrictions at all on the second-year films—they can be in any genre and on any subject. The school also allows collaboration on these films, which is something that it does not allow on the first- or third-year films. Groups of no more than three students may pool their resources and efforts to make a film that exceeds what each would be able to do alone.

Third year follows the same pattern as second: students bring in a screenplay on the first day, take three or four classes each semester, and have a completed film by the end of the year. The school does not tolerate long post-production periods. Students who are not finished with their thesis by the end of the third year are allowed to stay through the summer to complete it. But at the end of the summer, they are banished from the school and its equipment.

When a student's thesis is finished, Syracuse becomes very academic. Finishing the M.F.A. here is like finishing a Ph.D. program elsewhere. When a student has completed her thesis film, she chooses a four-member evaluation committee, including two professors from within the film program and two from other parts of the university. She screens the film for the committee and presents a paper that discusses and defends the thesis. She then has to go through an extended oral defense of the thesis, fielding questions and challenges from the four committee members.

The Price

60 credit hours at $503 per credit	$30,180
$10,000 a year rent and living expenses for 3 years	$30,000
Insurance and upkeep on a car for 3 years	$ 3,000
First-year-film budgets average around	$ 2,000
Second-year-film budgets average around	$ 4,000
Third-year-film budgets average around	$ 8,000
Total	**$77,180**

Life at Syracuse is inexpensive. Rents are cheap, with one-bedroom apartments running about $350 a month. A car is a necessity for moving equipment, cast, and crew around on shoots, though some students manage by befriending other students who have cars. The school offers no financial help with the films, so students are completely on their own financially when it comes to completing their projects.

The university funds seven half-TAships, each of which gives remission of half a year's tuition, plus pays a $3,000 stipend. That stipend almost covers the other half of the tuition, so basically each student who receives a half-TA position gets free tuition for the year. So nearly half of the fifteen students in the program at any time get free tuition. Generally TAships are not given to first year students—they are reserved for second and third year students, who usually need more money than first year students to pay for their films. Students may find TAships in the university outside of the film department, and there are work-study jobs available to those students who cannot get TAships at all.

Another money-saving feature of Syracuse the school is Syracuse the town, thanks to its dullness. There's nothing to do there.

Syracuse is a quiet, largely industrial town, so there is little temptation to blow large chunks of money on partying. There are few bars
around, so most of the social life revolves around house parties at
the local fraternities. Sleazy? Yes. Juvenile? Sure. But house parties
are a lot less expensive than trendy clubs, bars, or restaurants. The
downside is that eventually you will start to go insane, and you will
find yourself unable to fight the urge to party, and you'll take a road
trip to Toronto or Boston or Manhattan, and you will then spend all
the money you have saved by living in Syracuse, plus some of your
thesis film budget, plus half of your Visa card's credit limit before
you stagger back to Syracuse, exhausted and destitute.

The Lowdown

Along with your application and transcripts you have to send
three letters of recommendation and an original film or script. No
GRE is required, but the school will not consider any applicant with
an undergraduate GPA below 3.0. The school specifically looks for
people with experience making 16-mm films. While they will consider applicants without a background in film, there are so many
applicants now who do have film backgrounds that those without
are at a disadvantage. If you don't have any film experience at all,
you will have to show yourself to be unusually creative in both writing and some visual art such as photography or painting. If you are
accepted without experience in film, you will have to take a number of prerequisite courses before you can start the program. So if
you really want to get into Syracuse, you might want to go to a local
college or art school right now and take some courses in film. Make
a good film now to send with your application, and you will better
your chances of getting in—and you will also save yourself the time
and expense of taking the prerequisites once you are there. The faculty clearly aims to assemble an interesting mixture of people. They
usually accept a few applicants from other countries, and the people they accept from within the U.S. are interesting characters with
unique backgrounds. So don't play down your eccentricities.

The school is very strict about how long students can stay. It is a
three-year program, and you can only stay three years, plus the
summer after your third year if you absolutely need it to finish your

thesis film. Completing the program in less than three years is not possible, and staying for more than three years is not allowed.

The school has a good number of reasonably good camera packages, including two Arri SR-2s (one with video assist), four Arri BLs, and four CP 16s. Three of the BLs have internal crystal sync; one of them requires that an umbilical cord be attached to the Nagra recorder to make sure it runs in sync. The school also has an Eclair NPR, a sturdy old camera that also requires an umbilical cord for sync sound, a Beaulieu 16 that is mostly used for special-effects work, two Bolex ELs, and 20 Bolex spring-wound cameras. Most of the cameras use Angenieux zoom lenses. There are a few Zeiss prime lenses available, but they don't seem to get much use. Most of the lights available are Arri kits. There are some other lights— scoops and broads that are inconveniently massive but that do things the Arri lights cannot—and some grip kits.

The post-production facilities are fairly good, if somewhat dated. The school has one Montage Picture Processor, a nonlinear editing workstation, but most students still cut their films on film. The school also has two fairly new Steenbeck six-plate editing machines, one of which is reserved strictly for graduate use, and four older six-plate Moviola flatbeds. These are available for graduate use, but undergraduates also use them, so they can be hard to access come the end of the semester. The university also has a few low-end, non–broadcast quality, nonlinear editing systems scattered around the campus. These systems are not for the film department's sole use—they are distributed around the college in media centers and libraries, and may not be very practical for post-production of large-scale film projects. The school also owns an optical printer.

As a convenience, the school has a battery of VHS camcorders for students to use. These are meant to be used to tape rehearsals and are readily loaned to anyone who wants to use them for this purpose.

The school puts a heartening emphasis on sound, offering a class in production sound recording and providing production sound equipment to match. There are Nagras and DAT recorders, and a number of Marantz cassette recorders. A wide variety of microphones is available, from clip-on lavaliers to radio mics to Sennheiser shotguns. The school has a sound-transfer room for dubbing of recorded material onto mag film, and there is a sound-recording studio. Given the quality of Syracuse's production sound equipment, it has surprisingly rudimentary post-production sound equipment. The school's one interlock mixing facility has only three mag dubbers hooked into a mag recorder. Some students find ways to use this system by doing many premixes, but most find it necessary to go outside of the school to do their mixes, using sound houses in Boston, Toronto, or New York City.

There are no film-processing labs close to the school. Students usually send their rushes to Cine64 in Boston, Duart in Manhattan, or even Alpha Cine in Seattle. The school provides each student with a book of information about these and other labs but doesn't have any discount deals with them.

Syracuse is best suited to students who have ambitious projects in mind and want advice, not discouragement, from the faculty. The professors expect students to be ambitious and, because the school has a large supply of equipment, encourage them to make big, ambitious projects. In recent years students have even made feature-length films, and the faculty were happy to oblige. The only requirement is that the projects not be so ambitious that they can't be completed within the program's three-year-plus-one-summer time limit.

Some of the best things about the program: It is very small, making it easy for students to work closely with professors and other students. The small size also ensures that everyone can teach who wants to—just about every graduate student gets the opportunity to teach undergraduate film courses at some point. The school's two professors, Owen Shapiro and Dana Plays, try to make up for their lack of numbers with enthusiasm. As of this writing, they are looking for a filmmaker to become the department's third faculty member.

Some of the worst things about the program: The town of Syracuse is neither exciting nor attractive. Exterior locations in the area tend to be either industrial wastelands or northern deciduous forest. And the climate leaves much to be desired. On the other hand, in the words of one student we spoke with, "If you don't mind snow, it's fine."

The school does not do much to promote students at graduation. The school encourages students to enter their finished films in festivals and every fall holds a screening in town for locals to view the new works coming out of the school. But there are no trips to Hollywood, no introductions to agents or producers, no internship programs with TV or film companies, and no gala screenings for members of the film community to attend.

Nor is there an alumni organization. If you tell the school where you want to go after graduation, they will tell you which of their graduates are living there, what they are doing, and how to contact them. That's about the end of it.

Temple University

Department of Radio-
   Television-Theater
Annenberg Hall
Philadelphia, PA 19122
Department: (215) 204-1735
Admissions: (215) 204-1380
http://www.temple.edu/
   departments/fma/

**Equipment
Quality:** ☆

**Equipment
Accessibility:** ☆

Cost: $$

Annual Tuition:	**Resident: $7,263 Nonresident: $9,168**
Enrollment:	**15; 70 total**
Deadline:	**February 1**
Focus:	**Experimental/ Documentary**

The Program

Temple University is a well-funded school in the heart of Philadelphia. It is best known for its documentary filmmaking program, but in recent years students have also made good narrative and experimental films. The school accepts fifteen students each fall into the program. Two hundred apply. Two-thirds of all students have a television/film background.

The three-year program is currently in transition. The school is considering injecting more structure into its largely unstructured curriculum. At this writing, students must take fifty-four credit hours, including six hours toward the final creative project, within two years. The only required courses are Cinematography, Videography, Media Writing, Film History and Theory, Multi-media, and Colloquium, all taken in the first year. Colloquium is a one-credit course where all the film students meet to evaluate one another's work, screen films, or listen to lectures from visiting guests. It's also intended as an icebreaker for first- and second-year students.

There are only two technical classes—Cinematography, which students take in the fall of their first year, and Videography, which they take in the spring. Every technical aspect of filmmaking and video making is jammed into these two classes, including cinematography, lighting design, sound recording, editing, sound editing, sound mixing, and A&B rolling. It's a lot of work.

That's because the first year is filled with film exercises. In these classes, first year students experiment with shooting black and white film, editing in camera, and interior and exterior shooting. Students work in groups of four, so there is always some sort of production at work to be done on somebody's film. Exercise film supplies are provided by the school. Each student is given an account with a certain amount of money in it—$400 for a film, $200 for a video. And as a student gets supplies from the school, the value of those supplies is deducted from her account. Most students just make small projects that do not cost more than the provided budget to complete.

In one cinematography exercise, students duplicate a scene from the work of a favorite cinematographer in still slides. This presentation is accompanied by a written evaluation of lighting, mood, and ratios. In Media Writing they complete a script to shoot in cinematography class. At the end of the semester students are given 600 feet of black-and-white or 400 feet of color film and processing for this final project. Students who wish to complete a film through the answer print stage will do so out of their own pockets. Many shoot additional footage.

After finishing these required courses, students need only register for a second Colloquium. The rest of the program is tailored to the individual. Students are free to take courses outside the department or pursue independent study. Women's or African-American Studies are often pursued as minors. Some people take courses on a nonmatriculated basis to pick up some technical skills—in Avid, for instance. In addition to regular classes, there is the Women's Technology Workshop, a university-funded program designed to strengthen women's technical know-how in a user-friendly environment. They recently completed a university-funded short film about waitressing.

Students go through a lot of formal, written testing throughout the program. After finishing the required classes, each student puts together a committee for supervision of her comprehensive writing exam. She submits to this committee ten essay questions she would like on her own comprehensive exam. These questions have to be extensively researched and presented along with a listing of resources and readings done to support the questions. Students can devote an entire semester to preparation for this comprehensive. The committee chooses six or seven of the questions for the exam. Then the student has several days to answer the questions. Each question can require an eight-to-ten page response. Once the comprehensive exam is passed, a student can then start putting together a thesis.

Once the thesis is developed, the project must be defended before a second advisory committee. The thesis can be a feature-length screenplay, 16-mm film, a video project, or a work in a new technology (such as computer-controlled hypermedia).

The Price

RESIDENT

$269 per credit for 54 credits	$14,526
$9,000 a year rent and living expenses for 3 1/2 years.	$31,500
Average total film costs	$15,000
Total	**$61,026**

NONRESIDENT

$382 per credit for 54 credits	$20,628
$9,000 a year rent and living expenses for 3 1/2 years.	$31,500
Average total film costs	$15,000
Total	**$67,128**

Tuition at Temple is fairly inexpensive and only lasts for two years. After that, students need only pay for one thesis credit per semester to use the school's equipment. Most students take advantage of this rate to extend the program at least one additional semester beyond second year.

To be eligible for resident status one generally needs to have lived in Pennsylvania for a year prior to registration. A case could be argued if someone pays Pennsylvania taxes, owns or leases property in Pennsylvania, has financial holdings in the state, etc. If you have never lived in Pennsylvania before enrollment, you will not be able to become a resident—at least not before the end of the second year.

On the upside, there is a lot of funding floating around Temple. Every year there are about five fellowships awarded based on academic, creative, and professional credentials. These cover full tuition plus stipends of $12,000 to $16,000. Not a bad deal. Future Faculty Fellowships, covering three years of full tuition plus a stipend of up to $12,000, are awarded to qualified minority students (or students who have overcome some unusual obstacles) who have expressed interest in college-level teaching.

Finally, there are so many undergraduate film students that the remainder of students usually receive graduate assistantships (for which candidates assist or teach in the program) at some point. These pay $8,250 plus nine credits of tuition each semester in return for twenty hours of work per week. Part-time teaching is even available for some third-year students. Project Completion Fellowships of $8,000 and Project Completion Grants of $500 to $4,000 are awarded competitively each semester. So far every student who has made a thesis has received a Completion Grant. Many people work part-time.

The City of Brotherly Love has a lot to offer. There are several nice museums, decent movie theaters, good theater and art, lots of fine dining, and relatively safe streets . . . except in the area surrounding Temple University. Temple is basically a commuter school, and most of the students hail from the Philadelphia area and wouldn't dream of living on campus. Neither should grad film students. Temple is smack in the middle of one of the worst crime areas of the city. However, there is a lot of campus security and the actual buildings and immediate streets within the campus are safe. Students should join the commuter ranks and drive or take public transportation to the school. There is tons of available housing in many safe areas. Philadelphia is a city of neighborhoods, and apartments can be had in pricey Society Hill or Center City proper or any number of outlying areas such as Northeast Philly or South Philly or the Main Line. A one-bedroom can be had for as low as $450 or as high as $1,000, depending on the area and amenities. A car is not necessary, but it helps to have one. New York City is but a short train ride away for those who look for a bit more excitement.

In early May Temple presents the TUFAVA screening. This is a competitive juried festival organized by students and faculty.

The Lowdown

Applicants are chosen based on an essay, letters of recommendation, a creative portfolio, and GRE scores. Any type of creative material, film or otherwise, is considered. At Temple the message is more important that the medium. They look for content and strong opinions, not so much for experience in the technique of filmmaking. They search for people who have things to say and a strong drive to say them through the medium of film. This is the reason they do not spell out a number of requirements once students arrive.

The fellowships and assistantships take some of the financial burden off the first two years of school. As a result, most students cruise through the first two years with plenty of money, then lose steam, both financially and academically, during third year. Many students spend third year putting together their comprehensive exams and working to raise money for their thesis films, which they shoot in fourth year. The school tries to enforce an upper limit of five years. Though the assistantships and fellowships dry up after two years, every year the school hires a number of third- and fourth-year students as part-time teachers. The pay may not be as good as an assistantship, but since theses students are no longer paying full tuition, it works out to a good deal. It is also a great advantage for students who hope to teach after their M.F.A.s.

Although screenwriting is not the emphasis of the program, students single out their writing teacher as helpful. The cinematography teacher is also well liked. Some complain that since the majority of professors are documentary filmmakers, students feel they must mirror their instructors' work in order to be appreciated. Teachers don't necessarily volunteer their assistance. It must be sought out. The film theory classes lack direction, students say.

A fairly common practice at Temple is for students to shoot reversal filmstock, and treat the positive camera reel as if it were negative. They have the positive camera original processed, and then have a positive workprint struck from it. While unorthodox, it is inexpensive and it gives Temple films a unique high-contrast look. Some students have made feature-length films this way in recent years.

Filmmaking at Temple is cheapest for students who shoot black and white reversal stock. The school has a 16-mm black-and-white reversal laboratory that charges five cents per foot—much less than a professional lab. While students speak well of this lab's work, it cannot process color or negative film. So when shooting anything other than black and white reversal, outside labs are necessary. Unfortunately, choice in outside labs is limited. NFL Films (yes, as in National Football League) across the river in New Jersey has a deal with Temple for discount student processing but students sometimes grumble about their work.

This grumbling is nothing compared with grumbling about the equipment. There's simply not enough equipment to properly support the grad program. Equipment is shared with the huge undergraduate population and is assigned according to a course number hierarchy. The lower the course number (large, undergrad classes) the higher the priority. A thesis project is not a regular class. And they tend to shoot over longer periods. This makes them a low priority in this hierarchy. Temple is the only school that places grads behind undergrads. This situation is made worse by the fact that there is little communication between undergrad and grad faculty. Undergrad and grad classes often have to make projects simultaneously.

No equipment can be checked out unless a student is enrolled in a video, cinematography or thesis class. To assure a package, reservations must be made far in advance. Even then, students are not certain of what will be available. And what is available is in poor shape. A lot of people actually own their own 16-mm packages. Those who don't will have to scramble for everything. Students accommodate one another's schedules to share cameras when the packages are available. Projects are filmed according to when equipment is available, not necessarily when the director prefers.

There are nine sync camera packages, one of which is a grad-reserved Arriflex SR. There are sixteen Bolexes, one Arri M, some Hi-8 and S-VHS cameras, and seven Nagras. Cameras are not well maintained and are plagued by annoying and often costly problems, like faulty shutters and inconsistent motors. Once gotten, a camera can be kept for five days. The video situation is troublesome because video equipment is shared with the faculty and students of the entire school, not just film grads and undergrads. A few students have wisely invested in their own Hi-8 cameras. The equipment situation is further complicated by the tension between undergrad and grad faculty. Undergrads and grads often have to shoot class projects simultaneously. At times like this lights are especially scarce. In one instance, thesis students were unable to shoot for over a month because there simply was no lighting available. They are so short of lights that students pool their resources to purchase lights on their own. Those working on larger projects rent outside equipment from a couple of nonprofit co-ops in the area or even from as far away as New York.

Post-production facilities are also shared, so again there is not enough and what there is is not in the best of shape. Space is available on a first-come, first-served sign-up. Fortunately there are five VHS editing stations designated for grads. Unfortunately these break down all the time and can turn simple editing sessions into marathons. The school owns a number of Video Toasters. Fortunately there is also an Avid. Unfortunately the Avid is armed with the least expensive software so it is not really industry standard, and it breaks down frequently. There are two courses to teach the Avid but it is nearly impossible to get in. This is not so disappointing considering that the Avid is generally booked twenty-four hours a day seven days a week. Even if one is qualified, the odds of actually using the machine are slim. Many people choose to linear edit on the five flatbeds. This can be an inconvenience because there are no student storage lockers or editing bins. Students improvise bins with garbage bags, string taped to the wall, and clothespins.

There are an eight-track recording studio, an animation stand, and a contact printer. There are three TV studios with three camera setups and switchers and two screening rooms. The department is planning to move more from traditional video editing into the digital area. There is a dub rack that can take any format and convert it. For instance, a student could shoot in Hi-8 or Beta and transfer it onto a VHS workprint to use VHS editors.

Some of the best things about the program: Classes are intimate. Students are free to explore many different aspects of film. There is a real collaborative spirit at play. Temple is sort of an in-between school. It has some of the nicer small-school qualities, but it is still in a city environment. Students unite to support one another, so there is less stress or competition. The pragmatic philosophy means no one graduates with unrealistic expectations. The tuition is not extreme and the funding is substantial.

Some of the worst things about the program: There is far too much technical information imparted in the first-semester cinematography course. By the time students shoot their thesis films they often find themselves scratching their heads, trying to remember just what their professor said about sound recording (or sound mixing or negative cutting or whatever) in that one class at the beginning of the first year. Some graduate students take technical undergraduate courses to fill in areas like editing where the graduate school is lacking. The equipment is a real sore spot. Even the equipment room manager acknowledges the need for an overhaul. Major motion picture production is sporadic at best in Philly. Most of the film and video production in town is commercial or industrial. Students who want to work in production have a better chance of working in the few post houses that handle this type of work than waiting for a production to blow into town.

The most can be made of time spent at Temple by staying focused and even having a project to work on before arriving. Collaborate as much as possible. Try to get a camera whenever possible. Be patient and persistent and there is no reason you can't graduate with an inexpensive film. Be sure to contact the Mayor's Film Office. They can find great locations that can be used for free or close to it. Residents of Philadelphia are not jaded about film production the way those in Los Angeles or New York are. People are still excited about seeing films made and will give locations and assistance for free. Approach the undergrad population for crew assistance. There is a well-organized internship program that should be taken advantage of.

University of California, Los Angeles

Department of Film and
    Television
Box 951622
Los Angeles, CA 90095-1622
(310) 206-8504
http://www.filmtv.ucla.edu

Independent

Equipment
Quality: ☆☆☆

Equipment
Accessibility: ☆☆☆

Cost: **$$$$**

Annual Tuition:	Resident: $4,443 Nonresident: $12,837
Enrollment:	21 per year; around 70 total
Deadline:	November 1
Focus:	Independent

The Program

UCLA's Department of Film and Television offers M.F.A.s in four professional areas: Directing, Screenwriting, Producing, and Animation. The department as a whole is very large, including hundreds of undergraduates and graduate students in many other aspects of film like film theory and film preservation. But the segment of the school that most applicants want to get into, the directing specialization, is pretty small: only twenty-one new students are admitted to the program each fall.

UCLA's is one of the best-known film programs in the country, often mentioned in the same breath as USC and NYU. But compared with these other schools, its essence is elusive—whereas USC is well known as the ultimate Industry school and NYU as the ultimate Independent school, UCLA's identity is less well known. This is partly because UCLA defies expectations; despite its Hollywood-adjacent location, its direction is firmly Independent. But perhaps what makes UCLA's Department of Film and Television hardest to grasp is its breadth. While the program is clearly angled toward Independent filmmaking, it boasts a large and diverse faculty who provide specialized courses in many other kinds of filmmaking. Students may pursue interests in experimental and documentary filmmaking, in television, in New Media, and even in Industry-style filmmaking.

UCLA's is a three-year program which takes most students four years to complete. Because the school assumes no previous experience in film, the first quarter (UCLA is on the quarterly system) of first year is devoted to intensive studio courses in writing, directing, and the technical aspects of filmmaking. While taking these courses in the first semester, each student writes and directs a two-minute exercise film. Sync-sound cameras (CP 16s) are supplied, and the school provides each student with 400 feet of film, plus free processing and mag stock. The twenty-one students are split up into three seven-member filmmaking units. The seven members of each unit cycle through the various positions of a film crew, each in turn writing and directing her own film, and then acting as a crew member on the films of the other six. These films must be shot in a couple of hours and are then edited on flatbed editing machines.

In the second quarter of the first year students continue with more-intensive courses, including classes in directing actors and in television production. Each student writes an eight-page script and directs it. The seven-member groups shoot these more ambitious films, but no film or processing is provided by the school. Students have to pay for their own films—most spend around $2,500, while some spend as much as $8,000. The films are then edited, again on flatbed editing machines, during the third quarter of the first year. These films have to be completed by the end of the first year, otherwise students are not permitted to start work on their second-year films without first finishing these films.

The second year is less rigidly structured than the first. Students are required to take courses in writing, directing, and film theory and criticism, but otherwise they are allowed to choose their own focus. Having learned the basics of film production in the first year, students are encouraged to explore different facets of filmmaking in the second. They choose an area of filmmaking that interests them; documentary, experimental, television, New Media, or even directing for theater. Once a student has chosen an area of study, a faculty advisor who specializes in that area is assigned to her. This faculty member then acts as mentor, advising the student through courses and guiding her through the production of her second-year project, known locally as the Advanced Project.

Advanced Projects tend to run around twenty minutes, and on average students spend between $7,000 and $10,000 on them. The school does not allow students to find outside talent to work on advanced projects; students may only recruit crew members from within the school. While the advanced project is usually a film, it can be a television production, a New Media project, or even a feature-length screenplay. The students who make films shoot them in the winter quarter of their second year and work on them through the fall of their third year. Students are not allowed to begin work on their thesis films until they have finished their advanced projects, so most of them finish up their second-year films by winter break of third year. They then begin pre-production of their thesis films.

Classes continue on through the end of the third year. Thesis projects are shot in the winter or spring quarter of the third year and students do post-production on them in a fourth year. Thesis projects have only one restriction on them: length. Narrative films may not exceed thirty minutes; documentary films may not run beyond fifty-six minutes. Other than that, they can be in any medium and can be made by any crew—student, professional, or otherwise. Most students make narrative films for their thesis projects. Out of any class of twenty-one, two, or three are likely to make documentaries and maybe one will do a project in New Media.

The school has a firm policy that students may not stick around for more than four years; they either finish their films in that time or they are locked out of the facilities.

The Price

$12,837 non-resident tuition for three years	$ 38,511
$12,000 a year rent and living expenses for four years	$ 48,000
First-year films tend to cost an additional	$ 3,000
Second year films tend to cost around	$ 8,000
Thesis films tend to cost around	$ 15,000
$2,000 per year maintenance and insurance on a car for four years	$ 8,000
Total	**$120,511**

While this is typical of what students spend overall, most students get TAships or grants from the school that cover some of this expense, and many save a substantial amount just by being California residents. To be considered a California resident you have to live in the state for a year without being a student, so residency is not that easy to get if you don't already have it. But if you already live in California, UCLA tuition is a lot cheaper: over three years, resident tuition costs $25,000 less than nonresident tuition

UCLA is unusually well endowed with grants and fellowships; about $300,000 worth are distributed to students each winter. These are given to students according to the requirements mandated in each grant. Some are reserved for graduate students, while graduate students have to compete with undergraduates for others. Some are only for students who satisfy certain criteria. Most students get some sort of monetary assistance for their second- and third-year films, but it is far from uniform; in any given year some students will get most of the money they need to make their projects while a few will get nothing. There is one enormous grant, funded by the Bridges Larson Foundation. This $25,000 grant, given out every year, is the holy grail of grants at UCLA. The school plays this grant out for maximum entertainment value, first announcing a few finalists, and then making everyone wait to hear which of the finalists gets it.

Because UCLA has a large undergraduate population, there are a lot of TAships. Forty TAships are given out each year to graduate film students. First-year students are not allowed to have TAships, so most of the second- and third-year graduate students get TAships of some sort.

There are inexpensive ways to satisfy the requirements of the program. Second-year projects may be made on video, may be burned to CD-ROM, or may take the form of feature-length screenplays. Some students do very small second-year projects to conserve their resources and energy for their thesis films. The school pays for tape for television projects shot in one of the school's three television studios, so it is possible to come out of second year with a good-looking video project that cost very little.

A California resident who makes a nonfilm second-year project, an inexpensive thesis (or one funded by grant money from the school), and who finishes in exactly three years can in theory get through the program for less than $80,000, which makes UCLA one of the cheapest of the most famous film schools. But this takes discipline; it's easy to spend a lot more if you aren't careful.

A car is absolutely necessary. Unfortunately, car insurance in Los Angeles is exorbitant; basic insurance runs from $1,200 to $2,000 per year even on a rundown old wreck. One-bedroom apartments near campus are scarce, and what few exist are pretty expensive. But a mile or so away in West L.A. one-bedrooms can be found for around $650 a month. Most UCLA students find it worthwhile to share larger apartments or houses rather than rent one-bedroom apartments by themselves.

The Lowdown

For your application to be considered you have to have a Bachelor's degree, and you have to send the following materials: a statement of purpose, a two- or three-page description of a project you would like to make while at UCLA, and three letters of recommendation. GRE scores are not required. The school does not look at portfolios or reels of past work at this stage. Like most schools, UCLA is looking for articulate people with things to say; and though the materials they ask for are scant, they are your only chance to show that you have these qualities.

The school receives about eight hundred applications each year. Of these, the admissions committee chooses fifty or sixty applicants with whom to conduct personal interviews. If you make it to this stage, you will be asked to travel to LA, and bring a reel or portfolio of work with you. Your portfolio need not include films or videos: the school does not expect applicants to have any background in filmmaking. The school is not looking specifically for people who have made films in the past, and a large portion of the applicants who are accepted into the program in any given year are likely to come from law or business, or from other fields that have nothing to do with film. Your portfolio should include creative work that shows you have ideas and an ability to express them. When interviewing applicants, the admissions staff are not only thinking about finding interesting individuals; they are also thinking about putting together an ensemble. With each class they try to assemble a group of people who not only work well, but who will work well together and will learn from one another. Clearly this is something you can't have any control over in your application, but it might help to suppress any antisocial or sociopathic tendencies you might have.

First-year films are shot with CP 16 or Eclair cameras and Nagra recorders, and edited on flatbed editing machines. Second-year films are shot on Arri BLs, and thesis films are shot on Aatons, and on Arri SR-2s and SR-3s. Advanced films and thesis films are edited on Avids, or, less frequently, on flatbeds. Sound work is done in seven mixing studios, some of which still have mag film systems, while others contain more contemporary digital systems. (Many students don't trust the technicians in the mixing studio and have their mixes done at professional sound houses in the area.) The school has a huge stock of lighting and grip equipment, including three film soundstages and three television studios. It even has a remote television truck. UCLA has so much equipment that it takes nineteen people just to keep the equipment room running.

This is not to say that students have free access to the equipment: this is a large program, so the time students get with this equipment is limited. The faculty determines how much time each student needs with the equipment based on the size and complexity of her projects. While the time allotted is usually enough, some students wish there were more flexibility. Some students have found a way around the limitation by telling the faculty they are making documentaries. Because documentaries are by nature unpredictable, the school allows those students who want to make them much freer access to equipment. So some students have told the faculty that they are making documentaries, only to use the freely available equipment to make longer narrative projects. Some have gotten into trouble with the school for doing this.

The school also has a New Media lab where students can use a handful of powerful multimedia computers to experiment with programs like Adobe Photoshop, Adobe Premiere, or Macromedia Director. While the school's hope is that students will use the lab to create interactive projects and experiment with new forms of media, so far students mainly use the studio to supplement the old media. They create promotional materials for their films, or whip up simple special-effects or titles for their films.

Probably UCLA's greatest advantage is its location. Because it is near all the major studios, well-known filmmakers visit UCLA's classes and share their experiences with students regularly. Because it is near Hollywood's equipment-rental houses, film-processing laboratories, and sound-mixing houses, the limitations of UCLA's facilities can easily be surmounted. And there is always that great Southern California weather.

In the first year students work together closely and develop a sense of camaraderie. But because the school makes students compete for awards from the second year on, some of the friendliness falls by the wayside, only to be replaced by politics. Students say that the process by which the awards are distributed is very political: they rarely go to the most talented filmmakers and, instead, tend to go to the most shameless brown-nosers.

The man who is in charge of the graduate program is a controversial figure among the students. Students admire the time and energy he has devoted to the program but complain that he wields too much power. He has a seat on every student's thesis advisory committee and, as such, has complete power to dictate changes that students should make in their films before they can graduate. Students can be especially indignant when, this man, whose two films as a director, *Liberty & Bash* (1990) and *Angel of H.E.A.T.* (1983) are hardly monuments of cinematic art, tells them how to make their films.

UCLA works harder than most schools to promote student works. The school holds a widely publicized public screening of student films every year and has an office devoted to putting student works into film festivals around the world. The promotion seems to work better here than at most schools: some of the fourth-year students we spoke with were already getting paid directing jobs while completing their thesis films. There are a lot of UCLA graduates in the industry, so many networking opportunities are available for graduates.

Some of the best things about the program: Location, location, location. Situated at the edge of Beverly Hills and only a few minutes away from both Twentieth-Century Fox and Sony Pictures,

UCLA is closer to the business, and closer to the money, than any other school. This makes for great educational opportunities during school as working professionals stop by to teach classes, and often makes for great employment opportunities afterward. The equipment is top-notch, and the school gives out a surpisingly large amount of money to students every year. Students come out at the end with quite a few films under their belt, and usually also have some professional credits to their name. Students have a good track record of finding work in the industry soon after graduation.

Some of the worst things about the program: After a good first year, the program begins to lose focus and students start to fall into political battles for grants and awards. The process by which students gain approval for their thesis projects could be more democratic.

University of Miami

School of Communication
P. O. Box 248127
Coral Gables, FL 33124-2030
(305) 284-2265
http://www.miami.edu/com/
   programs/motion.htm

Independent

Equipment
Quality: ☆☆

Equipment
Accessibility: ☆☆☆

Cost: $

Annual Tuition:	**$742 per credit for 21 credits— $15,582**
Enrollment:	**15 per year, 30 total**
Deadline:	**March 1**
Focus:	**Independent**

The Program

While the University of Miami has offered undergraduate courses in film for decades, the M.F.A. program is fairly new. The program is divided into five areas of specialization: directing, cinematography, editing, animation (including computer graphics), and producing. Twenty students are admitted to the program each year out of around a hundred applicants; roughly fifteen of these specialize in directing. Admissions are only made in the fall semester.

Incoming students who do not already have experience with 16-mm film are required to attend the school's intensive summer institute prior to the first year. This lasts the entire summer, beginning in late June and ending in August, just before the fall semester begins. Generally, about half of all incoming students have to go through this summer session, which costs about $6,000. Students may skip the summer institute if they can show they have learned 16-mm filmmaking in similar classes at other schools.

The two-year program consists of a variety of film theory and film production classes that continue through both years. In the first year, students shoot short exercises in cinematography and animation. They also shoot exercises in directing actors on Hi-8 video. Beyond the classes, the program revolves around the making of a single thesis film. Work on the thesis starts at the beginning of the first year, when each production student writes a short screenplay. Directing students are encouraged to work with writing students in the creation of these screenplays. In the second semester the screenplay is completed, and each directing student puts together a package for its production as a film—including crew, shooting script, breakdowns, and budgets—and pitches it to the faculty.

After the faculty approves a student's project, the school gives that student enough 16-mm negative film stock to shoot it at a four-to-one ratio. (For a thirty-minute film the school provides 4,400 feet of raw film: about two hours' worth.) Once the film has been shot, the school pays for its processing. This may sound a bit like USC or AFI, where film and processing for student projects is paid for by the school. But whereas USC and AFI choose only a few student projects to receive these benefits, Miami gives them to *everyone*. And while the school covers much of the cost of students' films, it does not ask to retain any rights to these films. Unlike students at USC or AFI, students at Miami maintain all rights to their work and are free to enter their films in festivals or distribute them as they see fit.

These thesis films are shot late in the spring of the first year, or in the summer after the first year, with post-production taking up all of the second year, and, occasionally, some of a third year. The school pays for some of each student's post-production, providing processing, edge coding, and 8,800 feet of mag film. If the faculty are particularly impressed with a film, they may offer to pay to take that film to answer print. This might happen once or twice a year, or not at all, purely at the faculty's discretion. And again, it is only a benefit for the student, who does not surrender any rights by accepting the school's largesse.

Some students choose to make documentaries instead of narrative films. The school accommodates these students by supplying Beta SP stock and equipment all the way through off-line.

The Price

$640 per credit, with 30 credits required over two years	$19,200
$10,000 a year rent and living expenses for two years	$20,000
Thesis films tend to cost an additional	$ 1,000
$1,000 per year maintenance and insurance on a car for three years	$ 3,000
Total	**$43,200**

Don't forget that if you do not have a lot of film experience you will also have to pay $6,000 to enroll in the summer session.

One-bedroom apartments can be found in decent neighborhoods for $500 a month and less. Sharing a house or large apartment will make life cheaper still. A car is a necessity, both for moving shoot equipment around, and for everyday commuting.

It is also easy to make money in Miami. There are frequent opportunities to work on commercial shoots, and job opportunities often open up within the university.

There are six teaching assistantships available, which are usually split into twelve half-TAships. Only available to second-year students, the half-TAships pay a stipend of $3,750 plus a remission of half of the tuition in exchange for twenty hours a week of work.

One recent graduate told us life was so inexpensive, and jobs were so plentiful, that he did not know of one student who had bombed out of the program for financial reasons. In film school, that is saying a lot.

The Lowdown

Applications must include GRE scores, three letters of recommendation, and two written pieces: a 500-word statement on your favorite film and your response to it, plus a three-to-four-page idea for a film you would like to write or make while at Miami. You are not expected to send in samples of work. The admissions board looks for people who are good students and who can handle ideas. So while they look at the GPAs and GREs, they put more emphasis on the written materials.

Miami's is a two-year program, though it stretches out a bit at either end. At the beginning is the intensive summer session for about half of the incoming students. At the end is post-production, which for most students lasts through at least the fall semester of a third year. Students need not pay tuition to continue to use the equipment for this third year. Those who take longer still are kindly, but firmly, shown the door at the end of their third year.

Each student gets equipment to shoot her thesis film for up to five weeks. This is a surprising amount of time—many low-budget features are shot in less than five weeks. Most film schools cannot let students have the equipment for more than a week or two, so this is a real advantage of the Miami program. And if for some reason a student finds that five weeks is not enough time to finish, she can almost always get equipment for a reshoot.

Not every student makes a film. The school allows students to get their M.F.A.s in specialties like editing or cinematography. While these are slightly less expensive alternatives to directing, students who do this come out of the program with less to show for their time, effort, and money than those who completed a film or feature screenplay. And in a school where film and processing are free, even the expense is a poor excuse. It is much more beneficial to come out of the program with a feature-length screenplay, which might lead to an agent or a sale, than with technical credits on other students' films.

The atmosphere is friendly, and relations between students are supportive. The only divisiveness evident is between the students who want to be independent filmmakers working in the Miami area and those who want to move to Hollywood and make it in the industry. This split is largely between writing students and production students: the screenwriting students tend to move to Los Angeles after graduation, while the production people tend to stay in Miami, working on commercials and the odd feature while they plan how to raise money for their first features.

The faculty readily admit that two years is not the ideal amount of time in which to properly teach filmmaking. Miami now offers a two-year program so it can be inexpensive enough to attract students to a new and unproven program against stiff competition from better-known schools. The faculty are thinking of changing into a three-year program by 1999, by which time they hope to be better known and more in demand. Miami may very well be. This is a well-organized and well-equipped program. The student body is small enough so that every student gets personal attention; the equipment is functional and accessible; and the faculty, while limited, is solid and seems dedicated to building this into a world-class program. And the school seems to have money to burn. It is hard to believe they have so much equipment for so few students. It is even harder to believe that on top of providing all this equipment, they are also willing to give away film, processing, mag stock, edge coding—and for a few students even negative cutting and answer printing—without expecting any rights or royalties in return.

Miami's production equipment is not the newest, but it is functional, there's a lot of it, and it is readily accessible to students. The primary cameras are three Arriflex 16-BLs, each of which has a sound kit, tripod, and fluid head dedicated to it. Each camera comes with an Angenieux zoom lens, but prime lenses are available in a range of focal lengths. There are also two Eclair NPRs and some Bolex spring-wound cameras which are mostly used for cinematography exercises. The sound equipment is good: three Nagra 4.2 recorders and seven Sony DAT recorders are available, as are a wide variety of microphones, including some radio mikes. The university has one Avid, which the film school gets for half of every week (the Broadcast Department gets it during the other half). There is a separate Beta SP logging station so students can log their footage offline before they get onto the Avid. At this writing, of twelve students working on their theses, ten are using the Avid while two are using the flatbeds (the school has ten flatbeds, two of which are for graduate use only). While the school is pondering buying a Pro Tools system, at the moment sound mixing is still done on mag film in two eight-track mixing rooms.

The school has a good variety of lighting equipment, mostly in kits, though it also has four HMI lights, some single fresnel lights, some soft lights, and ample grip equipment. It has a Western dolly with pneumatics and a supply of curved and straight track. There is a soundstage available with a lighting grid and an ample supply of lights.

There are times in the school year when not everyone can get onto an editing machine who needs to, when both the undergraduates and the graduates have deadlines to meet. But there are other times—especially during the summer and fall—when every graduate production student can have her own dedicated flatbed to edit her thesis film.

Students suggest that you will get the most out of the program if you know what you want to do going in. Decide early what your goals are, both in school and in life afterward, and aim straight in that direction. The faculty will take you more seriously if they see you are focused and will be more likely to think of you when opportunities (jobs, internships, TAships, etc.) come up. Some of the professors are energetic, and really love what they do. If they see the same sort of energy, drive, and enthusiasm in you, they will be more inclined to help you out. Because classes are so small, students have a real opportunity to befriend professors. Professors often hold classes at their homes, or in other sites less formal and more pleasant than a classroom. Use that equipment! Miami has as much equipment as many programs four times the size—five good-quality 16-mm sync cameras for a total of twenty students. And the guys in the equipment room seem happy enough to let students use it. The school hands out film stock for the various exercises first and second year. One student suggests that if you plan well you can use some of this stock to make short films instead of little exercises, and learn a lot more.

In its literature, the school says of itself, "It is situated in the third-largest and fastest-growing film-producing area in the nation." It is true there is a lot of filmmaking activity in Miami and environs these days, and you can take advantage of this during your stay. While a number of features are now shot in Orlando, most of the production in Miami is commercials. You can get great experience by working for one of the local commercial houses. The school will often give credit for internships on these shoots, which can be a pleasant consolation for the minimal pay.

Paul Lazarus, the head of the program, appears to be the driving force behind the film school. Before coming to U. of Miami he was an agent, and a producer in Hollywood with major studio releases like *Westworld* (1973) and *Capricorn One* (1978) to his name. He came to the school to head the undergraduate program in 1987, and two years later founded the M.F.A. program. On top of running the program, he also teaches writing and producing. He has brought a great deal of energy and enthusiasm to the school, and the students seem to appreciate him for it. Once a year he chooses ten students (five graduate and five undergraduate) and takes them to Hollywood for a week to show them around. While it's been more than a decade since he lived in L.A., he still has some pretty good contacts (Quick: who directed *Westworld*?) and is happy to introduce his students to them. Students have to foot the bill for this trip.

Some of the best things about the program: Free film stock! Free processing! Free edge coding! Free use of an Avid and a Pro Tools! And all in a mere two years! Another good thing about the program is Florida itself, which has great locations—from tropical islands in the Caribbean to vibrant urban locations in the Cuban part of town; from stunning underwater spots in the Keys to scenes of Old South urbanity up around Pensacola. All this and great weather for shooting all year round. Just watch out for those hurricanes! The incessant commercial and occasional feature film shoots can pay well, and working on one for one day will teach you more about the process of shooting a film than will a solid year in a classroom. There is an active nightlife centered on the clubs in Miami Beach. And life lessons aplenty await students each spring in Fort Lauderdale. So you catch a social disease? Hey! You're a filmmaker! Grist for the mill!

Some of the worst things about the program: Students complain that some teachers seem to be coasting along on their tenure, doing only what needs doing, and showing little if any enthusiasm. Says one student, "They should be given coffee mugs that say 'I'm dead wood and there's nothing you can do about it.'"

While there is no formal alumni organization, there is an informal network—a tight community of graduates, both in Miami and Hollywood, who help one another out as best they can.

University of New Orleans

Department of Drama and
   Communications
University of New Orleans
Lakefront
New Orleans, LA 70148
(504) 280-6317

Independent

Equipment
Quality: ☆☆

Equipment
Accessibility: ☆☆☆

Cost: $$

Annual Tuition:	**Resident:** **$2,362** **Nonresident:** **$5,154**
Enrollment:	**6 per year,** **about 20 total**
Deadline:	**March 15**
Focus:	**Independent**

The Program

The University of New Orleans's graduate film program is a three-year program. In most cases it takes students two and a half years to complete the required classes, plus an additional semester to complete their thesis films. It is an inexpensive program, especially if you are a resident of Louisiana, but has state-of-the-art post-production equipment that puts most other film schools in the country to shame.

Until a year or two ago, New Orleans had only very rudimentary filmmaking equipment. Students shot films on aging, noisy cameras and edited on aging, unpredictable editing machines. Surprisingly, this has turned out to be a real benefit: the program recently received a large grant to upgrade its film facilities and, unencumbered by earlier investments in outdated equipment, has quickly acquired a large amount of the latest post-production equipment. Suddenly bristling with digital editing systems and digital audio workstations, New Orleans is now as well suited to introduce students to the new technologies of filmmaking as any school in the world.

The Universty of New Orleans's film course load takes two and a half years to complete. At the beginning of the first year students take the first of a three-semester basic production course. The three parts of this course teach the basics of filmmaking, as students start out making small exercise projects and building theoretical budgets in the first semester, leading up to the whole class cooperatively making a single short film in the second semester. The second semester of the course is devoted to the making of the Spring Film—a film usually written and directed by a faculty member. Students learn about the process of filmmaking by working as crew on this film. While students are free to make their own short films instead of crewing on the Spring Film, most opt to work on the Spring Film. It is easier, and much less expensive, than writing and directing a film. The Spring Film is different every year: one year it might be written and directed by students, the next year a faculty member might be at the helm. One year it might be twenty minutes long, the next it might be feature length.

In the first semester of the second year students take the final part of the three-semester production course. In this semester students write and direct short projects, or begin writing and preparing for their thesis films. At the end of this course, midway through second year, students go through comprehensive examinations. The comp exams are a big deal—a five-hour written examination, followed by an hour of oral defense of the examination in front of a three-person board. It is only after students have passed the comp exams that they are considered candidates for the M.F.A. degree. Once students are considered candidates for the degree, they can begin shooting their thesis films. While the school's cameras are older, clunkier models than some, there are enough of them that the school is pretty flexible about how much time students get with them.

Once their thesis films are completed, students have a few more things to do before they can graduate. Each must organize a public screening of her thesis, and must turn in a written thesis. The written thesis is a comprehensive history and analysis of the thesis film, including research, pre-production notes, shooting scripts, and schedules—the works. And it also has to contain an essay that analyzes and justifies the film. This written thesis is key to the program. While no one fails based on her thesis film, regardless of its quality, students have failed based on this written thesis: the board that reviews it can (and has) postponed students' graduation when their production books were not up to the school's standards.

Now, you probably know by now what we think of internships (if not, go look up *Internship* in the glossary), but we will still mention the internship program at UNO. In this program students are placed in film and television productions all around the country, and they receive three course credits for the work. These internships usually do not pay enough to live on, but by giving course credits for them UNO makes them somewhat more attractive.

The Price

NONRESIDENT

$2,577 per semester for five semesters	$12,885
$10,000 a year rent and living expenses for 3 years	$30,000
First- and second-year practice films tend to cost about	$ 2,500
Thesis films tend to cost about	$ 6,000
Total	**$51,385**

It is relatively easy to become a resident of Louisiana. Whereas some states require students to have lived in-state for a set amount of time before they can be considered residents, Louisiana's requirements are more bureaucratic—a Louisiana driver's license, paying resident state income taxes, things like that. This is not as much of an issue for students in a two-and-a-half-year program as it is for students in a four-year program, and not that many students in the graduate film program bother. But, just so you know, if you are willing to jump through the hoops, you can save yourself about $7,000 dollars that way.

Living is inexpensive in New Orleans. One-bedroom apartments can be found off campus for $400 a month and less. Some students choose to live twenty minutes away in the French Quarter. It is a bit of a distance from school, but it's a picturesque part of town, with good nightlife, and rents are similar to those near the school.

Jobs are plentiful in New Orleans, though many of those jobs are in the tourism industry. This can be a fun, flexible way to make money if you don't mind that kind of work, and if you can survive on that kind of pay. A number of digital post-production houses have opened up in the New Orleans area. Since UNO students learn how to edit on digital systems, many have found their way into jobs at these houses both during school and afterward.

Seven graduate assistantships are available to students in the graduate program—three in film, three in video, and one in new media. Graduate assistantships pay about $6,500 per year. Though these assistantships do not provide tuition remission, TAs who are not residents of Louisiana only have to pay resident tuition. Once a student becomes a graduate assistant, she remains one for her entire stay at UNO. This is nice for those who become GAs, for whom it is a bit like getting tenure, but it is unfortunate for those waiting to get one: they will not get a chance to become a GA until one of the current GAs either graduates or dies. There is a single full-tuition fellowship, which can go to a film student or to a writing student.

The Lowdown

At present, out of about fifty applicants each year the school accepts only five or six, and the number of applicants grows every year. Because of the ever-increasing numbers of applicants, the school now only accepts applicants with bachelor's degrees in theater, film, or TV, and who have strong, proven abilities in one or more of these fields. Others are discouraged from applying, though on occasion an applicant with little film experience but impressive skills or interests elsewhere will be admitted. The school also strongly discourages people from applying to the M.A. program in the hope of then moving into the M.F.A. program. It doesn't happen, so don't bother trying.

The school has an odd class requirement—forty-five units, which translates to five semesters of nine units each. Almost all students finish their classes in two and a half years and then take one additional semester to finish their thesis projects. No one has finished the program in less than three years, and few find it necessary to stay for more. Even the GAs usually finish in three years.

UNO has an impressive collection of state-of-the-art post-production equipment that complements a relatively small amount of film production equipment that is functional but aging. For editing, the school owns four brand-new broadcast-quality nonlinear editing systems; a Media 100 workstation; and three Matrox workstations. The school has plans to add an Avid to these by the time you read this and also plans to set up a media center with two dozen nonlinear systems that work at less than broadcast quality. Students may cut film if they prefer, using one of two six-plate flatbed editing machines; these machines are usually available since most students have moved over to the digital systems. For sound work the school owns a Spectral digital audio workstation.

The best cameras, which are reserved for graduate students and faculty, are four Cinema Products CP 16Rs. The CP 16R is certainly a reliable workhorse, but when it was built it was intended for use by television news programs, not by artists for creative expression, and it can be a frustrating camera for narrative filmmaking. It has a crystal sync motor, but it is noisier than most modern cameras, and it does not have a registration pin. (The Spectral audio workstation the school recently purchased can intelligently remove camera noise from a sound track, so the noisy cameras are less of an irritant than they once were.) There are only Angenieux zoom lenses to work with these cameras—the school has no prime lenses. The school owns a few Bolex cameras, some spring wound, some with motors. There are tripods with fluid heads and a small rubber-wheeled dolly. The school has a good assortment of sound equipment, including Nagras, Walkman Pros, DAT recorders, and a collection of good-quality microphones. The school does not own an animation stand or an optical printer.

Few students take their films to answer print anymore. They have found that the effects available on the new digital editing systems are much more impressive than what is possible on film. Also, a finished broadcast-quality tape costs only a few bucks, compared with a cost of thousands of dollars to have an answer print made, so the Matroxes have proved to be both much more powerful and much less expensive. The school is just as happy if a thesis is a good-looking tape as if it is an answer print.

Some of the best things about the program: It is a very inexpensive school. You can take all the money you would have spent on USC or NYU and make films with it. The atmosphere is noncompetitive. The faculty is open to students working in any kind of filmmaking and are as supportive of experimental or documentary films as they are of narratives. The film department is in the same building with the theater department, the music department, and the Video/TV department, so networking is easy if you need to find talented people to work on various aspects of your film. New Orleans is a wonderful town—small, quaint, but with great nightlife.

Some of the worst things about the program: There are no film-processing labs or post-production facilities on or near campus; students who want to work in film have to do their lab work via Federal Express and long-distance telephone. While the post-production equipment is great, much of the production equipment is functional at best. And the school does not have enough faculty to fully support all the new equipment. As of this writing students are encouraged to go ahead and mess around with the equipment and, if they find any especially useful tricks or features, to show the professors.

When you graduate, the school will show your work in its annual Media Showcase, a two-night festival of student films, videos, and animations. If you know where you are going to live after school the faculty can put you in contact with any alumni who might already be there, but there is no official organization for film school alumni.

University of Southern California

School of Cinema-Television
Los Angeles, CA 90089-0911
Department: (213) 740-3317
Admissions: (213) 740-2911
http://www-cntv.usc.edu

Annual Tuition:	**Approximately $12,600 (varies by program)**
Enrollment:	**100; 300 total**
Deadline:	**Fall: December 10 Spring: September 1**
Focus:	**Industry**

Equipment Quality: ☆☆☆

Equipment Accessibility: ☆☆☆

Cost: **$$$**

The Program

USC is the granddaddy of film schools: it offered its first screen-writing class in 1929 and its first cinematography class in 1932. It is now the largest film school in the country. Within the Cinema-Television Department there are five specialized graduate programs. Although we will concentrate on the film production division, some of the others are worth mentioning.

The Peter Stark Producing Program

This is a two-year program that focuses on the business of film-making. Twenty-five students are admitted each year out of around two hundred applicants. Students produce a number of short 16-mm films while in the program, which are paid for by the school. Some students write screenplays they want to produce, while others produce screenplays written by screenwriting division students. However, the program is not about the creative process. Students learn about entertainment law, union rules, contract negotiations, and other managerial topics.

Students work in internships during the summer between first and second years. Second-year students compete for one or two scholarships and a handful of teaching assistantships.

Stark program students earn their degrees by screening their thesis films for faculty and by presenting supporting materials such as shooting scripts, schedules, budgets, and complete marketing and distribution plans.

Screenwriting

Thirty-two students enter this intensive two-year dramatic writing program each year. Students learn not only the technique of writing for the screen, but also how to survive as screenwriters in Hollywood. Classes cover business and legal aspects of the screen trade and give students direct experience working with actors and film equipment. Electives cover specific genres such as comedy or episodic television. Thesis projects are feature-length screenplays.

Film, Video and Computer Animation

This is a relatively new two-year program which covers both classical and computer animation. Students work on large-scale animation projects as a group, and each creates a single animated thesis film. While there are currently thirty students enrolled in this program, the school plans to expand it to sixty in the next two years.

Film Production

One hundred students are admitted to the film production program every year, fifty each semester. First-year students start fall semester with a rigid course schedule. All first-year students take the same intensive production course and academic courses in screenwriting and the history of silent film. In Production I each student makes five short super-8 films. While the school provides film, students must provide their own super-8 cameras to satisfy the course's requirements. This course is rather archaic—there was a time when many people owned super-8 cameras and students could borrow the necessary equipment from friends or family. But super-8 cameras are rare today, and many students have to spend hundreds of dollars to buy good-quality super-8 equipment.

In the second semester of first year, students take Production II, History of International Cinema, and Intermediate Screenwriting. In the production class students pair up to make two short 16-mm sound films. On the first film one team member directs and records sound while the other shoots and edits. On the second film they swap positions. The school provides cameras this time as well as film.

The second year offers students more flexibility. There are fewer required classes, so students are free to choose electives that interest them. Classes that students may take include a wide variety of offerings in writing, directing, editing and cinematography. A number of courses in new media and nonlinear editing have been added in recent years.

Second-year students take Production III, more commonly known as course 546. In 546 students team up into crews and make larger-scale narrative films or documentaries. The school pays for the production of these films, including post-production costs and lab fees to take it through to answer print. Students taking 546 for the first time are only allowed to work as crew. They may not write or direct any of the films made in the class.

In order to direct a 546, students must have taken it once already, and must also have taken course 531, in which they prepare scripts or proposals for films they want to make at the school's expense. At the beginning of each semester students pitch their projects to a faculty committee in the hope of being picked to direct a 546. Each student has fifteen minutes to explain why her project will be the greatest film since *Gone With the Wind*. While some students pitch alone, others assemble teams and do the pitch as if it were a comedy act. Some screen video trailers or advertisements for their projects. Each semester the committee chooses four narrative and three documentary projects. The seven students whose projects are chosen become the directors. All of the other students in 546, including all second-year students and a number of third- and fourth-year students, must work as crew on these films. While the school pays for all of the film and processing, it does not pay for production expenses such as food, transportation, costumes or sets. All students contribute from $500 to $1,000 of their own money to the films they work on. Local etiquette dictates that directors match the total amount donated by the rest of the crew.

Projects made in 546 are shot, edited, mixed and completed in one semester. Because students are taking other classes full-time, shoots usually happen on the weekends.

In the third year students continue fulfilling their forty-six-unit requirements with electives and with repeated attempts at directing a 546. Those who have not made a 546 by the middle of their third year have to decide on a final advanced project. Some students write feature-length screenplays, but most make films in course 581.

Students work in pairs in this class to make ten-minute 16-mm films. Once students have presented the faculty with acceptable budgets and plans, the school loans them production equipment, but does not give them film or funding, to make these films. Students have two weeks in which to shoot these fairly ambitious films, which can cost anywhere from $5,000 to $20,000.

Students who don't want to take 581 can make a film in course 586, in which students work together in groups of five to create a single film. Each student is given a "chit," worth about $1,200, by the school. Students combine their chits and add money of their own to make these ambitious twenty-minute films. The school pays for film and processing. The student who directs the project usually contributes $10,000 to $15,000.

The final option for students who want to make a film is course 582. While students receive class credit for making a film in this course, they receive nothing else: no equipment, no insurance, no access to facilities—nothing. Films can be any length or format, but the filmmaker has to provide money, equipment, cast and crew. A faculty mentor oversees the project.

While courses 546, 581 and 586 are the most talked about, there are other opportunities for students to direct films. The Starkies always need directors for the projects they produce, and often post advertisements for directing students. Sometimes students will be hired to direct industrial films or commercials while still in school, and corporations that want to build relationships with USC will sometimes give opportunities to the students. One Japanese corporation provided high-definition video cameras and $200,000 for students to make thirty-minute narrative films of their choosing.

The Price

$679 per credit for 52 credits	$35,308
$12,000 per year rent and living expenses for three years	$36,000
$2,000 per year maintenance and insurance on a car for three years	$ 6,000
Average film costs for directors	$20,000
Total	**$97,308**

It is not uncommon for students to stay well past three years. Those who do matriculate by registering for two credits per semester. The financial-aid department is made aware of the additional expenses incurred by film students, making them eligible for more aid. Every semester there is a posted list of approximately thirty available teaching assistant and production assistant openings. These positions are open to second-year students. TAs receive eight to twelve credits of tuition remission and a monthly stipend. PAs receive an hourly wage ($8) and two to six tuition credits. Both positions perform ten to twenty hours of work per week. Assistants are selected from the applicant pool by the individual teachers. There are also quite a few industry-provided scholarships ranging anywhere from $100 to $10,000. Students apply for these on an individual basis, and the school selects recipients. Most students work part-time. Luckily, there is an abundance of temp employment opportunities, especially in production.

USC is a big school in a bad neighborhood. You can live near the school where rents are cheap and life is cheaper, or you can pay more money to live in a better part of town and commute. If you live near USC you can find a big apartment in a building that was built in the twenties with hardwood floors and moldings for very little rent. But get used to having all or part of your car stolen regularly. More students commute than don't.

First Look is the highly publicized USC screening held in spring, summer, and fall. For three nights, films produced in advanced film classes are shown first on campus and then the following week at the Director's Guild of America (DGA). The DGA screening is well attended by the industry.

The Lowdown

Five hundred applicants apply to USC each fall. There are fewer for the spring, so students stand a better chance of admittance at that time of year. In fact, if one is denied fall admittance, one should definitely reapply for spring. Along with GRE results and standard letters of recommendation, only written material is accepted for application. Creative portfolios should not be sent unless requested. They will not even be considered at this point so don't waste the postage. Writing samples must demonstrate creative expression. These consist of a one-page short film outline and a two-page prose piece, the topic of which is determined by the department. Previous film experience, especially an undergrad film degree, is not necessary.

The USC faculty is largely composed of former or currently working professionals. This does not mean the quality of all faculty is consistent. Unfortunately, there are still a great many "seasoned" professionals who have been around the school forever. While they had experience at one time and are more accessible than their more active counterparts, they could use a dose of the nineties. They are a bit sexist and set in their ways. On the other hand, the working types are often pulled in many different directions by their careers. It's hard to get the best of both worlds, but the school is trying to achieve some sort of balance. Celebrity lecturers are a real perk. Students are regularly treated to visits by Hollywood's filmmaking elite.

The equipment is good. There are fifty-two Arriflex Ss, sixteen Arriflex SRs, and a handful of S-VHS video cameras. The video cameras are usually used for documentaries. The packages include Arriflex cameras, Mole Richardson lights, Sennheiser microphones, and Nagra 3 or 4.2 recorders. The lighting is pretty skimpy for the beginning filmmaking classes, but the quality and quantity improve in the more advance courses. There is a fairly decent 16-mm black-and-white lab with a 16-mm optical printer.

All advanced films are posted on Avid or Lightworks and Pro Tools. The school owns ten Avids and four Pro Tools. Since it takes a large hard-drive to hold digitized information, most students provide their own hard-drive for the Avid. Earlier projects are edited on twelve Kem flatbeds or thirty-five Moviolas. The latter are old and temperamental but won't eat too much film if approached carefully. There is one 35-mm flatbed, S-VHS and CAVB on-line editing systems, and a digital Betacam suite. Each production class is allotted a certain number of editing hours per week. Time on these machines is reserved one week in advance. There's a real editing crunch at the semester's end.

The facilities are top-notch. Most are gifts from successful graduates. There are two soundstages and scoring stages and two great THX screening theaters. There are state-of-the-art DAT dubbing and mixing studios. D-Vision work station is expected by the year's end. Within the next few years a new post-production facility and three TV stages are projected to open.

Because of the location and industry exposure, many students are able to get free equipment at the numerous rental houses, studios, and post facilities in the area. Several students have talked their way into free 35-mm camera packages for their 546 projects.

There have been some real misconceptions about USC. The biggest is that the school pays for all student films. The school pays for some films, but students still wind up extending themselves financially to augment the school budgets. While 546 is still the most coveted directing slot, there are alternative classes in which students can direct films. And although narrative is king, documentary and even some experimental filmmaking are possible here. Another popular belief, one which is not a misconception, is that USC students do not own the films they make. The school claims ownership of all student films made with its equipment. Students may not enter their films in festivals or sell their films to distributors without USC's consent. Ant profits student films see belong to the school.

Some of the best things about the program: The proximity to the industry and the unique opportunities that come with it. The networking possibilities are endless for motivated students. The school hands out more than $2,000,000 each year. The scope of classes offered is excellent. USC is one of the few schools that seriously addresses television. The program is extremely flexible after the first year. The equipment is great.

Some of the worst things about the program: Those not chosen as TAs or PAs will incur some hefty debt. Many things at USC operate on political networking. Schmoozing is vital for both 546 selection and TA assignments. Competition for 546 is tough, and there is always bitterness at the end. The program's flexibility can be overwhelming. There are so many classes to chose from, it's easy for a student to get confused. Women still tend to be overlooked in a school that is trying to get past the "boys' club" mentality. Sexism is still evident.

Make the best of USC by availing yourself of the numerous resources. From internships to extracurricular projects to outside lecturers, this school is the hub of Hollywood. Students must be self-promoters in order not to get lost in the shuffle. Graduates will leave with a solid directing credit and will have the chance to parlay that credit into a real stepping-stone to their dreams.

USC has a great track record. The school claims that seventy-five percent of alumni are working in the film industry. Marcia Lucas, respected editor and former wife of Geroge Lucas, set up a Student Industry Relations office to promote student careers and build relationships with the industry. First Look is a big deal with a ton of PR behind it. USC films are seen by the right people.

University of Texas at Austin

Department of Radio-
  Television-Film
MCA 6.118
Austin, TX 78712-1091
(512) 471-3532
http://www.utexas.edu/coc/rtf/

Independent

Equipment
Quality: ☆☆☆

Equipment
Accessibility: ☆☆

Cost: **$$**

Annual Tuition:	**Resident: $2,460**
	Nonresident: $6,740
Enrollment:	**12 per year, about 30 total**
Deadline:	**December 1**
Focus:	**Independent/ Documentary**

The Program

The University of Texas at Austin's M.F.A. film program is a three-year program in which students learn through constant hands-on experience with film and video equipment. It is a small program in a large university, which provides the best of both worlds—the intimacy of a small school and the enormous resources and social life of a large one. While most student films are independent-style narratives, the program provides good training in, and equipment for, documentary filmmaking. The university tries to ensure that graduate students get a well-rounded education by requiring them to take courses outside of the film department. Students are not only required to take a number of electives; they are actually required to declare a minor in another field of study.

The first year revolves around two classes; one teaches the technology and aesthetics of film production while the other puts students in a studio where they get hands-on experience with the equipment. In this studio course students coalesce into teams and together make a number of group exercises. These exercises are shot on video in the first semester and on film in the second. For these exercise projects students submit short screenplays and then as a group choose a few to produce. In the first semester these exercises are shot on video; in the second they are shot on film. Students get an especially broad introduction to editing in first year: they edit projects on flatbed editing machines, then on linear video editing systems, then on nonlinear editing workstations. In the second semester the studio course continues, and students also take a class in screenwriting and the first of their electives.

Because the first year exercise films are either technical exercises or group projects, the first film that students get to both write and direct is the second year film or, in the local terminology, the prethesis. Pretheses are usually between ten and fifteen minutes long, and are as often made on video as on film. About a third of students in any given year make documentaries. At the beginning of second year, students choose a three-member faculty committee to oversee their prethesis projects. Once a student has chosen a committee, the committee reviews and ultimately approves her script. Students shoot their pretheses in the winter and early spring, and edit through the spring. Students continue to take a full schedule of classes while they make these films, including advanced courses in nonlinear editing and digital sound design, and they also continue to fill some of their elective requirements. The main production course and other required courses are scheduled to support students as they make their pretheses; the first semester courses center on writing and preproduction, while the second semester courses center on production, editing and sound design.

At the end of second year, each student shows a fine cut of her prethesis to her committee and also turns in a report about the project. This report includes the shooting script, budget information, and a discussion of the making of the project. Few students have finished their pretheses by this time. The school generally doesn't allow students to use the equipment during the summer, so most have to either rent editing equipment elsewhere or take the summer off and then resume editing and mixing when school starts again in the fall.

The school encourages students to use the summer, when they cannot use the equipment, to write their thesis projects, and to arrive in the fall with a script in hand. Once students have finished their prethesis films, they begin preproduction on their thesis films. Thesis films are ambitious projects that cannot run more than thirty minutes (though the school does not strictly enforce this time limitation). As in the second year, about a third of these films are likely to be documentaries, and many students choose to work in video rather than film. As in previous years, students attend a production class that revolves around the making of their thesis films, but they are otherwise free to complete their elective requirements.

Few students finish their films before the end of their third year. Most continue working on their films at least through the middle of their fourth year. While students usually finish all of their required coursework in three years there is one final course that students do not take until they are nearly finished with their thesis projects. This course guides them through writing their thesis reports, and prepares them to present those reports, along with their theses, to their faculty committees. The thesis report is usually about a hundred pages long. The faculty encourage students to discuss in these reports not only their films, but also how the program helped or hindered them. These reports are kept by the department, and are made available to younger students so they might learn some of the older students' lessons.

The Price

Nonresident tuition of $6,740 per year for three years	$20,220
Fees of about $600 per year for three years	$ 1,800
$10,000 a year rent and living expenses for three years	$30,000
First-year films cost around	$ 1,000
Prethesis films cost around	$ 5,000
Thesis films cost around	$15,000
Total	**$73,020**

It is not easy to become a resident of Texas if you are not one already. You have to live in the state for a year without taking any classes before you can gain resident status, so if you are not a resident you should not expect to be able to become one. If you do have resident status you can save nearly $13,000 off the above figure.

Either way, UT is a good value. The tuition is incredibly low even for nonresidents. And Austin is a fairly inexpensive town—rents for one-bedroom apartments near school run between $400 and $500 a month. It is a good idea to have a car, but it is not necessary. Most of what Austin has to offer is accessible by foot or public transportation, so you will mostly need a car for transporting cast, crew, and equipment during your film shoots. It is possible to survive by borrowing or renting a car on the occasions when you need one. On the other hand, if you do own a car you will be inordinately popular with your classmates who do not, especially around production time.

The graduate film department offers one all-expenses-paid fellowship per year. Because the school has a large undergraduate film department, it offers a lot of teaching assistantships to graduate students. The number changes from year to year depending on the amount of funds available: as of this writing, eleven of the roughly thirty graduate production students have TAships. There are two kinds of TAships: ten-hour assistantships, which require ten hours of work per week, and twenty-hour assistantships. Ten-hour assistantships pay a stipend of $3,600 per year; twenty-hour assistantships pay $7,200 per year. Both also allow out-of-state students to pay in-state tuition. There are a few more assistantships available to graduate production students in other departments. The Business School, for instance, has a communications unit with a lot of video equipment that requires the services of several technicians. To fill this need, the Business School gives out TAships to a few film students every year in exchange for their services as technicians. As of this writing, everyone who applied for a TAship received one, though this is unlikely to be the case in the future. The university offers a number of fellowships, which graduate production students have had a lot of luck winning in the past. Otherwise, the school offers no financial help with films.

There is a lot of entertainment in Austin; some of it is free, and most of it is very inexpensive. This is a town where music bars often have no cover charge, and where movie houses offer three-dollar tickets one night a week. Most nights there is entertainment on campus for free or nearly so.

The Lowdown

The school receives about one hundred and twenty applications a year. Of these, twelve new students are admitted. New students are only admitted in the fall.

For your application to be considered you have to have an undergraduate degree, with a GPA of no less than 3.0, and very good GRE scores. You have to send in two applications; one to the graduate school and one to the RTF program. You have to send to Graduate Admissions an application, transcripts and official GRE reports. To the RTF department, you have to send copies of all of the above, plus three letters of recommendation, a statement of purpose, a résumé, and samples of work. Officially, the sample of work should be a writing sample, but the admissions board will look at paintings, photographs, and even films and videos. The admissions board looks for applicants with a creative bent, preferably in writing, and not necessarily with experience in film. A sample of good writing counts for much more than anything else, including film or video work. The admissions board looks for applicants with broad interests. The program is designed to make sure that students study fields other than film; thus they look for people who will benefit from this breadth.

This is officially a three-year program, though many students have to stay beyond the third year to finish their thesis films. This is discouraged, but grudgingly tolerated by the school. It has been suggested that it might be possible to take the sixty hours of classes, make the two required films and write the final report in less than three years, but nobody has done it yet.

Students may work in either film or video—the school has ample equipment for both media. The equipment is of good quality, and there is a lot of it, though good-quality film cameras are in short supply. There is only one good film camera, an Arri SR-2, on which every prethesis and thesis film is shot. This is quite a good camera, mind you, which comes with extras like a video tap and a follow focus kit. There are other cameras of lesser quality—Arri BLs, a few Eclair NPRs, and some Arri Ss—which are mostly used for first-year exercises but can be used for pickups and reshoots if necessary. Students have to schedule time with the better cameras well in advance, first getting the approval of the faculty, and then the agreement of the equipment room. The time students get with the equipment is not set as it is at many schools: the faculty decide how much time each student needs with the equipment based on the complexity of the project she is making. The school has good video production equipment, including Ikegami cameras and an assortment of 3/4" and S-VHS recording gear. The school has three film soundstages, three television studios, and twenty-four editing stations.

The sound equipment is especially good. The school has a good complement of microphones, and a good collection of Nagra tape recorders. There are Nagra 3s, Nagra 4.2s, and a Nagra 4S—a stereo Nagra with SMPTE time coding.

UT is doing a good job of keeping up with new technology in film and video, especially in postproduction. The school has Steenbeck flatbed editing machines, off-line video editing workstations, and Avid digital editing workstations. Students are free to choose among editing on film, video, or computer. The Avids are reserved almost exclusively for graduate use, but even with that restriction they are still completely booked twenty-four hours a day for most of the year. The school recently threw out all of its mag film mixing equipment and replaced it with three Pro Tools digital–sound editing systems. All sound tracks are now edited and mixed digitally at the Pro Tools stations. The school has two animation stands—an old one that the school has had for years and a new one with nifty features like an auto-focus lens. There are also a number of title stands, so students don't need to tie up a full animation stand just to shoot their titles.

With such a large undergraduate department and three classes of graduate students, UT has films in production almost all the time. Students say that the way to get the most out of the program is to work on as many of these films as possible—it is the best way to learn how to make films, and it will give you a good preview of how your own prethesis and thesis shoots will run. Students have been heard to complain about the school's tendency to hire teachers for abilities other than teaching. Teachers are hired because of professional experience rather than professorial experience, and as a result the classes are not where they do their best work, or where students learn the most. Where the professors shine is in one-on-one communication—sitting in cafés discussing scripts, or sitting at editing stations discussing cuts.

The closest film processing lab is Allied in Dallas. Allied is expensive, and has a history of slow and careless service for student filmmakers. The faculty has put some effort into negotiating better service and prices for Austin students, but it's not clear whether this has had much effect. Some students grit their teeth and use Allied, others endure high shipping costs and long waits to use better labs in New York, Seattle or Los Angeles. Neither is a really satisfactory alternative, and many students never bother to take their films to answer print. As a result relatively few UT films make it into film festivals or competitions.

Partly in response to this, the school is now making an aggressive effort to market its students in Hollywood. Every spring the faculty choose about two-hours worth of student work and fly it out to Los Angeles, where they screen it for the industry. This is a new project—it's hard to say whether it has had an effect yet. But in general, thanks to the school's dedication to training students in new technologies, Austin students are well prepared to move into the job market.

Some of the best things about the program: The state-of-the-art editing and sound facilities. While this kind of equipment has largely supplanted the old magnetic film editing and mixing equipment in the Industry, few schools have the resources, or the know-how, to buy and use it. UT students are fortunate to have this equipment at their disposal, and have an advantage finding jobs after graduation. That the school is now actively promoting its students can only make matters better. The large undergraduate population ensures a lot of TAships for graduate students, provides many opportunities to gain experience working on undergrad films, and also makes sure there is a large pool of undergraduate technicians available to work on graduate students' films. Also great is the town of Austin, which with its good weather, picturesque locations and a teeming music scene is a great place to be a student.

Some of the worst things about the program: UT has offered a master's degree in film for two decades, but it was only a few years ago that it began offering an M.F.A. degree. The result is an M.F.A. program that has an established reputation for quality, yet is still in an early, formative stage of development. Every fall, students return to find different faculty and new policies. While these changes often achieve their intended goals of improving the program, students complain of being disoriented by the program's instability, and worry that their favorite professors might not be around a year or two down the road when they will need help with their thesis films. The school tells students that the main emphasis of the program is writing, but some students feel that this is not borne out in the faculty. If anything, writing seems to be one of the weaker aspects of the program. While the film production equipment is of good quality, because it is shared with the undergraduates it is spread pretty thin, especially the few good cameras. Students have to plan carefully around when they can have access to equipment, so there isn't the sense of freedom—that students can get a camera and make a film almost anytime they want to—that some schools have. While students work on a lot of exercises and group projects, most write and direct only two films.

University of Utah

Film Studies Program
203 Performing Arts Building
University of Utah
Salt Lake City, UT 84112
Application information:
    (801) 581-6448
Brian Patrick, director:
    (801) 581-6900
http://www.film.utah.edu/

Equipment
Quality: ☆☆

Equipment
Accessibility: ☆☆

Cost: **$$**

Annual Tuition:	**Resident: $2,298**
	Nonresident: $7,068
Enrollment:	**About 4 per year, about 15 total**
Deadline:	**February 15**
Focus:	**Independent/ Documentary**

The Program

The University of Utah's film program is a small three-year M.F.A. program. Out of about thirty-five applicants each year the school accepts between two and five new students. The program is geared toward documentary filmmaking, though it also provides all the necessary training and equipment for experimental and narrative filmmaking.

As of this writing, the film program is not an independent department; it is a program that resides within both the theater department and the art department. As such, when you apply you will do so either through the art department or the theater department. It is better to apply through the theater department (we'll explain why in the Lowdown section).

The University of Utah is on the quarterly system. While students are expected to have some film-related experience when they arrive, the first year begins with an introductory filmmaking course in order to level the playing field. This course makes sure everyone knows the basics of filmmaking and requires them to make several short projects on film and video. Students are also required to start taking courses in film history and criticism right from the start. In the second semester students move on to an intensive directing course. This is basically a dress rehearsal for filmmaking: students write scenes, cast actors, then team up into crews and shoot the scenes. They act as though they are shooting on film, but in the interest of saving money they shoot these exercises on video. After students finish the first-year courses they are free to make whatever films they want. The school does not have any requirements about the films students make—students are free to work in narrative, experimental, or documentary styles, and to make them whatever length is appropriate for the project.

Second year is fairly unstructured. Students continue taking classes in filmmaking technique and in film history and criticism, and they also make films on their own. The school suggests that students complete a short film early in second year and then begin working on their thesis films. In fact, most students spend the whole year on their second-year films and don't even start thinking about their thesis films until third year.

The school places an emphasis on film history and criticism. A number of film history and criticism courses are offered, from a year-long general history of film to specific histories of animation, documentary, or experimental film. Because Utah is on the quarterly system, instead of two long classes in a year students get three shorter classes. So what the film history classes can lack in depth the program makes up for in breadth.

The school puts less emphasis than most on the thesis film. The final film is not necessarily the most lavish production a student makes, nor is it the ultimate statement of a student's talents—it is just another piece that fits into a larger body of work. In awarding degrees the school takes into account a student's entire body of work, not just a single thesis film.

Although the school has historically been devoted to experimental and documentary filmmaking, it recently made an advance into the realm of Hollywood filmmaking with the addition of former child star Robby Benson as a visiting faculty member. Benson is still a player in Hollywood—doing voices for animation (*Beauty and the Beast* [1992]) and directing television situation comedies. He still works in Hollywood most of the year, but he spends part of the year in Utah. When he is around, he drops in at the school and helps out—he teaches occasional courses in directing, or he reads student screenplays and gives comments and suggestions.

Once a year the program head, Brian Patrick, takes a group of students to Hollywood and shows them around, taking them to the various studios and introducing them to industry professionals.

The Price

$7,068 nonresident tuition for two years	$14,136
$10,000 a year rent and living expenses for three years	$30,000
Upkeep and insurance on a car for three years	$ 1,800
Exercise films tend to cost around	$ 2,000
Thesis films tend to cost around	$10,000
Total	**$57,936**

If you are not already a Utah resident, it is doubtful that you will be able to become one during your stay. The university requires students to have lived in state for twelve continuous months, involved in activities unrelated to being a student. The university also requires students to establish a permanent domicile in Utah—this includes obtaining a Utah driver's license, car registration, and voter registration. In short, if you are not currently a resident, plan on paying the nonresident tuition for your entire stay. If, however, you are a Utah resident, the school is an awfully good deal. Paying the resident tuition of $2,298 per year will knock nearly $10,000 off the nonresident price.

There are four teaching assistantships available in the production program each year, plus four more in the film history program. Each TA receives full tuition plus a $6,000-per-year stipend. The school also gives out a handful of tuition scholarships each year. Thanks to all these forms of funding, of the roughly fifteen students in the program in any given year, about twelve will get at least free tuition from the school. The school also gives out a few hundred dollars here and there to students who need (and, in the faculty's opinion, deserve) money for their projects, and hires a few people to work in the equipment room. So almost everyone in the program gets some sort of financial help from the school at some point during her stay.

The University of Utah is a commuter school. Most students live far away from campus and drive to school for classes, so a car is virtually a necessity. And anyway, you need a car to take advantage of all the great exterior locations Utah has to offer.

The Lowdown

Of the pool of thirty-five applicants each year, between two and five are accepted. The school looks for applicants who have backgrounds in film or video. Once in a while an applicant will come along who doesn't have much experience but who shows promise. In this situation the school will sometimes tell the applicant to come to the university, take an undergraduate film course, and see how it goes. If the student lives up to her promise, the school will accept her into the M.F.A. program; if she does not, she will be sent on her way.

As we mentioned above, the film program is overseen by two different departments—the art and theater departments. When you apply to Utah you will have to apply through one of these two departments. This is an important thing to know—art and theater have very different requirements, and students who might not be admitted to the film program through one might be welcomed through the other. The art department's usual applicants—painters, sculptors, and the like—have typically worked in their media since childhood and have voluminous portfolios of work to show for it. On the other hand, the theater department's usual applicants, largely actors and dancers, may have a lot of experience but rarely have concrete evidence of their work to present in a portfolio. Likewise, most prospective film students have little to put in a portfolio. If they apply through the theater department that is not a significant handicap; but if they apply through the art department, it can be. On the other hand, students who are accomplished painters or sculptors who have a lot of visual material to present in a portfolio may be better off applying through the art department. Most applicants are better off applying through the theater department, so that is the address we have listed for the school. But if you think you would be better off applying through the art department, give Brian Patrick a call and ask his advice.

Considering the size of the program, the University of Utah is fairly well stocked with equipment. The equipment is not always the newest, but it is reliable and there is enough of it that students have virtually unlimited access at all times. The school's primary film cameras are three Arriflex BLs. Only two of the BLs have internal crystal sync; the third requires a cable run to the Nagra for double-system sync sound. For hand-held documentary work the school has an Eclair NPR and a CP-16R. There is also an assortment of smaller cameras for other purposes; Arri Ss, Bolexes, and a Beaulieu. On the video end, the school has a wide variety of high-quality beta and three-quarter-inch equipment. For sound recording the school has four Nagras, and for documentary sound work a Sony Walkman Pro with internal crystal sync. There is a selection of professional-quality microphones. Most of the lighting equipment available is in kits—either Arri or Lowell DP. The school has an assortment of larger, more unwieldy lights that get less use. There are two small dollies, but neither is of professional quality.

The school has four six-plate flatbed editing machines—two Moviolas and two Steenbecks—and a number of video editing workstations. They have just changed their sound-mixing facility from mag film to an eight-track Digital Audio Tape mixing system. The school does not have an optical printer or an animation stand, but it has several workstations for digital animation, including a Video Toaster. The school does not currently own nonlinear editing equipment.

The program recently received an endowment that will provide a good amount of money each year with which to purchase new equipment. So for the foreseeable future Utah should be able to keep up with the always-changing technologies of film and video, but check with the school to see exactly what they are buying.

There is one equipment rental company in Utah; Redman Movies and Stories. This company is owned and operated by a Utah film school graduate, and it has an ongoing relationship with the school. Redman will often give students good deals on equipment rentals, so if the school doesn't have the specific equipment a student needs Redman will usually be able to provide it at a good rate. Also, when Redman has extra equipment that they no longer need—old c-stands, grip equipment, lighting gels, etc.—they will often donate it to the school.

There are no film-processing labs in Salt Lake City. The closest Salt Lake City gets to a lab is Alpha Cine, which has an office there. Students take their exposed film to that office, and the office takes care of getting it to the lab in Seattle, making sure it is processed according to students' wishes, and getting it back to the students in Salt Lake City. The students who don't use Alpha Cine use Western Cine in Denver. The school has discount deals with both labs. There are no film services companies around—no audio mixing houses, no negative cutters. Students have to learn how to do these things themselves, and the school is pretty good about teaching them.

Some of the best things about the program: Utah provides almost absolute freedom in filmmaking. The school does not dictate the kinds of films students may make and provides nearly unlimited access to equipment. Students at Utah can keep up with all the latest trends in independent filmmaking by attending the Sundance Film Festival every year; and those with a lot of chutzpah can use it as a networking opportunity. Utah has incredible exterior locations—from the Salt Flats to the Rocky Mountains to landscapes down around Moab that look like Mars. And on the recreation end of things, it is a great place for hiking, mountain biking and camping in the summer, and for great skiing in the winter. Merely by his presence, Robby Benson provides a whole new angle to Utah's traditionally independent/documentary program. He is only a visiting professor, so he is not around very often. But when he is around he is willing to read scripts, give directing advice, and basically provide the viewpoint of a longtime Hollywood professional on all matters.

The program is probably best for documentary filmmaking—much of the equipment is especially good for documentary work, and the faculty have wide experience in all the problems involved in documentary filmmaking. As one might expect, Utah's documentaries tend to be about the American West. In recent years students have made documentaries about the wild horses that roam the West and about Native Americans reclaiming and reburying the bones of their ancestors. There was even one called *Nut Feed* about a culinary event that follows the annual castration of cattle on a ranch in Kansas. A Utah student won the Student Academy Award for documentary filmmaking in 1994 with a film about his father's experience entering Hiroshima immediately after World War II ended. With award-winning filmmakers like this coming out of the school, Utah's star is on the rise.

Probably the best thing that happens after graduation is the trip to Hollywood. The school also puts on a two-night festival of student films at the school every year. Utah graduates have a good record of finding work in the industry.

Some of the worst things about the program: A major minus is Salt Lake City itself, which is not exactly a lively metropolis. It is a quiet, deeply conservative community that revolves to a large extent around the Mormon Church. Bars and liquor stores close early, and clubs are all but unheard of. Some students and faculty choose to live far away in Park City, which, as a world-class resort, has more of the amenities students and academics seek.

University of Wisconsin at Milwaukee

Director of Graduate Studies
Film Department
UW-Milwaukee
P.O. Box 413
Milwaukee, WI 53201-0413
Phone: (414) 229-6015
Fax: (414) 229-5901
http://www.uwm.edu/Dept/
   SFA/Film/

Experimental

Equipment Quality: ☆☆

Equipment Accessibility: ☆☆

Cost: $$

Annual Tuition:	**Resident: $4,438**
	Nonresident: $13,322
Enrollment:	**Between 3 and 6 per year, 12 total**
Deadline:	**Graduate School: January 1**
	Film Department: February 15
Focus:	**Experimental**

The Program

The University of Wisconson at Milwaukee's M.F.A. film program may be one of the best-kept secrets in American film schools. It is not a school for novices, but experienced filmmakers who have projects they are dying to work on may find there is no better program for them.

This is an unabashedly unstructured program, with a tendency toward experimentation. Which is not to suggest that the program is unfocused or lazy. Quite the contrary, the professors are energetic and enthusiastic, and the equipment is (considering the number of students) plentiful and readily available. The idea behind the school seems to be to find a very few promising students, give them free access to a lot of equipment, and see what happens. It is a Film School Without Walls, where students are encouraged to follow whatever paths interest them and to make whatever projects they want, in whatever media they think best, on whatever subjects strike their fancy.

The school requires that students take two years' worth of classes. A three-semester graduate seminar forms the center of the program. Taught by a different professor each semester, students in this course discuss their projects and critique one another's work.

Students also have to take a number of film electives, and have to choose a Complementary Study. Complementary Study is almost like a minor—it is a separate field of study that students are required to choose and take four classes in while they are studying film.

Each student has to answer to a graduate review committee of four professors. Students meet with their committees after their first year, and then at the end of each semester thereafter. The committee reviews each student's work and discusses it with her. The student also has to propose her thesis to the committee, and gain their approval, before she can begin work on it.

The second semester of second year is supposed to be when students finish their thesis projects. In fact, many students only begin their thesis projects in this semester, and have to return for another year to finish. There is some pressure on students to finish in two years since the school does not accept new students until old students leave; those in their third year may begin to feel like guests who have overstayed their welcome. On average about half the students finish in two years, while the other half take longer.

The Price

Nonresident tuition for two years	$26,644
$9,000 a year rent and living expenses for three years	$27,000
Exercise films tend to cost around	$ 2,000
Thesis films tend to cost around	$ 4,000
Total	**$59,644**

This is assuming you are not a resident of Wisconsin. We make this assumption for two reasons: First, Wisconsin only has 4.9 million residents; second, it is not easy to become a resident if you are not one already. In order to be considered a resident you have to live in the state for a year without taking any classes. If you are a resident, or if you have a year you want to kill in Wisconsin in order to become a resident, tuition is a real bargain at only $4,438 per year. For a resident, the above total drops more than $17,000—to $41,876. But even at the higher nonresident rate, this is still one of the cheapest film schools in the country

The school offers at least three TAships each year. TAs get an $8,000-per-year stipend. If they are nonresidents they are only charged resident tuition (that $2,772 tuition comes out of the $8,000 stipend). The school also offers three Project Assistantships, or PAships, per year. These are what would be called graduate assistantships elsewhere—students are hired to work for the school, doing things like running the equipment room or repairing equipment. PAships pay about the same as the TAships—about $8,000 per year—but don't help with nonresident tuition. Between the TAships and the PAships, a majority of the graduate film students receive financial aid each year. There have even been years when every student had financial aid, though the faculty is quick to point out that there is no guarantee of that.

Life is inexpensive in Milwaukee. Nice one-bedroom apartments near the school run around $300 to $400 a month; smaller apartments, or apartments farther away from campus can be found for under $300. Many students choose to live in River West, an artsy community between downtown Milwaukee and the school with still-lower rents. It is a good idea to have a car, but it is not strictly necessary. A car is handy for moving equipment and crew to locations, but in the winter, when batteries freeze and roads and parking lots are buried under yards of snow, cars can be more trouble than they are worth.

The school has its own film-processing lab. Students pay a $20 lab fee each semester and then have access to unlimited black-and-white reversal processing free of charge. University of Wisconsin at Madison processes color reversal film for five cents a foot. Together these schools make a pretty good reversal lab; everyone we spoke to was happy with the quality of the labs' work. Students who want to shoot negative have to send their footage away to labs in New York, Los Angeles, or Seattle.

The Lowdown

The school receives about forty applications each year, out of which the handful of new students is chosen. Says one professor, "We're basically interested in people who are really cooking, who have some formal abilities and good ideas and don't look like they're going to dry up in a year or two." UWM looks for applicants who have some experience with film, and they generally only accept those who do. If the faculty see an applicant they think is particularly interesting, but who does not have experience in film, they might suggest that that person come to UWM, get a quick bachelor's degree in film, and then negotiate a transition into the M.F.A. film program. But that is fairly rare—they generally only accept people who have a working knowledge of, and some experience in, filmmaking.

On the other hand, the school will bend over backward to help students who are "really cooking." There are stories about students who were allowed to start using the school's equipment months before they started the program. There are stories about the school asking students what equipment they need and then spending thousands of dollars to buy that specific equipment.

The time requirements of the program are as nebulous as the creative requirements. It is not a two-year or three-year program so much as an as-long-as-it-takes program. Some students finish in two years, some in three, some in four. The faculty like to see students finish in a timely manner, but they also genuinely want to see students do the best work they can and won't complain too much if a student takes an extra year or two to make something really great. Students don't have to pay tuition once they finish classes. They just have to pay for one credit (a couple of hundred bucks) the semester they graduate.

Because Milwaukee stresses independent and experimental filmmaking, they make a point of not admitting people who seem to want to make Hollywood-type films. It is not that they hate Hollywood—only that they are not interested in teaching Hollywood filmmaking when there are so many other schools that are, and that do it well.

The Complementary Studies are crucial to the program. The school likes to find people who are interested in film and something else, and then encourage them to combine the two. So one student who is interested in painting and film is encouraged to find ways to use film to explore painting. Others who are interested in anthropology or Asian history are encouraged to make films that explore anthropology or Asian history. If you have other interests that you would like to explore through film, be sure to mention that in your application.

Considering its size, Milwaukee is reasonably well stocked with equipment. They have a few cameras—Arriflex 16S and CP 16R cameras that are shared with the undergraduates, and a single Arri SR, which is reserved for graduate students. The school recently bought some Zeiss prime lenses to go with the SR. There are tripods and fluid heads, but no dolly: the closest thing the school has is a three-wheel spider, which is not popular. On the video side there is a three-quarter-inch portapack, which is reserved for graduate use, and an assortment of VHS and Hi-8 video cameras which are shared by the graduate and undergraduate departments. There is so much equipment for so few students that students can always get a camera with a week's notice—and can usually get one with no notice, if necessary. The school does not place limits on equipment access the way most larger schools do.

Sound equipment includes Nagra 4.2s, DAT recorders, and sync cassette recorders. A wide variety of mikes—shotgun, hypercardioid, cardioid, and lavalier—are also available. For post-production sound work the school has six dubbers, which transfer over to an eight-track half-inch tape recorder that runs in sync with the projector. Students transfer their tracks to this tape recorder, then do their mixes on tape. The extra generation can result in a slight deterioration of sound quality, but it is not noticeable if the final product is a 16-mm optical track. All this equipment—projector, dubbers, and eight-track—is in one room; most people use the tape machine because it is a lot quieter than six dubbers running at once, making the mixing experience much more pleasant. Also, tape is more reliable than mag film, which has a bad habit of breaking right at the worst moment.

The school has two optical printers and, because of their popularity, is considering buying a third. The printers are not set up for color correction, so they are only for use with black-and-white stock. The school has an Oxberry animation stand, which is more often used for titles than for animation, a contact printer where students can do their own A&B rolling, and a machine to convert magnetic sound track to optical sound track.

There are eight flatbed editors available—one eight-plate, which is reserved for graduate use, and seven six-plates, which are shared with the undergraduates. The school also has a three-quarter-inch video post-production facility. The school does not have a digital nonlinear editing system and at the moment has no plans to buy one.

This program is best suited to self-motivated artists with clear visions of what they want to do. All the equipment is there for students to use, but there is little structure dictating when and how to use it. If you have found you work best under tight deadlines and strict guidelines, this probably is not the program for you. Likewise, if what you want in a film school is a pathway into the industry, Milwaukee is not the place for you. The school does not teach how to make Hollywood-style films, nor does it give any hints on how to get into the Hollywood system.

If you talk to the faculty about their students, they almost sound like proud parents. Any professor can name any student or former student and can tell you exactly what she did while at UWM, and exactly what she is doing now. This is not surprising considering the size of the program—only twelve students are enrolled at any one time. In any year the school only admits as many new students as graduated the previous year. The small size of the program gives students some big benefits. Students can check out production equipment almost any time they want. There are almost as many TAships as there are graduate students, so most students get financial aid, and almost everyone gets the opportunity to teach undergraduate courses. And because there are eight faculty members for those twelve students, students get an unusual amount of support and advice.

What Milwaukee does best is keep out of your way. It gives you access to equipment and moral support, but it leaves the rest up to you. If you have the vision and the force of will to make the films you see in your mind, if you want support and feedback from professors but don't need to be told when you are doing it all wrong, if you know what films you want to make and just need enough school to help you make them, then there is probably no better school for you than UWM.

Some of the best things about the program: The small size and the close communication between faculty and students. The ready availability of equipment. Everybody gets to teach. It's cheap!

Some of the worst things about the program: Winter in Wisconsin can be painful. And the school is so small it can feel claustrophobic. Just try avoiding someone you don't like—it can't be done. Because it is so easy to get reversal stock processed and so hard to get negative stock processed, many students never shoot negative and, thus, never learn the process of taking a film through to answer print.

After Film School

Okay, I've Got My Diploma. Now What?

Graduation from film school can be an exhilarating joyride, or more often it can be a depressing experience. After you screen your film, you may get interest from producers and agents. You may get meetings, representation, even interest in your talents as writer or director. The interest might lead somewhere, or it might lead nowhere. Or you may just find no one is interested, and nobody wants to read your screenplays.

No matter what happens, it will take awhile to adjust to life beyond film school. After a few years of being deeply involved in a tight-knit community of people as obsessed with film as you are, you will find yourself out in a world where the ongoing film conversations and the gossip and in-jokes no longer apply. The network will no longer be there to support you. The goals will no longer be common, the burdens will no longer be shared.

After graduation the world can be a lonely place. The important thing to remember about the real world is that there are no rules. If you want publicity, you have to make it yourself. If you want an agent or contacts in the industry, you will have to come up with original ways to get them.

If you ask someone who works in the film industry how he got his first break, he will inevitably tell you a story of incredible luck and/or incredible chutzpah. One story we heard from a successful cameraman went like this: He went to CBS Television City looking for a job as a cameraman even though he did not know anyone there and had, in fact, never touched a video camera in his life. He managed to find the person in charge of hiring new camera operators and lied that he had a lot of experience. The person in charge of hiring took him to a room where a video camera sat on a table. "Take it apart and come and get me when you're done," he was told. "When you've done that, you'll put it back together and come and get me again." He was left alone with a camera he had no idea how to disassemble. He left the room and wandered the halls for a while until he spotted an open door to a control room. He went in and found an old technician sitting at a console eating a sandwich. He explained to the technician the situation he was in, and the technician agreed to help him out. The technician disassembled the camera for him and left when the man in charge of hiring came to see it. When the man in charge of hiring left, the technician came back and reassembled the camera. Our hero got the job and had a long, happy career as a television cameraman.

We could tell you other similar stories we have heard, but you get the point: you should always keep an eye out for opportunities; and when they come, never let them pass you by. Never wait for the opportunities to come to you; and when they do, don't be afraid to tell lies, and don't be afraid to look silly.

That's if all you want is a job in the industry. If you want to direct or sell a screenplay, you need as much chutzpah, but much more luck. As you know, making a movie requires a lot of money. You can either try to get your money from Hollywood, or from somewhere else. If you want studio backing for your film, then you should try to get an agent to represent you. A degree from a respected film program might help you get in to meet the agents, but it won't compel them to sign you. A good short film will also help, but you will really need to show at least one really good screenplay—preferably a few—before an agent will seriously consider signing you. Once you have been signed, a good agent will send your screenplays around and try to get producers and production companies interested in you and your projects. If you are very lucky, an agent will find backing for your project. This is rare, though; there are tens of thousands of people in Los Angeles who want to direct movies, but only a few hundred films are made by the studios each year.

If you don't want to finance your film through Hollywood and instead want to go the independent route, then you should avoid agents at all cost. Hollywood filmmaking is the antithesis of independent filmmaking, and Hollywood agents will only try to make you compromise your independent spirit in order to make your projects more appealing to producers. As an independent you will essentially represent yourself. You will need to find wealthy people who want to invest in film and convince them that your film is the one they should invest in. You will want to apply for grants and enter your screenplay in competitions. You will want to get your student film in festivals, and you will want to stand around conspicuously after your screenings, hoping that some wealthy person will approach you.

Applying to film festivals can be rewarding (if they screen your film), or it can just be an annoying drain on what's left of your checking account (if they don't). Most film festivals charge an entry fee—some charge as little as ten dollars, others more than a hundred. If your film is chosen for screening at a film festival, you will probably have a great experience. You will be treated as a VIP, invited to parties, and fed large amounts of rich food. You will make contacts that are likely to be much more valuable than any you might get through film school. Certainly you should enter your film in a few festivals. Even if you can't attend, it is nice to know that your work is being seen somewhere. And if a few festivals reject your film, don't be discouraged—it only takes one to give you exposure. You might want to research each festival before you enter. It doesn't make sense to enter a romantic comedy in a festival that favors surrealist art films. You might as well wait to hear the winner's name and mail your entry fee directly to her. You can ask festivals for lists of previous winners' names to get a feel for what they like and determine whether or not you fit in. It pays to be particular: a Best Film Award from the Tumbleweed Festival might not be something you want to include in your press packet. An honorable mention from Sundance, on the other hand, would be. Don't be afraid to enter the more prestigious competitions. You are as entitled to try for Cannes as the next guy.

Some festivals are scams; make sure a festival screens films for the public before you send them your money—some don't.

After you graduate, if things are not progressing as quickly as you'd like, there are some alternatives you can pursue that might speed things up for you. If you want to write or direct, there are competitions you can enter. A production company called Chanticleer Films sponsors something called the Discovery Program, in which they choose a handful of short scripts and give the writers small budgets with which to make the scripts into films. Granted, it is only another short film, but this time you will be spending somebody else's money instead of your own, which is a step in the right direction. The Discovery Program is mainly geared for industry professionals who have never directed, or people who haven't directed in a long time. The program also favors celebrities—Daryl Hannah was recently accepted into the program. But film school graduates are sometimes accepted. It is good practice, and it can lead to new opportunities.

Screenplay competitions are another possibility. The competition is stiff, as hundreds of writers enter each of these competitions. Winners receive actual salaries (most seem to pay around $25,000 over the course of a year) and a lot of good feedback on their work from professionals. If you win a competition like this, you can concentrate on writing your screenplay without worrying about rent for a year. Disney sponsors one (which is geared toward giving opportunities to minority and women writers), the Academy of Motion Picture Arts and Sciences runs one called the Nicholls Fellowship, and Amblin Entertainment sponsors one called the Chesterfield Competition.

There are a lot of film distribution companies who will handle short films. Some handle the distribution of educational films to schools; others handle the distribution of more mature films to movie theaters and cable television networks. If your film is even remotely appropriate for children or teens you could earn back a lot of what you spent making it by distributing it in the educational market. New cable television networks like the Independent Film Channel and the Sundance Channel are broadening the market for good short films. And good money can also be made in international distribution, as many other countries still screen short films before features.

The profits you see from a distributor will vary depending on how the distributor handles your film. If the distributor is providing duplication of prints, publicity, and advertising, you should receive between 25 and 45 percent of their gross profits. If you are providing the prints and the distributor is not giving you any publicity, you should get somewhere in the area of 70 percent. Be sure to shop around to see which distributor can offer you the best deal. And be sure the rights revert back to you, preferably after two or three years. You worked too hard on your film to give it away.

It is rare for film students to make back all the money they spent on their films, but it does happen. Just make sure that the distributor you go with agrees to send you a quarterly progress report so that you can keep tabs on them. Some distributors will sign films but never distribute them. Unscrupulous distributors will distribute films but not report the income to the filmmaker. If after six months a distributor has not made any money with your film, try to break the contract and find another company.

Getting a Job in Film

So here you are. After all that time, work, and money, you find yourself no closer to working in film than you were before you went to film school.

Well, that's not entirely true—you know a great deal more now, and you have valuable technical skills. But you have to use those skills carefully. How you use those skills will determine how far you go. It's important to have a plan and a clear vision of where you want to go and how you plan to get there.

Film Work vs. Nonfilm Work

This may not sound like a very difficult choice, but it can be. Some people dive into the industry right out of film school, taking whatever jobs they can get on film shoots. Work like this will make them feel that they are in the industry, but it is so exhausting it leaves them with little time or energy for anything else.

The best thing you can do once you are out of film school is write screenplays, but if you are working eighteen hour days as a grip, you won't get much writing done. One alternative is to find a nine-to-five job that will pay your bills and allow you time to write in the evenings and weekends. It can be frustrating to be nowhere near the industry, but if you have the discipline to write in your free time (and perhaps even on the job), it can be a good way of paying the bills while you write. If you do choose the office work route, it is important to maintain a support group. Weekly writing groups can keep you focused and help provide a sense of purpose. Without this kind of support, it is easy to be sucked into the world of business and to lose track of your film aspirations.

But for now let's say you just want to move to Los Angeles and get a job in the industry. What jobs are available?

Entry-Level Jobs

So, you've got your degree and have made the big move to Los Angeles only to find that your door is not being broken down by agents and producers. Once you have resigned yourself to this, you will be ready to join the ranks of the gainfully, if not happily, employed. The next fact you need to resign yourself to is that whatever job you wind up in, you probably could have gotten that job without an M.F.A. In fact, it is quite possible that you will find yourself working as a veritable slave to someone younger, less skilled, and less educated than yourself. You should also become resigned to the fact that even though these are low-paying, drudgery-filled positions, they are highly coveted and competition to get them is tough.

You need to think about whether you are interested in working in film or television. Although the positions may be similar, the philosophies behind them are not. Established writers and directors can easily move between film and TV, but when you are first starting out you will be pigeonholed in one or the other. So if you want to work in TV, start out in TV. And if you want to work in film, start out in film.

You will need to get used as quickly as possible to the paltry wages that you will be receiving, and the obscenely huge amounts of money your higher-ups will be receiving. We don't expect you to ever like the fact that you are surviving on $500 a week while your twenty-two-year old boss is taking home $15,000 a week, but it is the way the industry works, and the sooner you learn to grin and bear it the better off you will be.

At any given time there are usually more television shows being produced than films, so there are usually more jobs in television than in film. But a lot of the positions listed below occur in both television and film. Where you wind up often depends on your interests and how badly you need a paycheck. Again, keep your eye on your goals. If you find you are not advancing, start looking for work elsewhere. Learn to recognize when it is time to cut your losses.

So have we made these jobs sound terrible enough yet? Well get this: You will probably need good connections just to get a shot at one of these jobs. If you do not have any connections, you might try starting at the Human Resources Department of the major studios and production companies. If possible, get the name of someone you can contact directly. If you talk your way into an interview, you will be required to take some sort of test. Strong typing and computer skills are a must. You can also be bold and contact specific producers and writers personally, saying something like "I saw your episode on such-and-such-a-date and I would sell my family to Gypsies to be where you are . . ." Flattery works very well. If you have a favorite television show, try calling their offices directly and flattering the hell out of whoever picks up the phone.

Line producers are good to buddy up to. An inventive letter to a line producer followed up by a phone call can often get you at least an interview. But almost anyone at any production office from the PAs on up will know if there are any entry-level positions available. If you cannot speak with one of the higher-ups, don't hesitate to talk with the lower-downs who know what the job entails. They are on the inside, and if they like you they can often give you helpful tips and leads. Most important, be congenial and follow up on all of your calls. Persistence really pays off.

Writers' Assistant (TV)

Writers' assistant jobs on situation comedies are popular for people starting out in the industry, especially for those who want to write. Television shows always have teams of writers who brainstorm ideas for episodes. As a writers' assistant on a TV show you will sit in a room with the writers, take notes as they brainstorm, and then make revisions to scripts based on the ideas they come up with. You, along with two or three other assistants, will be responsible for putting together each week's script based on the notes you take.

A great deal of your time will be spent in a room filled with writers who acknowledge your existence with warm sentiments like, "Did you get that?" You will have to remain on your toes during this time "in the room." You have to be able to take quick, concise notes that you can later transcribe accurately. Some shows actually have writers' assistants type while in the room, thus strengthening that writer-assistant bond. You will be asked to read back dialogue and scene descriptions, so acting skills are a plus. The staff will count on your dramatic interpretations to determine if scenes work, so if you read their scenes in a remote monotone they will not be pleased with you. If you are shy about this type of thing, you will have to get over it—you will be expected to perform like this every day, for every script. You will need to have a good grasp of grammar and spelling, basic computer and typing skills, a great deal of patience and stamina, and enormous resources of humility. The hours are very long—ten to twelve per day is common, fourteen or more is not uncommon. On new shows and pilots, weekend stints and overnight sessions happen regularly.

The pay will vary according to your experience, as will the depth of the pockets of the producers behind the show. A standard salary is about $500 per week, but assistants with a lot of experience can earn $1,000 per week.

Most studios have a pay system that is cost-efficient for them, and painful for their employees. After you agree with them on a salary, they will then break that salary down into hourly pay for sixty hours: forty hours of straight time and twenty hours of over-time. This brings their pay practice within spitting distance of the law, but it still amounts to slave labor for the writers' assistant, who *must* work sixty hours every week, and who cannot hope to earn any overtime pay until *after* sixty hours. Be sure to ask about overtime before you take any position. There are some shows that do not offer it at all, and you should avoid working for these shows if you possibly can. Otherwise, after that seventieth hour kicks in, you'll be making a lower hourly wage than your average fast-food server.

A small perk for writers' assistants is that most shows provide free lunch and dinner. That's because writers' assistants are ex-pected to work through the lunch and dinner hours without taking breaks. But it does save money, and the food is often from very ex-pensive restaurants.

On the upside, you are surrounded by people who are doing what you want to do. You will learn a great deal about the business, writ-ing, and getting ahead. If you befriend the writers, they may allow you to pitch jokes and make script suggestions. This is your chance to dazzle them with your comic talent, and perhaps even make them think of you as a writer rather than a slave. After endearing yourself to your executive-producer bosses you will want to write a spec script and request feedback. Follow this up with a request to "pitch" ideas for your show—it is the only way you might move up into one of the writer positions. If your show runner is reluctant to promise a script assignment, move on. Far too many assistants go on working slave hours for slave wages for years without ever getting the chance to write an episode. You must find a show that believes in nurturing your talent.

The pay is terrible, the hours are hellish, the prospects grim. So why do the job? Well, it's dues-paying. And you can make good connections. And it can lead to a script assignment.

Production Assistant

You do not know the meaning of hell until you have worked as a PA.

This is not a job for the weak of heart, body, or spirit. The hours are just as long as those of writers' assistants, but the pay is substantially less and the work is grueling. In television, production assistants are at the beck and call of everyone who works on the production. Writers, producers, line producers, even secretaries and writers' assistants turn to PAs to do their grunt work.

You will be asked to do everything from taking and picking up meal orders to delivering scripts in the wee hours of the morning after the rest of the crew has gone to bed. Basically, any unpleasant work that needs to be done falls into the PAs' hands. Don't believe us? We know of one male PA who, while working on a popular show several years ago, was sent to buy a full-length lace bodysuit for the executive producer's girlfriend. All this for somewhere in the range of $300 per week—sometimes even less.

Even though PA work is a worse job than most people can even imagine, it is still difficult work to get. There are always hundreds of youngsters who want to get into film badly enough that they are willing to work as PAs.

The only people who can actually survive doing PA work are young people who are still living at home with their parents; $300 a week is only enough money for people who do not have to pay for room and board. Are there good things about PA work? Well, yeah. It gives you the opportunity to meet and speak with technicians in every field on a shoot. If you schmooze well enough you may be able to convince a gaffer or a sound recorder to hire you for the next shoot as his assistant. If you are good, you won't be a PA for long.

The single best thing about PA work: Whatever jobs you find afterward will seem wonderful by comparison.

Producer's Assistant—TV

A step above production assistant. A producer's assistant's job description can vary widely depending on how involved a producer wants his assistant to be. Producer's assistants are usually responsible for scheduling the boss's meetings and making sure her calendar is up-to-date. But sometimes producers will include their assistants in many aspects of their work. Producer's assistants can wind up taking notes during run-throughs of shows or attending meetings with industry professionals.

Producer's assistant can be a good job for those who want to write because there is often a lot of downtime that enterprising writers can fill with their own work. While the job usually only pays about five or six hundred dollars a week, the hours are relatively normal: most assistants are out of the office by six and are thus actually able to have a life. Which is not to say producer's assistants do not get stuck running their bosses' embarassing personal errands. One producer's assistant we know was made to do research for his employer's eleven-year-old son's science project. Of course the next season that assistant received a sitcom script assignment. But producer's assistants are slightly more appreciated and slightly better paid than PAs or writers' assistants. And producer's assistants have the opportunity to make connections with other producers and agents, and quickly learn how the power structure in Hollywood works.

Producer's Assistant—Film

If you want to be a feature producer, it is a good idea to latch on to someone already doing the job. Producer's assistants in film work longer and often more hectic hours than their counterparts in television. Film producers rely heavily on their assistants. So while producer's assistants have to manage the boss's calendar and run her personal errands, they gain invaluable firsthand producing experience.

Again, vital industry connections will be at your fingertips. Often you are responsible for running the office and making key decisions while your boss is away. Sometimes you get to travel to various sets and locations during filming. If you play your cards right, you might be able to eventually parlay your work into an associate producer credit. This of course depends on your relationship with your boss and how benevolent she is, but it is something to work toward. Working for a film producer is the best way to grasp what the job of producer entails. While the pay is nothing to write home about (roughly $600 a week), the experience can make it worthwhile.

Development Assistant (TV and Film)

One thing you need to know: Development is evil. Development serves no function except to make sure that any film that gets made contains no original thought, no emotion, no human truth whatsoever.

Officially, development people are supposed to take promising screenplays and tighten them up. But what development people actually do is take interesting screenplays and strip them of their interest. If a screenplay contains anything that has not already been seen in a thousand other movies, they remove it. If a screenplay contains a writer's strong personal voice, they hire a dozen script doctors to excise it. In Hollywood one often hears writers boasting, "I have a script in development at Disney (or New Line or Paramount)." Though the tone of their voices indicates they expect to be admired for this achievement, in all but the rarest cases they deserve only pity.

Assistants in development are often referred to as "D-Girls." Although there are a few token men in the field, the majority of development people are women. Many would-be writers make the mistake of thinking that these are great jobs because they get to deal with scripts and writers. WRONG. What they wind up doing is surrendering their lives to reading bad screenplays.

While reading a lot can help your writing skills, in this position you'll never have time to do any of your own writing. You will read screenplays and write coverage on them every waking hour, seven days a week. In television the job is a bit easier because television scripts are shorter, faster reads. At feature film production companies, D-girls will carry home a stack of feature film scripts to read every night and every weekend. As a writer it can be frustrating to spend all your time reading other writers' work and trying to figure out why your scripts aren't being read.

The upside of this job, once again, is that you'll learn a lot about how this system works and you'll have the opportunity to make contacts. And if you're interested in producing features, development can be a great way to build relationships with writers and agents. Many development people move on to be producers. They find a screenplay that others have passed on and turn it into their first credit. Salaries for development assistants range from $400 on up, again depending on the company.

Temp Jobs (TV and Film)

In Los Angeles, temping can be a way of life. And, if you're with a good agency it can be a not-unpleasant way of life.

There are several agencies that specialize in placing temps at companies in the entertainment industry. Working through these agencies can give you an idea of what it is like to work in various menial positions within the studio system, allowing you to choose which menial position you want to commit yourself to. Sometimes a one-day stint can turn into full-time employment. A lot of people choose not to take a permanent position, preferring to work in a variety of menial positions to commiting themselves to one menial position. Agencies can provide surprisingly steady work, and can even get you placed in the offices of high-level executives.

Most temp agencies won't place you unless you have excellent office skills. You'll need to be able to type very fast, and you'll need to know how to use both IBM and Macintosh computers. Temping only pays about $12 to $15 per hour, depending on the wealth of the company where you are placed and on your skills and experience.

Try to be as professional and enthusiastic as possible when you go out on a job. Dress and act as if you're an executive. Appearances are everything in Los Angeles, and the better first impression you make, the better your chances of getting hired and moving up.

If you want to take some time to get your bearings in the industry and don't want to be locked into a position right away, temping is not a bad gig.

Benediction

Now comes the hard part.

Going to film school is a tough decision, and a real sacrifice. We have tried to arm you with as much information as we could—it may not be much, but it is a lot more information than we had when we applied. Many people apply to all the schools and go to whichever one accepts them (we both did this, and, as it happens, we both got into NYU). We hope that now you will be able to decide whether or not a school is right for you before you move there and give them your money. No matter which school you choose, you have to be committed for the long haul, financially and personally. To get through film school, your commitment has to be so strong that you may find yourself alienating friends and loved ones.

Film school is all about the student film. You may dedicate several years of your life to bringing your thesis film into existence. But no matter how much time, money, and sweat you put into this film, it is important to remember one thing: *It is only a student film.* It will not make you an internationally known filmmaker. It will not get you a three-picture deal. It is just one small step at the beginning of a very long journey. Don't go into it intending to re-create cinema; just intend to tell a good story, and to tell it well.

Remember that there are many more graduates each year than there are jobs. You can't count on directing anything for a very long time, or on getting a high-end production job. You will be stuck assisting somebody somewhere, doing humiliating work for sixteen hours a day for a tiny salary. Or if you don't get a job at first, you will spend long months searching, schmoozing, and interviewing. You will be told that you are overqualified for jobs—often by people much younger than you. More than likely you'll wind up taking a job you could have gotten without your degree. That's where endurance, determination, and confidence have to come into play. You may be answering phones for some studio executive, but you must try to continue writing and making connections. It is very easy to become despondent as you watch another class graduate and debut all bright-eyed and hopeful. Each year it gets a little harder. But if you believe in yourself and you want it badly enough, it can happen. It just might take a few years longer than you imagined. But when it does happen, you can throw one heck of a party. (Be sure to add our names to the guest list. We don't get out much.)

We can only hope that we've helped provide some insights into what lies ahead for you in film school. Maybe we have saved you a lot of heartache, or maybe we have confirmed your convictions. In whatever choice you make . . .

Good luck!

Glossary of Common Film School Terms

A & B rolling. Also called conforming or checkerboarding, this is a process for hiding the physical cuts in a finished film by splitting successive shots onto two separate reels. In addition, A and B rolling makes possible effects like dissolves, wipes, and fades.

Actor. A difficult person.

Answer print. A final print of a film struck from the negative after it has been cut and A and B rolled, and after the sound track has been mixed.

Arriflex. Arri is short for Arnold and Richter, German manufacturer of high quality 16-mm and 35-mm cameras. All Arri cameras have a registration pin, so even the bottom-end models provide a very steady image. Arri cameras include the 16S (non-sync); 16 BL (crystal-sync); 16 SR, 16 SR-2, and 16 SR-3 (internal crystal-sync with microprocessor-controlled movement).

Arri kit. An Arri kit is a light kit very popular with film schools. It consists of four 1,000-watt tungsten lights, with stands and scrims, all in one box. Each kit is the size of a thirty-inch TV and weighs about twice as much. To show off their strange Teutonic sense of humor, the Arriflex company put a flimsy little handle on the box, like what you'll find on a Samsonite makeup kit, and dubbed it "portable." If you care about your back, you will not try to lift an Arri kit by the handle.

Assistant director. The AD has to keep communication flowing among everyone in the cast and crew, no matter how much bitterness may have developed. The AD has to butter up the people who are being difficult and make sure the shoot stays on schedule. In many ways it is the hardest job on a film crew.

Avid. Refers to any of the digital nonlinear editing systems made by Avid Technologies. These include Media Composer, Film Composer, NewsCutter, Media Suite Pro, and Video Studio.

Best boy. On a film crew, the first assistant electrician who answers directly to the Gaffer.

Boom. On a shoot, the person who aims the microphone at where the sound in a shot is coming from. Gets to stand around chatting nonchalantly with actors and actresses during the long lighting setups. As a result, tends to be oversexed.

Cinematic masturbation. See *Experimental film.*

Cinematographer. The person on a shoot who is in charge of how the film looks. The cinematographer dictates the kind of stock to be shot, the position and intensity of lights, the gels and filters used, and all the other details that determine how the overall appearance of the film will be.

Conforming. See A & B rolling.

CP 16. A 16-mm camera made by Cinema Products Corporation. Small, light and quiet, this camera was designed to be used by television news crews in the days before video. When video made them obsolete every television station in the country did the same thing—they donated their CP 16s to the local university and took hefty tax deductions. As a result the CP 16 is still the most common camera in film schools. Cinema Products' newer models include the GSMO, a small, microprocessor-controlled, crystal-sync 16-mm camera.

Crystal sync. No two machines ever run at exactly the same speed. So to make sound and image run together as one, motion picture cameras and sound recorders have to be forced to run in sync. One solution to this is crystal sync. It is a unique property of quartz crystals that they oscillate at an extremely precise rate when an electric current is sent across them. Manufacturers of motion picture cameras have put motors into their machines that use the oscillations of quartz crystals to dictate the speed at which they run.

Dailies. On a shoot, the workprint of a day's footage. On a typical film shoot, exposed negative film is rushed to a film-processing lab at the end of a shooting day. Late that night the lab processes the negative, exposes a workprint off of it, and processes that workprint in time for the DP and director to see it first thing the next morning. Also called rushes.

Daylight spool. A metal spool with 100 feet of raw 16-mm film wound on it. The metal spool blocks all light from reaching the film, so it is not necessary to use a darkroom or a changing bag to load it into a motion picture camera.

Director. The person ultimately in charge of all artistic aspects of a film's production.

DP. Director of photography. See *Cinematographer.*

Double System. The use of separate equipment to record a scene's sound and picture; i.e., a Nagra recording the sound and a camera recording the picture. Some cameras, like the CP 16 and the Arriflex 16 BL have the capability of recording sound inside the camera, directly onto the film. This is known as single system sound. Single system was developed for documentary work, especially for news in the days before video. Single system sound is poor in quality and hard to manipulate. It is rarely used in documentary films these days, thanks to high-quality, compact, crystal sync sound recorders like the Sony Walkman Pro.

Eclair. Eclair International makes a variety of good quality film cameras. The model most often found in film schools is the NPR, a rugged 16-mm crystal-sync camera. A more recent camera you might come across is the Eclair ACL.

Editor. A person who can be happy spending all day every day locked in a small, dark room squinting at the small, dimly lit screen of an editing machine.

Experimental film. If it doesn't tell a story, if it isn't a documentary, if it isn't animated, if it's so strange that you can't think of a single thing to say about it—well, it's an experimental film. Many students making their first film want to make a film that will redefine the medium of cinema—that will defy the audience by not telling a story, that will assault them with shocking images, and that will challenge them with dense, inscrutable symbolism. These are, well, um, experimental films. (Okay, we admit we're being a little disingenuous. In fact, experimental film is an offshoot of painting and photography, not of cinema. Taken in that context, these films can be quite interesting [we admit a particular fondness for the films of Maya Deren]. But too many filmmakers, when they are just starting out, use experimental film as an excuse for laziness: Why go to all the trouble of inventing intriguing characters and putting them in a thoughtful story when you just can splash cool images across the screen?)

Flatbed. An automobile-sized (and -priced) machine on which reels of picture and sound film run in sync across a broad, flat tabletop. Digital editing systems are quickly making flatbeds obsolete, just as flatbeds once made the upright Moviola film editor obsolete.

Foley. Sound effects created in a recording studio.

Gaffer. The chief electrician on a film crew, who oversees the setting up of lights according to the Director of Photography's instructions.

Great screenplays, examples of. For examples of screenwriting at its best, please contact Karin Kelly about her screenplays *Crossover Summer* or *King's Ransom,* or Tom Edgar about his screenplays *Cahoots* and *Alcatraz Avenue.* These are fine screenplays that would make fabulous, groundbreaking, hugely successful motion pictures if only someone were to give these talented filmmakers the money to make them.

Grip. Grips are in charge of anything that moves on the set. On student shoots, almost everyone has to be a grip.

Internship. Slavery. Here is how film companies regard interns: "We take in interns because they do work that nobody else wants to do and don't even expect money in return. If interns get uppity and start asking for enough money to live on, we just sack them—there are always hundreds of other kids willing to work for free at a film company." We know many people who have swept floors, taken out garbage, walked dogs, picked up and delivered baby food, driven producers' children to and from school in Beverly Hills, bought lingerie for producers' girlfriends, and so on, all for less than subsistence pay. But we know of no one who has ever gone from an internship into a decent paying job. Avoid film internships if you possibly can.

Mag film. Magnetic film. This is 16-mm or 35-mm film that is coated with magnetic baiting like audiotape. It is traditionally used in the editing and mixing of films, though there are now a number of high-tech alternatives to it using computers, videotapes, DAT, and/or laser disks.

Mise-en-scène. This is a French term that means both "everything in your film" and "I know more obscure film terms than you do." For example, if a fellow student says of your film, "I liked the *mise-en-scène*," she is giving you a compliment, and also trying to show that she knows more film terms than you do. Thank her. If she says "I didn't care for the *mise-en-scène*," she is putting you down, and also showing that she knows more film terms than you do. Kick her in the shin.

Moviola. Moviola editing machines come in two types; upright and flatbed, though when someone refers to a Moviola she usually means an upright. Upright Moviolas are compact machines, about the size of a small refrigerator, that allow for the editing of one image track and one soundtrack simultaneously. Upright Moviolas were replaced as an industry standard by flatbed editing machines, which allow editing of more soundtracks at once and provide a larger viewing screen.

Narrative film. This is a film that tells a straightforward story in a straightforward way. It is the kind of film most schools want students to make, and the kind of film few students want to make when they are starting out (see *Experimental film*).

Negative. Film that exposes a negative image. A lab processes the negative, exposes a positive "workprint" of it, and processes that workprint. The advantage of shooting negative stock, as oppposed to reversal stock, is that the negative remains untouched while you cut your workprint. When you have finished editing your workprint, you then go back to the negative and, wearing cotton gloves, cut it to match your edited workprint. Once your negative is cut, you can make answer prints of your film for distribution.

Nonlinear. For most of their history, films have been edited in a linear fashion. That is, one shot is placed after another in a single, very long strand of film. Computer technology has made it possible to edit in a nonlinear fashion: A nonlinear editing system allows an editor to order and reorder shots and scenes the way one can rearrange words and sentences in a word processor.

Producer. The person ultimately in charge of all of the business aspects of a film's production.

Pro Tools. A powerful digital audio editing system made by Digidesign, now owned and distributed by Avid Technologies.

Registration. A term that refers to how steady the image is that a motion picture camera exposes. Good registration is achieved by cameras that hold the film firmly in place in the exposure gate for the fraction of a second while an image is being exposed. Some cameras use a registration pin—a small pin in the exposure gate that thrusts into one of the film's sprocket holes and holds the film absolutely still during exposure. All Arriflex cameras have registration pins. Other cameras, like the CP GSMO and the Eclair NPR use a spring-loaded plate that presses the film firmly into the gate. Cameras that have no registration mechanism can give you a shaky image. This can be unnoticeable on small screens or video, but it can be nauseating when projected on large screens.

Reversal stock. The opposite of negative stock. Reversal stock exposes a positive image inside the camera. Processing is quick and cheap, because no workprint is necessary, but any cut you make on the film cannot be undone. Reversal film saw its heyday in television news before the advent of portable video equipment; it could be processed quickly and cheaply, and could be edited in time for the six o'clock news. Now that all news is shot on video, reversal stock is used almost exclusively by film students, who want to shoot a lot of film but don't want to have to pay the high cost of shooting negative.

Spielberg Game. A popular film school game for killing time on set. You name a celebrity, and everyone else needs to link that person to Steven Spielberg, getting points for brevity. So if you said, "Katherine Ross," someone could respond, "Katherine Ross was in *Butch Cassidy* with Robert Redford, who was in *All the Presidents Men* with Dustin Hoffman, who was in *Hook*." But that person would lose to someone who responded, "Katherine Ross was in *The Graduate* with Dustin Hoffman, who was in *Hook*." Try it. A popular variant—the Kevin Bacon Game.

Steenbeck. A common-brand flatbed editing machine.

Walking film. A film in which an unnamed character walks around a city glumly looking at stuff—a perennial favorite with film students, who are traditionally good at organizing actors, locations, and camera equipment, but who are traditionally bad at writing actual stories.

Writer. A bright, quiet person. Writers make great dates. Honest!

"You just don't get it, do you?" The archetypal bad line of dialogue: it means nothing, nobody ever says it in real life, and you can't turn on the TV without hearing it at least once. When you come across this line of dialogue in a film or screenplay, you can know with certainty that you are dealing with the work of a bad writer—one who does not listen to how people really talk, one who does not watch how people really interact. Runners-up for the archetypal bad line: "Are you nuts?" "What is it with you?" "Wait a minute, let me get this straight!"

Appendix: Two Examples of NYU Thesis Films

We, your humble authors, both went to NYU. While we know our experiences don't apply to everyone at every school, we thought they might be helpful to some. And, anyway, we felt like writing them down. Please humor us—they may be the last films we ever get to direct.

Wildwood Nights
by Karin Kelly

Wildwood Nights began as a thread of idea based in the filmmaker's annual family vacations at the South Jersey shore. If you are working from your own original material, we cannot emphasize strongly enough that it should be from your own experience. Write what you know. It will make your job a whole lot easier, and your film a whole lot more watchable.

The film was one of three one-page treatments handed in for a January deadline. All were given approval (which, honestly, doesn't matter at NYU if you have the money to shoot), and I chose *WWN* for what I then believed to be greater cinematic qualities than my other choices. The story centers on fourteen-year-old Stephanie's attempt to escape the boredom of a family vacation by accepting a date with an older boy. The couple goes to Wildwood, New Jersey, and the wackiness ensues.

From January through May, the script was revised nine times. You need to have people read your work who aren't afraid to be honest. It helps. And don't take anything too personally. Film students are notoriously critical of other people's work and notoriously closeminded about criticism of their own work. But, you'll survive the criticism and will probably wind up with a stronger story because of it (not to mention all that character-building stuff). This is not to say you need to be a sponge that absorbs every suggestion and winds up a confused mess. Listen, evaluate, and take what works for you. One of the smartest things I ever did was to remove a voice-over, based upon a fellow student's suggestion.

I always knew that I would have enough money to shoot the film. By making relatively inexpensive first- and second-year films, ($6,000 total), I had managed to save up the $5,000 I would need to get the film in the can. This is a very small budget, considering that I would be shooting on location in South Jersey and Philadelphia for the entire shoot. With careful planning, I believed it feasible. However, with a twenty-nine-page script I also knew that it was going to be tiring. The rule of thumb for film is roughly one minute per page—and that's for a well-written script that doesn't deal in ambiguous time frames like "Then Bill and Mary make love." Looking back, I should have cut the script by several pages to make for an easier schedule. Film students expect to be abused on a fellow student's shoot, but everyone has their limits. If the weather and beaches hadn't cooperated on mine, I think perhaps that limit would have been reached.

I begged for an early June shooting date. Normally dates are chosen by chance drawings, but if you want an early date that no one else wants you can get lucky. Or if another student needs a different date, you can switch. I needed June for several reasons. First of all, shore house rentals, of which I needed at least two to house my cast and crew, would be less expensive up until July Fourth. At this time of year the summer attractions would be open without the massive summer crowds. And last of all, the "Senior Week" advantage. A tradition in the Philadelphia area, "Senior Week" is when, upon their graduation from the local high schools, students head to the shore for a week of reckless abandon—often rowdy, but usually harmless. I knew that during those two weeks I would be able to cheat the look of a crowded summer resort frequented by teens. Luckily, most of my fellow film students were pushing back their shoot dates. My self-imposed deadline gave me the cream of the equipment and a large pool of nonexhausted crew choices.

It is vital to choose crew members who are not only adept at their jobs but also in sync with your sensibilities. When things get rough, and inevitably they do, you want to feel comfortable around your crew. They should be a support system that wants to see you succeed as much as you do. If you're thinking *Risky Business* and your Director of Photography is more *Last Year at Marienbad,* we can guarantee problems. And with all the stress you'll be under, you just can't afford it.

I highly recommend finding a producer other than yourself. Once you're actually filming, the burden gets to be too much if you have to worry about performances as well as all the millions of other little things that can go wrong. If you can't find a producer, a strong production manager (PM) is vital. In the film school realm, your producer/production manager handles everything from your budget to location scouting. Once on the set, the PM makes sure that it all runs smoothly for you. I can't tell you how much I longed for someone else to worry about costumes and meals, bringing the right props and maintaining relationships with the many people helping us along. Ultimately, everything fell on my shoulders.

Because I was acting as my own producer I began location scouting and pre-production in January. This included a lot of letter writing, phone calls, and groveling. I often think students would greatly benefit from a "Groveling 101" course. It's a skill you need to learn and perfect. Not everyone is good at this. If it makes you uncomfortable, or you know that you aren't good with people, find a production manager who is. You can save yourself a lot of money. You should always try to get everything for free. You'd be amazed at how much you can get if you really try. I didn't pay for one location. I managed free costumes, food donations, several props, and even the use of a police patrol car. Looking back, if I'd had more time, I would have tried for even more. Just try not to ruin it for those who follow you. Most people have no idea of what a film shoot entails. The time, mess, and aggravation are monumental. It is extremely easy to become jaded by a reckless crew who leaves your rugs soiled and torn and numerous patches of missing paint on your walls from hastily removed gaffer's tape. Locations should be left as you found them . . . better, if possible. And be honest about time frames. Better to finish early than to have to beg for another four hours. By being honest, polite, extremely grateful, and conscientious you can ensure that another film student will not be frowned upon because of you. Don't abuse the kindness of others, even if you are paying them. Eventually someone else will need that diner or mansion or library. If you've behaved responsibly, they'll be able to get it.

Since I would not be filming in New York and I was hoping to afford dailies for at least a portion of the film, I elected to go with NFL Films in South Jersey. I still relish the thought of my little fourteen-year-old star frolicking on the same screens as those hulking football types. But they were convenient and cheap. Besides, I figured if it was good enough for Troy Aikman, it was good enough for me. They were extremely understanding and helpful and gave me a student discount that's unheard of at any of the New York labs. And because of their proximity to my locations, I was able to finagle a free pickup and drop off of negative and dailies. In addition, I didn't have to pay up-front for anything. Try working out that arrangement in the Big Apple.

In March I advertised for actors in *Backstage,* the local New York film/theater newspaper. As with my other films, the ad gleaned about two hundred and fifty responses. I auditioned roughly seventy-five of those applicants. Out of that group I didn't find anyone I felt met my requirements. So, I advertised again. I needed two parents, three kids, one dream date, some rent-a-cops, and numerous extras. I suggest you try to find someone to help you or at least keep you company during these auditions. They're time-consuming and exhausting when you do them alone.

You should know that it is quite hard to find talented actors in the forty-to-fifty age bracket. By that age, many of the really good ones no longer have to do student films. You just have to filter through the rest to find those late-bloomers. On the other hand, if you have the time and stamina to search through it, the eighteen-to-thirty age bracket is a veritable gold mine. The fourteen-to-sixteen age range is another story—especially when you need to take a kid away from home for several weeks. My film was dependent upon finding the right "Stephanie." I decided that although I could work around the rest of the cast, I wouldn't shoot if I didn't feel I had found the right lead and if I didn't have time for at least one month of weekend rehearsals. After three tries in *Backstage,* I tried the performing arts high schools . . . then regular high schools in Philadelphia and New

Jersey . . . then acting schools. It was in the smallest of these acting schools, in the most obscure of towns in the outskirts of Philadelphia, that I ultimately found my Stephanie, after over a hundred auditions and two months of searching. I made my one-month rehearsal schedule with two days to spare. If you really get stuck, don't be afraid to call talent agencies. They are always looking for exposure for new talent. If you are professional enough and you have a solid script, they often cooperate. For actors, experience is really the name of the game. Videotapes of a good performance can be a real asset.

Excluding the parents, I cast the other roles with actors whom I had worked with in my performing days or on my other films, and from my relatives. I've made good use of my eight siblings and numerous neices and nephews! Hey, you do what you gotta do.

Along about this time I submitted my script to the annual Grad Film Grant/Scholarship Awards. Never having won so much as a handshake in the previous two years, I was shocked to receive a Warner Bros. Grant (and fall fellowship) for my script. The $2,500 would enable me to pay for my dailies, and in the fall I would be production assisting on a TV show. Also, along with three equally poor students, I applied for the "Princess Grace Grant." NYU had never even heard of this organization which patronizes the arts. In a desperate search for money we found their name in the Yellow Pages. Eventually we were awarded the $25,000 grant, which we split equally. I'm convinced there is money out there if you just figure out how to find it.

I shot for twelve days, three-quarters of it exteriors. We started with days and, mid-shoot, moved into nights. By the end, I'm sure my crew felt like hostages. Beaches and sunshine only compensate for extended hours of tough work for so long. At times like these you need to have plenty of food on hand. Your crew will rebel on pizza and Chinese takeout. I had most of my meals prepared and frozen ahead of time. The rest were prepared by my parents who graciously agreed to stay for a week and cook for us. Surprisingly enough, they still speak to me.

Feeding fifteen to twenty exhausted, cranky people for two weeks is not an easy task. And takeout gets expensive. If you can trade off cooking duty with a fellow student, do it. I often thought about starting a film student catering service to make some extra money, and fulfill a major need. The quality and quantity of food can make or break the morale of your crew. If you want a hundred percent from them, they need to be treated properly. I really tried to provide good food, lots of snacks, and at least seven hours of sleep. But I'm sure if you interviewed my crew today, they would still tell you I fell short. Don't take this lightly. It will affect your film. At the very least, no one will want to work for you again. Gossip flies fast and furious about who's serving peanut butter and jelly and who's barbecuing on the patio.

Basically we had a relatively trouble-free shoot. Of course there were the minor setbacks. One crew member had to pay a visit to the hospital to remove boardwalk splinters. Another had to be shipped back to New York with a severe case of sunburn on his feet. And we did have to deal with our "date car" blowing up en route to the location. Fortunately Wildwood, New Jersey, happens to be the Camaro capital of the world, so I was able to convince one of the jubilant graduates to "loan" us his car for two nights. Never underestimate the bargaining power of a case of beer. We also were delayed in shooting a large party scene when none of the extras showed up. My wonder PA combed the beaches and once again those senior week graduates came in handy.

The major complication occurred when an angry, somewhat immature film student tried to sabotage my film by canceling an equipment rental. This is not the norm at NYU. For the most part students really help one another out. It's the only way you are able to crew your film. In this instance I had chosen a DP who backed out of my film because of a prior commitment to another student whose shooting date changed. When the other student changed his dates, he wanted to hop back onboard. At this point I'd already hooked up with another DP, who happened to be a good friend of the first DP (Are you still with me?). I then agreed to let both very capable cinematographers shoot my film together. A very bad, extremely foolish error on my part. As pre-production progressed, it became apparent that my initial DP was more committed to the project. I could not have one person do all the work and allow the other, who was busy working on other projects, to just cruise on the set the first day and complicate my shoot. After much soul-searching I called and explained this to him. Unfortunately this happened to be a few days before the shoot. Another bad error on my part. As soon as I had begun to have doubts, several months earlier, I should have ended the partnership. In spite of my stressing that this was not based upon talent, simply preplanning availability (i.e., storyboarding, location scouting, etc.), he didn't handle it too well. I remember standing alone in a phone booth on the boardwalk, in the middle of my shoot, trying to confirm my equipment package pickup back in Philadelphia, only to be told the package had been canceled by the former DP. Yikes! Although a supposed friendship was ruined, my preplanning paid off and I was able to remedy the situation rather quickly. When I hear of some of the other problems students must overcome (i.e., losing actors or locations at the last minute), I feel very fortunate. But, I pre-produced like nobody's business so that I could avoid any unnecessary problems. Pre-production can give you a well-scheduled, realistically budgeted, and successful shoot, or it can send you reeling with costly mistakes and delays. It can make the difference between finishing your film quickly or enrolling on the ten-year program. Don't leave anything overlooked. Spending the extra time prior to your shoot will save you time on the set, when you'll really need it. If you don't feel ready to go out, for any reason, then don't do it. Trust your instincts.

After the shoot was complete I handed the dailies over to a fellow student who agreed to edit my film in return for my producing his. Having suffered through the editing of my second-year film, which was optional at that time, I realized that editing was not my forte. My editor did a superb job and there began to be a buzz around the school about *WWN*. This "buzz" enabled me and my film to be submitted for the newly developed Paramount Pictures Fellowship—sort of a national discovery program. I was one of four film school graduates selected to participate. Essentially they gave us a year of employment and access to everybody and anything on their lot. It got me out to California and helped me make some more connections. As the guinea pigs of the program, we soon discovered that it was not designed to lead to much of anything else at that time. Still, I was thankful to be chosen and found the year to be beneficial in numerous other ways. We were given offices and computers and I was able to at last concentrate on writing the script that I should have had upon graduation.

Poison
by Tom Edgar

I am originally from California. I had never lived in cold weather—and I had never lived in squalor—before I moved to New York. So while I enjoyed NYU film school, I hated New York with a passion.

All my first-year films at NYU were dumb comedies. For my second-year film I decided to do something different; I wrote a screenplay that reflected my feelings toward New York. I portrayed the city as cold and evil and its inhabitants as wicked and selfish. Sure it was a downer, but it was a pretty good story, I think. The problem is, the story called for emotion, and I directed it in the same flat, deadpan way I had directed all my comedies. The final product was all but unwatchable. I decided to leave it behind me and take everything I had learned from that horrible experience and use it in my thesis film.

I knew that many NYU students took years to make their thesis films, and I swore to myself that I would finish my thesis as fast as was humanly possible, if for no other reason than that I desperately wanted to leave New York. I had about $8,000, some of which I had saved up by working at Saks Fifth Avenue, and some of which I had borrowed from my parents. I determined that I would spend no more than that on my thesis. I spent the summer and fall trying (and failing) to write a story good enough—and cheap enough—to film. Fall turned to winter, and soon I was up against the January script deadline with no script in hand.

I was faced with a choice between delaying my shoot until the following year or finding an existing story and adapting it. I was damned if I was going to stay in New York for another year, so I started going through my book collection, looking at my favorite short stories and pondering their cinematic qualities. What I decided on was a story by Roald Dahl called "Poison."

"Poison" tells the story of Timber Woods, an Englishman in colonial India who comes home late one evening to find Harry

Pope, with whom he shares his bungalow, calling quietly to him from bed. When Timber goes to Harry's bedroom, Harry whispers that a krait, a poisonous snake, has crawled over his chest, under the sheet, and onto his stomach, where it is now lying in the warmth, probably asleep. Timber calls a local doctor, Dr. Ganderbai, and the three try to find a way to remove the snake without killing anyone.

I adapted the story into a screenplay and presented it to my writing class. It is a very suspenseful story, and everyone seemed to like that, but there was a problem. Everybody hated the ending. Dahl's story ends ambiguously: after pouring ether on the bed to put the snake to sleep, Timber and Dr. Ganderbai pull the sheet down to find that there is no snake. Dr. Ganderbai asks Harry if he was sure he saw a snake, and Harry suddenly turns on him, hurling racist slurs. Dr. Ganderbai leaves, hiding his anger and humiliation. Timber runs after him to apologize. But Dr. Ganderbai doesn't accept the apologies—he says, enigmatically, "All he needs is a good holiday," and disappears into the night.

"You have to have a snake!" I was told repeatedly. "After all that suspense, if there isn't a snake, your audience will be angry!" If only one or two people had said this to me I could have laughed it off. But every single person in the class—including the teacher—insisted that there had to be a snake. I couldn't ignore such unanimity, and I rewrote Dahl's ending so that there was a snake after all.

I was still not completely convinced, though, so I planned to shoot the original ending as well as the new one, and decide which worked better in the editing room.

The school assigns thesis shoot dates in January; they are determined by lottery. Everyone wants to shoot in the spring and summer—the weather is better and it allows more time for pre-production—but dates as early as mid-April are assigned. People who get April dates often decide to cancel their shoots and wait until fall or the following spring. But I was determined to get the hell out of New York as soon as possible, so I went to a professor and asked to shoot in early April—before the first lottery-assigned shoots began. I was planning on shooting on a soundstage, so the weather didn't matter, and I knew that if I shot when nobody else was shooting I would have access to more equipment. And I would be able to leave New York once and for all by summer. The only drawback was there wasn't much time.

I knew I couldn't make the film without two people: Juliet was the best production manager in the school, and Keith was the best assistant director in the school. I had worked on shoots for both of them, so they "owed me," but they were also good friends. Unfortunately, they were less than available to help me—they were getting married about three weeks after my shoot. I asked Juliet if she would be able to do it, and she told me no.

I was lost. Not many people were willing to work on my shoot—everyone knew I was leaving town, and thus would not be around to work on their shoots—so I had counted on Keith and Juliet. A few days passed, and I was beginning to recognize that I would not be able to make my thesis after all, when I ran into Juliet on the street. She told me she and Keith could work on my film, but I would have to give them a few days off during the shoot to work on preparations for the wedding. It was a deal.

I placed adds for actors in the local trade papers. Middle-aged actors are hard to find: most of the actors in New York are in their twenties. But I got very lucky; at an open casting call, Timber and Harry walked in the door, almost exactly as I had imagined them. Eric and David were both fine actors, and they worked very well together.

Dr. Ganderbai, however, did not walk in the door. Not a single Indian actor responded to my advertisement. I put signs up in Little India, and when that didn't work, I started asking shopkeepers in Little India if they knew anyone who acted, and learned some interesting things. For instance, that there are very few Indians in New York. All the Indian restaurants are run by Muslims from Pakistan or Bangladesh (which is why you may notice they all serve beef but not pork). Drama is widely taught in schools in India, Pakistan, and Bangladesh, so almost all of the men I met had acting experience. But they are in New York to work and send money to their families—none of them has time to act in a film. I was pondering other alternatives when I met Masum.

Masum owned a spice shop in the East Village. He was quite a presence—he spoke softly, but when he entered a room everyone knew it. He liked the story and, as his own boss, had the time to do it. His English was not great, but I knew that could be fixed by dubbing his lines after the shoot was over. After sitting and talking with him over tea in the back of his shop for a few hours, I knew this was the guy. Lucky thing, too—we were two weeks away from production.

My roommate, Geoff, designed the sets. We built the inside of the bungalow on one of NYU's soundstages and shot there for a week. Then we built the outside of the bungalow and shot for three more days. The heating system on the soundstage was out of control—it was about ninety degrees on the set for the entire shoot. Lucky thing the film was set in the tropics; the sweat looked natural.

It was only after the shoot was over that somebody said to me, "Hey, didn't Alfred Hitchcock make this film?" I checked a reference book, and to my dismay found that "Poison" had been made into an episode of *Alfred Hitchcock Presents* in the late fifties. This depressed me profoundly: anyone who had ever seen that episode would think I was remaking a Hitchcock film. Months later, after I had finished cutting the film, I went up to the Museum of Broadcasting in midtown and watched Hitchcock's version. It was an interesting exercise, seeing how Hitchcock directed the same story. But—forgive me for saying this—I liked mine better.

I moved back home to California in the summer and edited the film there. I tried both endings and it was obvious that Dahl's ending was the best. With the ambiguous ending it was a story about the decline of Empire, about the best and worst of colonialism. With a snake in the ending, it was just a story about a couple of guys and a snake. (Hitchcock had put a snake into the ending of his version, and his, indeed, is just a story about a couple of guys and a snake.) When I took the finished film back to New York and screened it for professors and classmates, it was a big hit. Nobody remembered the snake controversy. *Poison* was named a finalist in the big end-of-year awards and was given a very good time slot in the festival—Thursday at 8:00 P.M.

It didn't win any of the top awards, though, and it was not shown at the Directors' Guild screening in Los Angeles. I put it in a number of festivals, where it won some awards, including one that qualified it for the Academy Award short film competition. Two things seem to have hurt me in the festivals, though: 1) Some festival programmers had seen the Hitchcock version and dismissed my film as a remake; and 2) Todd Haynes, an independent filmmaker based in New York, made a film called *Poison,* which won the top prize at the U.S. Film Festival that same year.

A few production companies contacted me and asked to see a screenplay, but when they read the one I sent them they lost interest. This always baffled me—it was a good screenplay. Perhaps it wasn't commercial enough. Perhaps they wanted to see a snake at the end.

The people who won the big awards in the NYU festival that year haven't done much better than I have. I now live in Hollywood, as do many of my classmates from NYU. We all work day jobs to pay the bills, and write screenplays in our free time. Sometimes we get together and read one another's screenplays. We go out for drinks and complain about our jobs and ponder whether any of us will ever direct another film.

Deep down we all still believe we will be making films again sometime soon. But, the truth is, time is passing and film school is receding into memory. And a few thousand more film school graduates move into town every year and compete for the same directing jobs.

We try not to think about it too much.

But Wait! There's More!

Things change quickly in the film industry, and film schools have to change quickly to keep up. In an effort to assure that *Film School Confidential* provides the most up-to-date information on these ever-changing programs, we have put up a site on the World Wide Web. The *Film School Confidential* site includes information that came in too late to be included in this book, and links to the web sites of all of the M.F.A. film programs in the country. You can even send us comments and criticism. Stop by anytime! Just point your browser to:

http://www.lather.com/fsc

Ratings at a Glance

	Equipment Quality	Equipment Availability	Cost	Focus
American Film Institute	☆☆☆☆	☆☆	$$$	Industry
Art Institute of Chicago	☆☆	☆☆	$$	Experimental
Bard College	☆☆☆	☆☆☆	$	Experimental
California Institute of the Arts	☆☆	☆☆☆	$$$	Experimental
Chapman University	☆☆☆	☆☆☆	$$$	Independent
City College of New York	☆☆☆	☆☆☆	$$	Independent
Columbia College	☆☆	☆☆	$$	Independent
Columbia University	☆☆	☆☆	$$$$	Independent
Florida State University	☆☆☆☆	☆☆☆	$$	Industry
Howard University	☆	☆	$$$	Independent
New York University	☆☆☆	☆☆	$$$$$	Independent
Northwestern University	☆☆☆	☆☆	$$	Experimental
Ohio University	☆☆	☆☆	$$$	Independent
San Francisco Art Institute	☆☆	☆☆☆	$$	Experimental
San Francisco State University	☆	☆☆☆	$$	Experimental
Savannah College of Art and Design	☆☆☆	☆☆☆	$$	Independent
Southern Illinois University at Carbondale	☆☆	☆☆	$$	Experimental
Syracuse University	☆☆☆	☆☆☆	$$$	Experimental
Temple University	☆	☆	$$	Experimental
University of California, Los Angeles	☆☆☆	☆☆☆	$$$$	Independent
University of Miami	☆☆	☆☆☆	$	Independent
University of New Orleans	☆☆	☆☆☆	$$	Independent
University of Southern California	☆☆☆	☆☆☆	$$$	Industry
University of Texas at Austin	☆☆☆	☆☆	$$	Independent
University of Utah	☆☆	☆☆	$$	Independent
University of Wisconsin at Milwaukee	☆☆	☆☆	$$	Experimental